D1388135

DAVID RABE

GARLAND REFERENCE LIBRARY
OF THE HUMANITIES
(Vol. 795)

DAVID RABE

A Stage History and
A Primary and Secondary Bibliography

Philip C. Kolin

GARLAND PUBLISHING, INC. • NEW YORK & LONDON
1988

Library of Congress Cataloging-in-Publication Data

Kolin, Philip C.
    David Rabe: A Stage History and A Primary and Secondary
Bibliography / Philip C. Kolin.

    p. cm.—(Garland Reference Library of the Humanities: vol. 795)
    Includes index.
    ISBN 0-8240-6611-1 (alk. paper)
    1. Rabe, David—Stage history.   2. Rabe, David—Bibliography.
I. Title.   II. Series.

PS3568.A23Z7   1987   812′.54—dc19   87-21155   CIP

Printed on acid-free, 250-year-life paper
Manufactured in the United States of America

FOR DAVID RABE

PLAYWRIGHT AND FRIEND

CONTENTS

PREFACE

This is the first published book on David Rabe. Given Rabe's importance in the American theatre, it is surprising that other books have not preceded this one. For the last twenty years, Rabe has been in the vanguard of playwrights who have shaped our theatre. His career crisscrosses paths with some of the most influential artistic directors and producers of our age—Joseph Papp, Mike Nichols, Robert Altman. Although not as prolific as some of his compeers (Mamet or Shepard), Rabe has nonetheless produced eight extremely important plays, including his so-called Vietnam trilogy (*Basic Training of Pavlo Hummel*, *Sticks and Bones*, and *Streamers*), which have earned him a high and permanent place in American theatre history. It was Rabe who brought the Vietnam War into the American theatre and who steadfastly kept it before the American consciousness in the 1970s. Rabe fits squarely into the American tradition of playwrights—one thinks of Williams and Albee—who have blended the lyrical with the grotesque. He has delved deeply into the American dream to uncover the nightmare. Rabe's most recent work, *Hurlyburly*, has been perceptively labeled a horror comedy. Given Rabe's relative youth, there are many more plays—and doubtless books about him—to be published.

As the first full-length work on Rabe, this book appropriately provides the groundwork for many later critical and biographical studies. This book is divided into three parts. The first part—a 100-page essay—attempts to do three things. First, it offers a short biography of the playwright, with a decided emphasis on his early life. This biography is interwoven throughout the essay. The second part of this essay summarizes and evaluates Rabe's journalistic work for the *New Haven Register*, the paper he worked for from 1969 through 1970, at one of the most formative periods of his life— between Vietnam and Broadway. The 26 stories he wrote for the *Register's* magazine—the *Sunday Pictorial*—and the many book, play, and movie reviews he wrote for the *Register* proper provide a key to his plays or in some instances a source for them. In many of these stories journalist Rabe wrote about the same topics and events (drugs, the war, the struggles of an urban existence) that he dramatized on stage in his plays. The third (and major) part of this essay presents the first detailed and cohesive stage history of Rabe's plays in this country and abroad. I have traced Rabe's fortunes as a playwright, surveying the high points in his career, from his very first play (*Chameleon* in 1959) through the closed New York production of *Goose and Tomtom* in 1986 and the Dartmouth production of *Hurlyburly* in 1987. I have also recorded major productions of Rabe's plays abroad. While I have tried to be vigilant and include everything, doubtless I have missed some performances. But I do believe, however, that this survey offers a relatively accurate picture of Rabe's achievements and reputation up to mid-1987.

The second part of this book presents the most comprehensive and authoritative primary bibliography of Rabe to date. It includes all of Rabe's early published poetry and fiction done at Loras Academy and Loras College in his hometown of Dubuque, Iowa, a chronological listing of his stories and reviews for the *New Haven Register* (which, alas, has yet to be indexed!), and a record of his screenplays and plays (both published and unpublished). I have divided Rabe's writing into genres, and organized entries chronologically within these genres. I have tried to list the various anthologies where Rabe's plays have been excerpted or reprinted, and I include the published texts of his plays.

The third and final section of this book contains a secondary bibliography, including a section on biographical studies. It also includes an annotated list of critical studies—articles, chapters of books, dissertations, but not reviews of specific performances of Rabe's plays. Following this annotated list of criticism are nine sections, devoted to Rabe's plays, the film *Streamers*, and his one produced screenplay (*I'm Dancing as Fast as I Can*). Each of these sections includes reviews of productions done in this country and abroad arranged in alphabetical order by the author's surname (with anonymous reviews being listed according to the first key word in the title). I have recorded the original pagination as well as the pagination for reviews included in the *New York Theatre Critics' Reviews*, abbreviated *NYTCR* in this bibliography. When a review does not specify an exact company or a specific major New York production, I have included a short annotation listing the name of the theatre company to which the review refers.

Even a quick glance at these nine sections shows that Rabe's work has been performed all over this country—by professional Broadway companies, at regional theatres (the Goodman, Long Wharf, the Arena, the Academy, Trinity Rep, etc.) and by student troupes on campuses large and small. The good number of foreign reviews found in each section testifies to

Rabe's growing international reputation. Obviously, I make no claim to have provided a complete, exhaustive listing of all reviews of all Rabe productions. Some productions of Rabe's plays were workshop performances where no reviews were given and other productions and reviews of them may have unfortunately slipped through my net.

I could never have completed this book without the help of numerous individuals. Bibliographies, especially of living, productive authors, can never be safely compiled in the comfort of one's own university library. Given the far-flung places where Rabe has been produced, it has been a challenge to gather and verify the reviews. I have been the beneficiary of much kindness. My gratitude goes to the many theatre companies who answered my questions about their productions and then sent me copies of playbills, programs, and reviews. And my gratitude goes to the many librarians (at universities and newspapers) who also answered my questions and who supplied me with the missing page numbers that clipping services (an apt name) cruelly excised from the reviews they gathered for their theatre company clients.

I happily record my debt to the following librarians who have greatly assisted me: Serge Mogilat at the New York Shakespeare Festival and Margaret Goostray at the Special Collections division of Mugar Library at Boston University where some of Rabe's papers are housed. To the two archivists at Rabe's alma maters go my profound thanks—Michael D. Gibson at Loras College and Father Dennis Gallagher, O.S.A. at Villanova University. I am also grateful to Loras College President Pasquale Di Pasquale for his assistance.

The following individuals helped me to track down reviews domestic and foreign—Ralph Black, Philip J. Egan, Anthony Fichera, William Kleb, Colby Haight Kullman, Jim Davis, Susan Harris Smith, Walter Meserve, Ken Watson, Ferenc Kerenyi, David Phelan, and Tony Roche. To Barbara Lonnquist at the University of Pennsylvania goes the order of merit for her valiant assistance. I also thank the linguists who helped translate reviews, playbills, and newspaper stories—Jozef Figa, Irmgard H. Wolfe, Martha Hammond, Georges Pilard, and Marie Kai.

I am also grateful to the University of Southern Mississippi and President Aubrey K. Lucas for a summer research grant which enabled me to get started on this book; and I thank Thomas J. Richardson, Chair of the English Department, for his continued support as I completed it. To Scott Nations, my research assistant, goes my gratitude and respect for many jobs well done. Thanks also to Karolyn Thompson of USM's Interlibrary Loan Department.

Extra special credit goes to Ellen Neuwald, David Rabe's agent and friend, for giving me invaluable information about foreign productions and wise counsel on how to obtain them and information about Rabe performances in this country, too. She unhesitatingly opened her files to me, and I profited immensely.

Beyond doubt my greatest debt of gratitude is reserved for Marsha Rabe, the playwright's sister, and for David Rabe himself. They read my introduction and saved me from grievous error, supplied me with clippings and copies of publications, and put me in touch with the very individuals I needed to speak with about sundry matters. Generously and patiently they answered every one of my numerous phone calls and always gave me the encouragement I needed to keep going with my work. Marsha is the most careful bibliographer of the American theatre I know; and David is characteristically kind and cooperative.

Finally, I thank my wife Janeen, who assisted me at every stage of this book, and my offspring—Eric and Kristin—for their patience and prayers; they gave unboundedly of both.

Philip C. Kolin
June 3, 1987

DAVID RABE

A BRIEF BIOGRAPHY, A REVIEW OF RABE'S WORK FOR
THE *NEW HAVEN REGISTER*, AND A STAGE HISTORY

EARLY LIFE AND EDUCATION

David William Rabe was born on March 10, 1940, at St. Joseph Mercy Hospital in Dubuque, Iowa, to William and Ruth (McCormick) Rabe. At the time the Rabes lived at 716 1/2 Ries Street, in the German neighborhood on the north end of Dubuque.[1] The playwright's father taught high school history and coached freshman football at Loras Academy from 1945 to 1955. But he left teaching to find more lucrative employment at the Dubuque Packing Company, where he had moonlighted a few years before. The senior Rabe worked for this company for 22 years. A writer himself, Rabe's father worked on a couple of novels, including *The Killing Time*, which (alas) were never published. Rabe's mother worked for 18 years at the local J. C. Penney's. In 1955 the Rabes moved from 1411 1/2 Lincoln Avenue to 2065 Lincoln. Rabe's parents still live in Dubuque. The Rabes had a daughter Marsha born in 1948, seven and a half years after David.

Of his early years, the playwright tersely noted in a *New Yorker* interview published in 1971: "I'd had a Catholic childhood in Dubuque, played football, gone to Loras College out there, and then to Villanova, in the East." The Dubuque of Rabe's boyhood—pretty much as it is today—is a Roman Catholic town. It is the seat of the Archdiocese of Dubuque, and in the 1950s was the home to 10 parochial schools, 11 convents, a Trappist monastery and two highly respected Catholic colleges— Loras for men and Clarke for women. "The 'locals' jokingly described their city as 'little Rome,' since it was built on seven hills, each topped by a Catholic institution of one kind or another."[2] Rabe attended Holy Trinity grammar school, just a few blocks from his house, and played outfield on the school baseball team, beginning an interest in sports that has continued throughout his life. According to a boyhood friend, the young Rabe showed an early interest in film, going to the movies frequently and making a number of short films with his 8mm camera.[3]

3

Holy Mother Church, sports, and literature were strong and abiding influences on Rabe. From 1954 to 1958 he attended Loras Academy, an archdiocesan preparatory school where students had to belong to the ROTC program and wear military uniforms on drill days. Rabe played trumpet in the school band and was involved in intramural baseball and basketball. As a first-string fullback on the varsity team, Rabe distinguished himself as a valuable player. He won a freshman letter in his first year at Loras Academy and a junior varsity letter in his sophomore year. *The Log* (the Loras Academy yearbook) for 1957 singles Rabe out as a "very capable replacement" for an injured player and points with pride that, in the Loras game against Dowling, "It was a scoreless game until the third quarter when Dave Rabe scored from the four yard line." Over a 17 game series in his junior and senior years Rabe gained more than 1,000 yards, averaging about six yards per carry. In a 1973 interview with Robert Wahls of the *New York Sunday News* Rabe looked back at his high school football days and noted: "When I was, oh, 16, I wanted to go to college and play football, all that. But something happened when I was 18. I lost all that and it didn't come back until I left the Army almost 10 years later. I thought I had to give up football to be a writer. But now I know I can do both."

While in high school Rabe wrote short stories and poems and earned recognition for both. In May 1955 he won first place in poetry in the Annual Loras Academy Literary Contest, presided over by the Rev. Eugene J. Wiemer, Head of the Loras Academy English Department. Rabe's winning poem was entitled "Night," a 10 line, two stanza poem about the power of night "Engulfing all with deadly, quiet hand." The next year Rabe won first place in the Annual Literary Contest in the short story category for his "Walls of Blackness," a rather eerie tale about a young man who is blinded in an automobile accident by a "sniveling drunk" guilty of a hit and run. Nurturing bitterness and revenge, the young man (Jim) is befriended by a man (Bill Allen) who becomes like a father to him, taking the boy on a fishing trip to the Florida Keys. An unscrupulous ship's captain reveals the truth to Jim that it was Bill Allen who was the driver of the car that blinded him. Pleading for forgiveness, Allen asks for a chance, promises to be Jim's eyes, and says they'll fight together. Jim accepts the challenge in love, stretching his hand out to Allen. Juvenile and sometimes pathetic, Rabe's first published story contains significant references to dreams, betrayals, and barriers—(blinded and angry, Jim in his mind "built up an almost invulnerable wall behind which he tried to hide from the earth"). The young Rabe saw possibilities for happiness arising from suffering; a later Rabe would present a different view in his blinded veteran David.

To no one's surprise, Rabe was offered a football scholarship (he was a fullback) to Loras College. He did enter Loras in 1958 but changed his mind about football after summer camp. Rabe graduated from Loras with a B.A. degree cum laude in English in 1962. Like the Academy, Loras College was run by the diocesan priests, but the philosophy department was controlled by Dominican Fathers, the Order of Preachers, known for their effective teaching and intellectual rigor. As in high school, Rabe distinguished himself as a writer. One of his most significant accomplishments came at the end of his freshman year. Together with some high school friends, Rabe founded an amateur theatre company called Ralako, an acronym formed from the names of David Rabe, John Lang, and Jim Kostle; it is a name Rabe still uses judging from the copyright notation in his recently published *Goose and Tomtom*. Their first offering was a play written by Rabe himself, *Chameleon*. Initially, Rabe showed the play to the Rev. Thomas Carpender, who taught at Loras Academy. Father Carpender sent Rabe's script to Professor George Herman who taught drama at Clarke College. Herman was so impressed by the Loras freshman's play that he submitted it to the National Catholic Playwright Circle for their scrutiny. Rabe and his Ralako cohorts persuaded the Rev. Terrence Thomas, Rabe's pastor at Holy Trinity, to let them use the school auditorium for a performance.[4]

The reviews of *Chameleon*, in the *Lorian* (Loras College newspaper) for April 8, 1959, and the Dubuque *Telegraph Herald* for April 12, 1959, were the first theatre reviews Rabe was to receive. As these reviews pointed out, *Chameleon* was a large success. It dealt with a man who, under the domination of a possessive mother, suffers a mental breakdown. Tom Tully (the reviewer for the *Lorian* and who was also in charge of publicity for Ralako) said one reader compared Rabe's first drama to the play that launched Tennessee Williams's career—*The Glass Menagerie*. Rabe himself played the leading role in *Chameleon*. Supposedly, in this role and others Rabe played he was imitating the acting style of James Dean.[5]

Rabe also played a leading part in the *Spokesman*, the Loras College literary magazine. He was on the editorial staff in 1959-1960 and assumed the editorship of the magazine during his junior and senior years (1961 and 1962). In addition to evaluating work for the magazine, Rabe was a fairly regular contributor. He published seven poems and 13 short stories in its pages. One of his *Spokesman* poems—"Deathbed"—was reprinted in the *Annual Anthology of College Poetry*; and two of his short stories ("Napkins and a Coke Straw" and "When You're Eighteen") were reprinted in *Today*, a Catholic magazine published in Chicago. The *Lorian* (for Mar. 9, 1960) described "When You're Eighteen" as "a study of adolescents in and out of love," an honest assessment. "Napkins" is told from the point of view of a

16-year old girl in love with an 18-year old football star who tells her he needs to date other people. Crushed, the young Cathy "felt the cold emptiness grow inside of me." She makes a date to see a movie with a friend and rushing to that date hears the family cat scream. Her father had mistakenly stepped on it. The story ends with these words about the cat:

> I touched my finger to his head: the skull seemed so fragile.
> You had to try. When some hideous thing inside you wanted to kill love. What you had to do was fight. There would always be need. There would never be enough love.

Rabe's story is filled with obvious symbolism—the cat, the straw with "balled up" napkins that Cathy places at each end to suggest herself and her lover Larry, the arrogant football player—and its stated moral suggests the loveless world in which Rabe's later characters would also encounter fragile skulls.

For his work in the *Spokesman* Rabe won several literary contests on campus, although ironically he never captured first place in any of them. Twice he won a prize in the Gerard Manley Hopkins Poetry Contest, receiving second place ($15.00) in 1960 for "Boy, Seven" and third place ($10.00) in 1961 for "Yes, I Remember." He also won the Gilbert Keith Chesterton Short Story Contest twice—third place in 1961 for "When You're Eighteen" and second place in 1962 for "Jack Be Nimble." These awards no doubt encouraged Rabe to pursue the writer's craft and no doubt pleased his creative writing teacher, Father Raymond Roseliep, the moderator for the *Spokesman*. Rabe's interest in poetry was unquestionably strong under Father Roseliep's guidance. In November 1961 Rabe and one of his classmates (Paul Fransen) interviewed the visiting distinguished poet John Logan who came to Loras as a guest of Father Roseliep. In a December 1971 interview with Vincent Panella of the Dubuque *Telegraph Herald*, Rabe said: "As far as encouragement and even thinking of myself as a professional . . . Father Roseliep was very influential. He taught me a concern for words." In this same article, Father Roseliep recalled Rabe's work at Loras: "There was always a painful honesty about David's writing. The dark side of David came out in his work. He was quiet, and one never knew what he was thinking."

Rabe's early work—the short stories and the poetry—have the earmarks of youthful enthusiasm, of the writer testing his craft, experimenting with forms, points of view, weary symbols and metaphors. There are a few places, as "Napkins and a Coke Straw" suggests, where we can hear distant rumblings of Rabe's later, more cynical voice. In his poem

"Boy/Man" (1962), Rabe speaks of the faded youth of an alcoholic—he is "battered like a tin can cup" and lives "in dark hope." A poem from 1960— "Yes, I Remember"—explores the sad events of a couple in a "dying house/ dustshadowed by the years." After too much self plundering, "too much flesh/ unclothed our urgency/ and made us die/ like dandelions snowing death/ in early May." As we might expect from a teenager, a recurrent theme in Rabe's early work is "fuzzy love." Losing a lover presented the young Rabe with numerous occasions to speculate about life. In his poem "I Loved Her," Rabe sentimentally records "For remembrance/ sketches only lightly/ outlines grey on white/ and nothing more" and distantly anticipates David's tenderness for Zung: "She was a fable/ of sex soft escape into snow/ that I,/ too afraid to touch,/ dreamed on sand sprinkled/ towels of imagination . . . ." In "When You're Eighteen," the young protagonist "Dave" is jilted by a girl and escapes his family ("Darn Mom anyway") and his town by speeding away at 82 m.p.h. "You know you're doing exactly what they'd do in some Hollywood movie and you wish you could stop, but you don't," Dave confesses to himself as he tries to "find something to fill the emptiness," preferably "sympathy" from the community on his "loss." More maturely somber, Rabe's poem "Deathbed" confronts the cruel reality of the dream, a frequent dilemma in the plays: "My life is gone it seems . . . The rest is dreams." But perhaps more than any other early work, Rabe's poem "Knight Errant: 1960" reflects his later views on the hollowness and self destructiveness found in myths of military heroism and lofty romanticism:

> His grey eyes, when men on mirror turn
> from flesh to glass reflecting murdered
> dream, carve his thought. And he cannot learn
> the young girl with lips so stranger burned
> they fear to meet a snow flake. After
> stars he finds the promise of ribald
> dancing, or the light carnal laughter,
> both lies—and brown like paper crackle.
> His void will numb from love (or quick gin);
> and when time dyes with the blooded sun,
> he mounts a drunken horse: hoofs beat thin
> as pale drumming on a broken drum.
> He wanders: a child of Quixote
> crying *Dulcinea and the sea.* [6]

Purgold, The Loras College Yearbook for 1962—the year Rabe graduated—lists among his accomplishments and affiliations that he was a member of the Young Democrats and the St. Vincent de Paul Society. The goals of these two organizations, one secular, the other religious, are complementary. The Young Democrats in 1962—in the heyday of Kennedyism—sought to increase social justice by attacking injustice. The mission of the St. Vincent de Paul Society is to find the destitute, the needy, and to relieve human suffering through charity and self-sacrifice. His membership in these two organizations suggests much about David Rabe's values in 1962 and the later manifestation of them on the stage.

After graduating from Loras College in June of 1962 Rabe left "the heartland of America" (a phrase later used by Joe Papp) to work on an M.A. degree in the theatre department at Villanova University in Villanova, Pennsylvania, outside of Philadelphia. Rabe's Villanova roots would run deep; over the next ten years or so some of his most successful plays would premiere at Villanova's Vasey Theatre, and Rabe himself would return to the university to teach courses in film history and playwrighting. But in 1962 he was employed as a graduate assistant working on a variety of university productions. In 1963 one of Rabe's own plays received a workshop production.[7] Rabe has informed me that the play was entitled *Bridges*. While at Villanova Rabe shared a dorm room with Leslie Lee, himself destined to become a distinguished black playwright.

In 1976, the two established playwrights shared the bill at the Philadelphia Company which staged Rabe's *The Crossing* and Lee's *As I Lay Dying, A Victim of Spring*, both "one-act plays harking back to their student days in the 1960s" as Jonathan Takiff pointed out.[8] These short plays dimly prefigure the later, more successful works of both authors. Interestingly enough, Robert Hedley, the director of the Philadelphia Company, taught both Rabe and Lee. Of *The Crossing*, Takiff states: "The Rabe play, being apolitical and sometimes comic, is much farther removed from his later work than is Lee's play . . . *The Crossing* concerns a pair of Wisconsin youths, who awaken from a drunken fling to discover themselves 250 miles from home, in a fleabag Chicago hotel." The boys encounter the evil frolics of the hotel manager—a sadistic pimp—and a hooker who lives there.

After two years at Villanova, Rabe left without taking his degree. He lacked only one or two courses. For a year (1964) he took a series of odd jobs ranging from driving a cab to doing substitute teaching. He told Jerry Tallmer of the *New York Post* that at this time in his life, "I was interested in writing but I just couldn't seem to do anything." He did try to rework his father's unpublished novel, *The Killing Time*.

RABE IN VIETNAM

In January of 1965 Rabe was drafted at the age of 25. He could have easily obtained a deferment; he had done substitute teaching in the last year in New Haven and might have taken a teacher's contract to the draft board. He might also have re-enrolled at Villanova to finish his master's degree. He might even have pursued his ideas about becoming a conscientious objector, as the editor of *New Haven Register*'s *Sunday Pictorial* said Rabe once pondered. But as Rabe later told Robert Wahls about the war, "I thought of it as a cause." He lacked the experience that would disprove the government rhetoric he heard.

Like Pavlo, Rabe took his basic training at Ft. Gordon, Georgia. His athletic interests and prowess served him well during this arduous phase of military life. He informed Charles Michener of *Newsweek* in 1971 that "I turned down the job of squad leader because I was willing to go along with the system, but not enforce it." In February of 1966 Rabe was sent to Vietnam where he completed an 11-month tour of duty. He recalls that his trip to Vietnam took 22 days by boat and gave him an opportunity to catch up on his reading. A slow reader, he took a lot of time to savor *War and Peace*, a novel he had not read before.

"I saw no combat," Rabe pointed out in a *New Yorker* interview of 1971. Like Pavlo, he was assigned to a support group for a hospital unit where he performed a host of duties. As he told Jerry Tallmer in a March 11, 1972 interview:

> I think generally what I did over there was be a flunky. I did a tremendous amount of building, a tremendous amount of driving, a tremendous amount of guard duty. And then at the end a tremendous amount of clerical work. One time I got traded with another guy to another company for a jeep.

Like Pavlo, too, Rabe initially wanted to see combat. "I had wanted to go on the line. After two months I changed my mind. It took about two months for a lot of things to start going sour—a lot of attitudes I went over with."

Although Rabe himself did not see combat, he did encounter firsthand the ravages of the war. Attached to a hospital unit, Rabe watched as the casualties came in. In a July 10, 1976 article by Ira Simmons of the *Journal-Courier/Louisville Times* Rabe is quoted as saying: "I tried to get on a stretcher detail to get closer to the war, but never made it. I didn't want to be put in the position of shooting people, but, yeah, I guess I was prepared to." He recalls that sometimes these casualties had received some type of medical attention before he had seen them; and at other times they came in covered with blood and gore. As Rabe told Robert Wahls: "I had seen truckloads of human limbs and piles of green uniforms. The impact was terrific on anyone who was over there."

Rabe also witnessed the cruel effects of nightly bombing raids. In the 1971 *New Yorker* interview he stated: "I was stationed at Long Binh, near an ammo dump, and I can remember the strange excitement and sensation of watching the other side go after that dump." Recalling the same experiences for Tallmer, Rabe noted: "You'd sit up there and watch it. Like a tennis match." Rabe was also a careful observer of his fellow soldiers. "You don't realize how young most of our army is over there until you see them, troops fresh off the line, standing around some bar like teenagers at a soda fountain, talking coolly about how many of their guys got killed in the last battle." Echoes of *The Basic Training of Pavlo Hummel*!

In his Introduction to the Viking Press edition of *Pavlo* and *Sticks*, Rabe asserts: "I kept no journal and even my letters grew progressively more prosaic, fraudulent, dull, and fewer and fewer. Cliches were welcomed as they always are when there is no real wish to see what they hide" (p. xvii). He carefully (and, in retrospect, painfully) explains why—"writing requires a double focus that I could not then quite handle." Rabe elaborated: "Not only to see the dead and crippled, the bodies, beggars, lepers, but to replay in your skull their desperation and the implications of their pain . . . seemed a lunatic journey. I did not go upon it. I was living then in a high, brittle part of my mind. I skimmed over things and hoped they would skim over me." As Rabe points out, "All I knew in Vietnam were facts, nothing more" (p. xvii).

In January 1967 discharged Specialist Fourth Class Rabe left Vietnam for an 18-hour plane trip home to Dubuque. Rabe contrasted the slow 22-day journey to Vietnam by ship with the light-wave quick return home. In less than one day he went "from getting out of bed in Vietnam to being in my living room" in Dubuque. The journey took a day but brought the veteran light years back to an American culture that was now strange and confusing to him. He felt estranged, lost, and ready to record his experiences. Rabe told Jody Brockway in an *After Dark* interview of 1972 that "When I first came home . . . I found that not just my family but *nobody* wanted to hear about what actually happened over there. People were only interested in the debate on the war, not the war itself, or any evidence of it." Vietnam—and the veterans of the war—will always be in Rabe's blood. As he told Walter F. Naedele, in an April 2, 1972 interview, when referring to his Villanova days after the war: "Even if I run into a veteran or if I meet somebody whose brother just came back from Vietnam, I'm terribly drawn to them. Or if I meet somebody in a bar who's been there. I just want to know more, want to know different things about Vietnam."

In an important interview with Markland Taylor of the *New Haven Register*, on the eve of the world premiere of *Streamers*, Rabe reflected on the role his army experiences had on his writing. Admitting the complex significance the military life had on him, Rabe stated: "I think that without the army experience I'd have written the plays but written them differently. No, I really don't know. It's hard to say." A little later he confessed that the army was "clearly a catalyst" in his life and that it provided the "crucible" for his plays.

"Coming home was traumatic, finding business going on as usual. For a while I couldn't talk to anyone who hadn't been over there," so Rabe told Robert Wahls. Rabe wandered around for some time but really wanted to return to Vietnam, perhaps as a civilian construction worker or, better yet, as a war correspondent. He did apply to a number of newspapers for the job, including the *New York Times* and the *Hong Kong Standard*. Failing in the attempt, Rabe returned to Villanova where he still had a masters degree to finish. Fortunately, one of his professors and head of the theatre department—Richard Duprey—had wanted Rabe to return long before then. He had tried to secure a fellowship for Rabe earlier but because of his military commitment the playwright could not return to Philadelphia, obviously. But in 1968 Duprey was able to give Rabe the benefits of a Rockefeller Playwrighting Fellowship for a year and a half; the student who had originally won the fellowship had left Villanova and given up the award. This was a wonderful break for Rabe, for it allowed him to work on *Bones* and *Pavlo*. (Interestingly enough, in 1981 Rabe was one of eight individuals to receive a prestigious Rockefeller Foundation Fellowship Award for Playwrights—carrying a $9,000 stipend; the wheel had come full circle.[9]) In 1970 Rabe was recommended by Bobbs-Merrill for a scholarship to the highly acclaimed Bread Loaf Writers' Conference at Middlebury College, and he attended the workshop that summer.

WORK FOR THE *NEW HAVEN REGISTER*

From May 1969 through approximately August 1970 David Rabe (sometimes signing his name David W. Rabe) worked for the *New Haven Register*, a newspaper then having a Sunday circulation of about 125,000.[10] Rabe was primarily employed as a staff writer for the *Sunday Pictorial*, the *Register*'s highly respected rotogravure magazine. In his stint at the paper Rabe contributed 26 stories to the *Pictorial* in addition to a few scattered miscellaneous pieces (captions and announcements of forthcoming stories). Rabe also wrote ten book, movie, and theatre reviews for the "Arts and Leisure" section of the *Register* proper. The budding playwright quickly established his reputation as an award-winning journalist. He won one of the "writing awards of merit" (capturing third place) from the New England Associated Press News Executives' Association for his in-depth look at the draft, military stance, and conscientious objectors, three stories that filled the pages of the *Pictorial* for December 14, 1970. Rabe also won acclaim for his coverage of the Daytop drug rehabilitation program—four stories spanning two issues of the *Pictorial* (June 14 and June 21, 1970).

The years (or months, more accurately) that Rabe worked for the *Register* marked a tumultuous time in American history. It was a time of great social unrest as one turbulent decade exploded into another. It was the time of the Mai Lai massacres and the growing public outrage, shock, and shame over the war, the Manson murders, the closing of universities, and the civil rights protests. Fear of insurrection haunted the land. Rabe could not have selected a more incendiary city than New Haven in which to work. Going on there during 1969-1970 was the trial of the Black Panthers and their leader Bobby Seale, the formation and fomenting of various draft resistance groups, and the very closing of Yale itself in the face of waves of student protesters ready to rock the venerable school to its foundations.

If the years 1969-1970 were crucial for America they were equally important for Rabe. He came to practice journalism at an important juncture of his life. Behind him lay his wartime experience in Vietnam and a few years of experimentation at Villanova (see pages 29–31; 51–52). Ahead lay further experimentation at Villanova and the fame and success at Joseph Papp's Public Theatre and Broadway. The *Register* experience gave Rabe an opportunity to see America's domestic troubles—its rituals and protests—firsthand; he found the writer's workshop at the journalist's desk. Listening to Robert Asahina, journalism and not the theatre supplied the reigning voice of the age, the key source of information about the Vietnam War.[11] Rabe was writing both. At the *Register* Rabe had a laboratory in which he could gather information, test his ideas, and postulate a few answers.

His 26 stories for the *Pictorial*, therefore, have great importance biographically and critically. The stories reflect his approach to a host of contemporary topics that repeatedly surface in his plays. In many ways the *Pictorial* articles acquire the status of sources or commentary for understanding ideas raised dramatically in the plays. In fact, we might say that Rabe's stories for the *Pictorial* are the journalistic counterparts to his plays. These stories also shed light on Rabe's developing style as a writer, his sense of the power and decline of language to express meaning. The choices that Rabe made as a journalist—using metaphor, analogy, personification, dialogue, and shifting points of view, for example—demand comparison with the stylistic decisions he made as a dramatist.

Rabe's stories cover a variety of topics, events, places, and people in the New Haven area, a rich center of culture and also of dissent. It may be that as Rabe himself said "a free-lance writer . . . does not pick his subjects according to taste and love so much as they are chosen for him by the opportunities of the market" ("Life of Ordered Singularity" [Feb. 8, 1970]). But, undeniably, the subjects of Rabe's articles are remarkably relevant to a young writer's interests and intentions. We might profitably divide Rabe's articles into seven categories: (1) the war and dissenters, (2) the drug scene and drug rehabilitation, (3) the arts, (4) writers and the craft of writing, (5) issues and abuses in the legal system, (6) sports, and (7) journeys—symbolic and real. Two of Rabe's articles—"Merchants' Quest for Quality" (Oct. 19, 1969) on the struggle and differences between New Haven's downtown stores and those in the mall and "Architects of Webs" (Oct. 12, 1969), a short introduction to a photoessay on spider webs—do not comfortably fit into any of the above categories. What I shall do here is briefly review the articles in these seven areas, pointing out the major themes Rabe found and emphasized in the sights and sounds around New Haven. The ideas that captured his imagination in this highly formative period of his career no doubt spilled over into his plays, and vice versa.

Rabe's AP award-winning three stories about the war appeared in the December 14, 1969 *Sunday Pictorial*—"Three Faces of Dissent and How They've Changed," "The Military Stance," and "Conscientious Objector." Don Sharpe, the Editor of the *Pictorial*, thought these stories so significant that he supplied his own detailed introduction ("The Draft and A Reporter's

Reasons") providing background information about correspondent Rabe and explaining his motivation and approach to the complex topic. Sharpe pointed out that as a veteran Rabe was "fascinated" by the "phenomenon" of the conscientious objector and even thought about becoming a C.O. but changed his mind after being drafted. Rabe originally intended to do a short article, a "personality piece on a couple" of conscientious objectors, but "as he tested the levels of the story he found it growing larger and larger, more complicated and subtle." Rabe spent a great deal of time interviewing a variety of individuals in the draft resistance movement, for whom New Haven was the hub of meaningful action at this time. Although Rabe pierced through the perceived contradictions in the approach of these groups, he nonetheless respected their "openness, emotion, reasoning and intelligence" and decided to report what he heard with "as much balance and objectivity as he could manage." Rabe's goal was "to go toward dealing with the voices—the people and what was said and done by them. Judgments were not to be passed."

Rabe's objectivity generally wins the day. It is interesting to note, though, that a few years after Rabe's stint on the *Register*, his friend (and then director of *The Orphan*) Barnet Kellman offered this view of the playwright's reactions to 1970 New Haven:

> David was outraged and viscerally upset by much of what he
> saw in New Haven that year. He found himself in a uniquely
> lone position amid the broil of the times. A veteran of the war,
> he had little sympathy for its apologists, but at the same time,
> he was appalled at how little the war protesters understood the
> reality of what they were protesting.[12]

The first (and longest) of Rabe's three stories traces the evolution of the beliefs and the effects of the symbols on the draft resistance movements in New Haven. Rabe links the parts of his story by interweaving short biographies of three well-known radicals—Doug Rosenberg, Bill Morico, and, most prominently, David Tobis. At first, notes Rabe, the "sensibilities" of the radicals "were innocent of the true nature of the struggle they had entered." They saw themselves as "singular sacred entities" waging a holy war against an unholy law that would strip them of their moral rights. A major symbol of their protest was the draft card turn-in at Yale's Battell Chapel where the radicals fervently tossed draft cards into a collection basket forswearing allegiance to a corrupt system. But, as Rabe carefully pointed out, Tobis and others learned that the draft card turn-in was a futile gesture, an empty symbol. It was meaningless to the very people to whom it was directed. Said Rabe analyzing the symbology: "No amount of wish, will or hope on the part of the sender can make it moral if the receiver sees it as dangerous, foolish, arrogant, trivial, immoral, silly or sinister."

Living up to his promise of objectivity, Rabe explains the reasons why the radicals opposed the Selective Service System and why they believed the power structure behind the draft was evil. Rabe quotes Tobis as saying "We run toward isolation" in corrupt America. In his dramatic conclusion, Rabe describes the scene at Yale when a film of war-ravaged Vietnam is shown to resisters and he supplies an eloquent analogy summarizing the relationship of the resisters to their country. America is like a woman who does not know she has lost her innocence and still claims to be good. The resisters are "the childen of the illusions" of this country. They have "the rage of duped and frustrated love . . . in them, the will to vengeance of the scared child."

The army point of view is represented in the second story of Rabe's journalistic trilogy—"The Military Stance." Rabe interviewed three Vietnam veterans—a colonel, a major, and an enlisted man—whose "diversity of experience, attitudes and expectation" fall within "the accepted discipline and life-style" of the army. Rabe insists that each man offers a "unique and valuable" perspective. Most attention is given to Col. Richard Irving, then the head of the ROTC program at Yale. A veteran with more than 36 years service, Irving quite expectedly takes a hard line on dissenters whom he castigates as "social outcasts, misfits," individuals who suffer from "their own inability to gain recognition proportionate to the value with which they regard themselves." Curiously enough, at least from Rabe's point of view and interest in symbolism, the colonel does not want a formal retirement ceremony, preferring a quiet exit into civilian life.

Major Raoul Alcala, Rabe's second interviewee, expresses less predictable views about dissenters. The major is concerned about the lack of communication between different segments of society, gloomily observing that "when your adversary is someone incapable of change [it] leaves you talking to yourself." Worried about labels, Alcala feared that the army was being made into a "subculture" that splits away from "the masses of the people."

Perhaps the most penetrating comments about the war come from the anonymous sergeant who lost an eye in Vietnam. He admits that the boys are "getting killed learning things I already know" and believes the problem is not Vietnam but America. He bitterly ruminates on battlefield casualties—"It's like we shot' em here and took' em over there." Expressing an idea central to Rabe's plays, the sergeant discredits the army's adherence to symbolism—"It's like everybody over there thinks they're symbols, all the boys who are dead, they're not—they don't mean anything but themselves, and they're good."

"Conscientious Objector," the concluding article, is the shortest and perhaps the bleakest of Rabe's stories on the war. Rabe allows the story of one man, Jeffrey Rawn of Port Chester, New York, to illustrate and explain the motivations and problems of all conscientious objectors. Selecting key details from Rawn's high school and college days, Rabe explores the process by which the young man became a conscientious objector, of how he was involved in the "struggle to know the speaker within him." Never expecting to become a conscientious objector, Rawn ultimately came to hate the ugly futility of war (especially nuclear war) and fear the bombs which would "blow out the lives" of his children. Rabe explains the procedures Rawn (and many like him) had to follow with their draft boards to be considered for the C.O. classification—the paperwork and the personal appearances. Meticulously choosing the words for the essay that would justify his objection to the war for his draft board, Rawn was met by the indifference of "five strangers reading papers behind a desk" who branded him a liar. Legally the board did not have to give a reason for their rejection and left Rawn feeling betrayed and baffled. Ironically, Rawn did receive a deferment—for hardship as the father of a family—but as Rabe ends the story he leaves Rawn, alone in the woods near his house, pondering the consequences of honest moral indignation.

The enticement and deadly entrapment of drugs is a recurring motif in many of Rabe's plays, most especially in *I'm Dancing as Fast as I Can* and *Hurlyburly*. It is not surprising, therefore, that the other major series that Rabe did for the *Sunday Pictorial* focused on the Daytop drug rehabilitation center in Seymour, Connecticut, a few miles northwest of New Haven. The four stories that Rabe wrote on Daytop dominated the two issues of the *Sunday Pictorial* for June 14 and June 21, 1970. Judging again from Don Sharpe's explanatory note to this series, Rabe was obviously interested in and deeply moved by what he saw at Daytop. "Rabe's extended visits to Daytop left him literally shaken and unsure—shaken by the intensity of the addicts' feelings and unsure of the exact worth of the program itself." As with his study of the war, what started out to be a short article for the *Pictorial*, explained Sharpe, turned into a group of "uncommon articles [illustrated] with uncommon pictures" by photographer Joseph Pettis.

Rabe's "surgically precise look" at Daytop (as the headnote to the June 21st *Pictorial* describes his approach) resulted in powerful writing and expressed a number of themes found in Rabe's plays. Images of despair and desperation explode in the collection of narratives that make up a large share of these stories. Laced with penetrating quotations from addicts, ex-addict expeditors (Daytop trustees), and moderators (some of whom are also ex-addicts), Rabe's stories give readers multiple perspectives of the hell of addiction and its subsequent rehabilitation. Key themes of the Daytop stories concern the identity of the individual, the assaults on self, and the sham of false, destructive dreams. Losing oneself is essential for addiction; finding oneself is crucial to rehabilitation. The "real power" of dope "to infect," says Rabe, "is in the area of the will, the feelings, wish and fantasy." The junkie, searching for gratification of the high, feels himself superior to a society of straights and values the "exclusivity of his image." But the junkie's door to fantasy opens the way to self-annihilation. Expressing a paradox of contemporary existence, Rabe points out that in satisfying themselves, the junkies "were killing themselves." Heroin users have "huge black pupils" and their dead bodies "look like hunks of stone."

It is the addict's pernicious self that Daytop seeks to combat and destroy. To give his readers a sense of having visited Daytop themselves, Rabe explains its history, philosophy, staff, operations, funding, outreach program, and successes. The Daytop philosophy maintains that drug addiction is not the real problem but only "the symptom of a thing deep and wrong within the personality itself" (see "Hostility Encounter"). Devoting most attention to the Daytop approach, Rabe describes how its advocates engage in "turning man's mind around, making right into left and up into down." To cure, Daytop is cruel. Any ambivalence Rabe may have felt about the Daytop approach surfaces in this description: "Nearly militaristic in its rigidity, the daily pattern of pressure, responsibility, and punishment is meant to give the Daytop resident a structured world in which to move and live with the constant knowledge that his acts have consequences" ("Hostility Encounter").

To help the addict survive and rejoin the world, Daytop makes him or her go through "the most uncomfortable" encounters. In sentences that smart from the strokes of Daytop's punishment, Rabe describes the "pattern of daily life" at the facility (from "the day of arrival" onward to the end of the addict's two-year stay), the "voices and insults" of the staff, and, most of all, the humiliation inherent in the rehabilitation process. The slightest infraction of the harsh rules causes "explosions and repercussions." One addict is forced to wear a sign saying he is a baby because he stole a cigarette, another is publicly degraded for not refilling a sugar bowl, and another has his head shaved for showing signs of violence. Such gruesome punishment is necessary, Daytop feels, to have the addict "uncover the new edges of himself," to peel away the "layers of lies," and to dissolve "the protective wrapping of self-deceit."

As Rabe points out, the treatment is highly effective—the "halls and rooms of Daytop are filled with people who have lost their sacred lies." There is no place to hide. "Surveillance is constant. Each person watches and is watched." A crucial part of the treatment is the hostility encounter group. Forced into submission for most of the week and harnessed to unbending rules of communication, the addicts are formed into hostility groups three times a week with people (addicts as well as moderators) of their own choosing. In these groups addicts are free to unleash the built-up frustration and anger of the preceding days, returning insult for insult, raving jibe for jibe; they can express any feeling or fear to whomever they wish (addict or staff). Anything goes except violence. In other group settings addicts are taught to see the error of their ways and are exhorted to change. Rabe's visit to Daytop documents the price contemporary souls pay for their addiction.

The arts (sculpture, painting, architecture, ceramics, drawing, and theatre) surface in many of Rabe's *Pictorial* stories, but four in particular focus exclusively on the arts and the artist. In Rabe's earliest story on the arts—"The Fine Art of Shaping Obstinate Clay" (July 13, 1969)—he visits the Creative Arts Center in New Haven, appropriately meeting in a Jewish temple, a place of reverence and mystery. The focal center for Rabe is Lynn Canterbury, the resident artist, whose comments and style give the story its direction and shape. Rabe writes about the relationship of the artist to his materials ("the creator with the thing created") and the issue of form (Canterbury, notes Rabe, prizes the Japanese "aesthetic of roughness"). Rabe delineates Canterbury's reasons for sculpting—"to personalize the world"—and his firm belief that art need not be "moralistic." Demonstrating his own interest in the artistic process of shaping clay into exquisite creations, Rabe concludes with a lucid and lively description of how pottery is made, how it grows into a thing of wonder.

In "Artist Cimaglia's Obsessions" (April 26, 1970), Rabe offers a masterful portrait of local artist Judy Cimaglia who creates drawings in lead pencil. This in-depth piece is interesting for the view of art and the artist's relationship with self, family, and society that Rabe reports on. Obsessed with her art (her drawings), Cimaglia is "like a person who will be blind if she does not look with her fingers, see with her hands." Perhaps Rabe was reminded of his own David, son of Ozzie, who sees with his blind hands and perhaps, too, he was reflecting on his own drive to create. Emphasizing Cimaglia's "persistence," Rabe describes her compulsive pursuit of perfection, her "crying pictures," and her goal of capturing not just the exterior but the interior ("the terribly human") aspect of her subjects. He also describes Cimaglia's "violent" art, her coveted privacy, and her fame (Bette

Davis owns one of her drawings). Perhaps most intriguing of all for Rabe is Cimaglia's avowed belief that she paints "ghosts" (trying to capture the quintessence of the individual), and in a carefully wrought sentence about the artist's battles Rabe writes, "It is the things she is told by what she sees that she struggles to draw." Struggle and violence, which characterize Cimaglia's art, have also informed Rabe's.

In the "Arts and Leisure" section of the *Register* for February 22, 1970, Rabe interviewed actress Katherine Houghton, then starring in Hartford Stage's production of Shaw's *Misalliance*. The occasion gave Rabe an opportunity to listen to some highly provocative views about the history, substance, and function of theatre from a very popular actress. Rabe was provocatively jostled and approvingly enthralled at the same time by her remarks. What struck him as out of the ordinary was the course of Houghton's career. She returned to little theatre from a highly successful Hollywood career, which, as Rabe points out, was "the reversal of the traditional procedure." Discussing the Hollywood scene, Houghton very well anticipated Rabe's own response five years later. In Rabe's recollection of her words, "The days when a young actor signed a contract with some big company and vanished into the myths it produced about them were gone . . . . They would turn you into nothing but a phantom, a symbol of brainless flesh." Returning to the theatre did not involve "idealism" for Houghton as much as a "selfish" desire to perfect her craft. She grew disappointed with the commercialism of agents and announced that "most of the scripts I read are garbage."

Affirming that "theatre is important to me," she conversed with Rabe about her beliefs in the art form. For Houghton it was erroneous to regard theatre as "entertaining" or offering "universal appeal." Although she regarded the playwright as a "metaphysician," she stressed to Rabe that the theatre should strive for magic and produce "plays of language." She deplored the contemporary "worship of facts and logical positivism" as well as the cult of Freud. No doubt pleasing to Rabe, she assaulted the establishment, "the rhinocerous faction," in this country and in Russia.

Amid such heady discussion, drinks, and plates of food, Rabe records his own reactions. At first he is angry. "I expected the knowledge but not the seeming ice." Listening to her expostulate on the direction theatre must take, Rabe winces: "My head is busy with all I have had happen. I feel extremely unknown and throw up a flare." Rabe's conclusion focuses on Houghton's love of Fellini, Antonioni, and Bergman films and how to see them she had to visit porno houses, the only places that showed such films. He ends with this grand compliment to her: ". . . she must touch the world and see evidence of her touch."

In his article on the New American Theatre Ensemble (July 12, 1970), Rabe reports on the health and importance of a progressive New Haven theatre company. Among the last stories he wrote for the *Register*, this relatively short piece for the "Arts and Leisure" section gives us insights into Rabe's view of the function and power of the theatre arts, as did his earlier story on Katherine Houghton. He applauds the stamina of the N.A.T.E. which, "grantless, aidless, living off box office receipts," is providing numerous cultural benefits to New Haven. Rabe congratulates the company for not wallowing in self-pity or mourning "the unattended, unseen beauty of their work." Instead they have a keen sense of the real world, an enviable perseverance in struggle, a characteristic Rabe had so often applauded in other artists. Rabe contrasts the complementary views of the N.A.T.E.'s co-directors—Sergei Retivov and Barnet Kellman. (Four years later Kellman would direct *The Orphan*.) Retivov is more European in his views of art and artists, seeing the theatre as "a community of people." Kellman is more American.

A full half of Rabe's article is devoted to reviewing Nancy Fale's *How They Made It*, which Kellman had just directed. Rabe is in awe of this play which he says "assaulted" him. A collage of scenes and crimes from America's past and present (Yankee Doodle, cowboys, Indians, cops, and teenagers), Fale's play goes "through time into history and beyond into uniquely American myth." To Rabe it is "both shocking and beautiful." Reviewing *How They Made It* provides Rabe with yet another suitable opportunity to voice his own views on the salutary power of drama to shock, to provoke, to inspire, and to examine our national sins and symbols. He concludes by recalling his response to the fireworks he heard and saw after he attended the play on July 3 and how the explosions outside the theatre profoundly reminded him of the moral explosions in Fale's play inside the N.A.T.E.

In less than ten months (October 1969 to July 1970), Rabe contributed four probing articles on writers and the craft of writing to the *Register*. These pieces contained capsule biographies of local writers who attained national reputations. Their achievements no doubt captured the admiration of the fledgling playwright deeply involved in his own work while he was preparing these stories. In them we find recurring themes that occupied Rabe at this time—the relationship of the writer to the environment, the writer's lifestyle and social views, and, most important of all, the craft of writing itself. As we will see again in his articles on sports, Rabe stresses the struggle in the accomplishment. Writing for him is an agonizing search for self-fulfillment which explores the self along the way.

The first and perhaps most valuable (biographically speaking) of Rabe's stories about writing, "Strenuous Test for Writers," appeared in the October 5, 1969 *Pictorial.* In this piece Rabe explores the Bread Loaf Writers' Conference, on the campus of Middlebury College in Vermont, where participants can visit and be inspired by Robert Frost's famous rough cottage from which the poet wrote "of terror and unfulfillment." (As we saw, Rabe would attend this conference himself in the summer of 1970.) Rabe gives his readers a poetic guided tour of the landscapes of the conference and then (as at Daytop) outlines a typical day's activities. He scrupulously reports on the origins of the conference, the history of its directors (John Ciardi was then in charge), its "severe" curriculum and reading schedules, and the students who attend for wisdom but frequently endure the scalding "sarcasm of the staffers." One student responds as if "she had been told she was ugly."

The main point of the conference—one with which Rabe no doubt must have agreed from his own experiences—was that writing at Bread Loaf is regarded as hard, demanding work, more drudgery than magic. The conference, states Rabe, is a "crucible" in which the students' work, their self-worth, and their ability to withstand the onslaught of criticism are tested. If the neophyte writers are not found wanting, their work might lead to fame. As he would do in his articles on sports, Rabe pays dutiful respect to "the bits of rules and notions of craft" that the conference emphasizes. An absolutely delightful part of Rabe's story is his description of poet Ciardi and his frisbee-catching dog. Ciardi's voice, observed the poetic Rabe, "thrashes about in his stomach before emerging." Having a "karate green belt in poetry," Ciardi is a tough combat-seasoned veteran in the writer's war for success. In the Ciardi vignette and in others in "Strenuous Test for Writers" Rabe displays his keen eye for colorful and lively detail. Rabe the athlete interested in physical struggle intuitively recognizes the necessity of struggle in the writer's craft.

In "A Life of Ordered Singularity" (Feb. 8, 1970), Rabe illuminates the contributions of the Rev. Mr. Alexander Winston, aged 60 at the time. A local pastor and former president of the New Haven Council of Churches, Winston earned a national reputation as an author of sermons, articles, and a book on piracy (*No Man Knows My Name*). Winston is a highly attractive figure to Rabe who praises the clergyman for his discipline, scrupulousness, endurance, and energy. A historian who is also a novelist, Winston saw research as "the real agony of his task." Yet Rabe acknowledges that all of Winston's laborious research among old documents had "been concealed beneath an easy and smooth-flowing narrative." Rabe respectfully describes Winston's habits (he is an avid runner and squash player), the room in which he works (reflecting his "relished singularity"), and the symbolic journey he had taken. Searching for the clue to the man and the writer, Rabe concludes that "some central puzzle occupies" the preacher intrigued by pirates and that "complication and contradiction are frequent in the man."

If the ghost of Frost greeted would-be writers at Bread Loaf, then the voice of Faulkner echoes in the house of the Essex, Connecticut, writer Brian Burland whom Rabe studies in "Time Machine For Words" (Mar. 22, 1970). Burland plays a record of Faulkner's Nobel Prize address for guests and also for Rabe who liberally weaves Faulkner's comments into the last third of his story about Burland. A novelist, Burland inhabits "the purgatory of fiction." Rabe opens the story dramatically with events from Burland's past—a boyhood in Bermuda, a dangerous journey to England across the submarine-infested Atlantic of World War II. It is of his boyhood, of initiation rites, of mistreatment of blacks that Burland has written. Rabe movingly speaks of Burland's pain in writing, of the difficulties in placing his book (*A Fall from Aloft*) with an American publisher but of his success with a British one, of his praise by Anthony Burgess, and of the similarities between Burland's life and Malcolm Lowry's. Always offering loving devotion is Burland's wife, Edwina Ann, hoping to see his second work (*A Few Flowers for St. George*) bring additional fame to her husband. Mindful of a writer's sense of place, Rabe describes the "brown blank cabin called his [Burland's] studio." Reverently Rabe points out that this cabin is "a kind of time machine. Only he [Burland] is allowed to enter."

In "Survivor of a Difficult Trip," included in the "Arts and Leisure" section of the *Register* (July 5, 1970), Rabe profiles the life and contributions of John Clellon Holmes (of Old Saybrook) who with Jack Kerouac and Allen Ginsberg founded the Beat School of Poetry. Rabe's short biography also dips into the poetics of dissent. As Rabe admits, the three founders "banged, in the youthful seeking after life for themselves, against the antiseptic silence of Eisenhower's '50s. . . ." Rabe looks at Holmes in the 1970s to see how he has met the challenge of going beyond the legendary establishment of the Beat School. A survivor, Holmes may have received less "notoriety" than the other members of the triumvirate, but according to Rabe he deserves special attention for his four books and for his poetical ideas of great timely interest. Rabe examines Holmes's pacifism, his opposition to the Vietnam War, and his dedication to the moral principles of nonviolence, even in the face of deadly threats. One of Holmes's works—a novel—is concerned with violence, "the background of the Sharon Tate murders" setting the tone. Needless to say, these ideas interested the author of *The Orphan*, too. Rabe calls Holmes's latest work—*Nothing More to Declare*—a book of "exquisite prose, the product and expression of his precise mind."

Two of Rabe's stories report directly on issues of social injustice—inequities in the legal system, hollow legal rituals, and racism. In pieces about criminologist Ahmed Sharif (Sept. 7, 1969) and lawyer-author Dan Horowitz (Aug. 9, 1970), Rabe provides as much a short biography of these defenders of justice as he does an expression of his own outrage at social evils. Sharif, an internationally respected scholar and at that time a professor at New Haven College, decries the lack of attention paid to physical evidence in American jurisprudence. He calls for a "new language of physical evidence" and opines that sometimes a legal case is seen as a game, "lawyers playing tricks." Reporting on Sharif's use of handwriting as evidence, Rabe is amazed to learn that "a man's state of mind could fall through his fingers and enter not only into the content of the words he selects but even into their written shape." Consistently attuned to the symbolic, Rabe concludes that there was "something judicial in the barrenness" of Sharif's sparsely decorated office. When Rabe records Sharif's own bewilderment at America's gun laws, we catch a horrifying glimpse of the playwright's vision of America in the following question: "Is not the belief that a man must have a gun in his house rooted in an expectation of the enemy who comes from within one's own boundaries . . . ?"

In his story on Horowitz, Rabe's indignation at the system seems to rankle in the very journalist's prose he uses to discuss the topic. Horowitz left a lucrative law practice (filled with moral "deceits and failures") to write a book (in his house in Branford, Conneticut) about inequalities in the law directed against blacks. It is these blatant prejudices, says Horowitz, that "legitimize" all other evils, for as the lawyer-author notes, "what is legal is respectable and moral in this country." Offering examples from Horowitz's practice about the horrors of shady (but legitimate) legal deals at the expense of black clients, Rabe emphasizes what Horowitz calls the "emotional conspiracy" in this country that refuses to admit that blacks really care about their lives. Horowitz, himself aware of the treachery inherent in received symbols, observes that judges in black robes and buildings that architecturally look like they "have endured from antiquity" do not automatically promise fair treatment. In his conclusion, Rabe stresses that the "true insidiousness and sickness" of racism is "much more subtle" than name calling and stereotypes would have us believe and consequently he pleads for reform. As Rabe the playwright-journalist realized only too well, racism "stands on the legs of assumptions that go unchallenged and hold up whole communities that are seemingly healthy, solid and virtuous in every other area." Rabe had already written about Ozzie and Harriet.

At least five of Rabe's stories deal with sports. The athlete-playwright has had a long and glorious love affair with sports going back to his football career in high school. Even today Rabe has a picture of himself from his high school football days on his mantle.[13] Two of his sports stories examine rugby, one for the *Philadelphia Magazine* (April 1969) and the other for the *Sunday Pictorial* (April 25, 1971). As a member of the Philadelphia Rugby Club (the City Club), which began at Villanova, Rabe had more than an ephemeral interest or superficial knowledge of the game. A highly speculative story on boxing appeared in the *Sunday Pictorial* on August 10, 1969, and two lighter pieces on sporting events also appeared in the *Pictorial* on January 25, and June 7, 1970. In covering sports Rabe the journalist, like Rabe the dramatist, is fascinated by the rituals of combat, the ceremony of struggle. Whether playful or analytical, Rabe's articles on sports reveal his interest in the struggle between combatants and the effects of the struggle on the psyches of players and spectators alike.

Rabe's two stories on rugby, which have much in common, are aimed at two different audiences. In the Philadelphia story, Rabe is full of information about local teams in Plymouth, Villanova, Bryn Mawr, Whitemark, and other Philadelphia environs. For New Haven readers he charts wins and losses of teams in places such as Hartford or Newport, Rhode Island. In both stories Rabe discusses the history of the game, its "rhythms" and "moves," its playing fields and terminology, its seasons and its laws and punishments (he speaks of the "controlled" violence in the *Philadelphia Magazine*). Especially lively are Rabe's remarks on the camaraderie of the game—the post-game challenges, parties, and songs ("often wild and vulgar"—*Sunday Pictorial*). On deeper reflection, Rabe muses about the effect of the game, played without "protective gear," has on the player: "The pleasures are the pleasures that come from risk, from defying the wills of others, and dealing with difficult physical tasks within a context of precise rules" (*Sunday Pictorial*). Players must learn the venerable "gestures of respect and defiance, the two emotions that are at the center of the game."

The *Pictorial* editor's headnote to Rabe's article on boxing reads: "*Pictorial* staff writer Rabe attended the Quarry-Frazier heavyweight championship bout with the idea of looking into the reality of this one event and comparing it with the theory of philosopher Paul Weiss's book *Spirit: A Philosophic Inquiry.*" Quotations from Weiss, interspersed throughout the story, are the leaven for Rabe's own comments. In one of his most speculative articles (one is sorely tempted to label it an hermeneutical essay), Rabe probes to find the meaning behind, and the truths of existence in, this famous fight. He discusses the system in which the fighter works, the capitalists of boxing (the "arrangers and watchers" whose "dark dollar had power"), and the loss and acquisition of reputation (including how a victor earns the reputation of all the fighters his opponent once defeated). Most important, Rabe distinguishes the "real" fight from the "ceremony" of the fight ("the entrance of the participants into the ring").

Using Jerry Quarry as a salient example, Rabe offers thought-provoking generalizations about what goes on philosophically in the ring. In that ring Quarry was "exorcising the ghosts of other men's voices that had derided his previous efforts." The fighter "was walking into reality embodied in this vision of himself"; he had to confront the changing identity of his opponent and his own knowledge to "become himself." Chronicling Quarry's lapse into defeat (his decision "to touch the dark side of the dare"), Rabe speculates about the "confrontation with defeat." He concludes that the fighter's choice to suffer defeat is noble and forges a new relationship with his opponent. Victory is less important; the bout is important "more for what he wanted to feel than what he wanted to make happen."

As elsewhere, journalist Rabe reports on the "combat" of men, the hollowness of ceremony, and the ability of the combatants to learn from defeat and transcend the meager rewards society can offer them. Appropriately enough, one of the epigraphs to *Streamers* is Sonny Liston's immortal observation: "They so mean around here, they steal your sweat." Jerry Quarry knew this and other matters about the ring, too.

Two playful pieces on local sporting events reveal Rabe's sense of humor. In "The Great Inner (Space) Race" (June 7, 1970), he reveled in the antics of the Sixth Annual Swiss Ski Club gathered at the peaceful, old Housatonic River near Cornwall, Connecticut, to crawl, run, splash, and slide down the river in an odd assortment of inner tubes, balloons, and bathing outfits. Rabe's description sparkles with comedy in the Stephen Crane vein. At the starting point on the river bank, the participants looked "like a bunch of frontier yahoos gathered for the start of an 1880's land rush." The starter's hat resembled a piece of "angel food cake made of straw." And then, in the chaotic splashing to win, the Swiss Ski Club seemed like a "herd of doughnuts." In the short "High Expansion Winter," Rabe offers a few melodious paragraphs on the joys children experience when the fire department sprays snow-like Jet X high expansion foam at the Pine Rock Field in the middle of summer. Printing this article on "winter in summer" in the January 25 issue of the *Pictorial* is, moralizes Rabe, "a sign of how we wish for what we do not have."

The symbolic possibilities of a journey interested Rabe so much that he devoted three of his *Pictorial* stories to trips—"A Wanderer Passes Through New Haven" (June 22, 1969), "On Different Journeys" (Aug. 24, 1969) and "Return to the Orient" (Mar. 15, 1970). Of course, descriptions of journeys of one type or another run throughout other Rabe stories, but in these three articles it is the journey itself and what it teaches the traveler that critically occupy Rabe's imagination and powers of analysis.

In the two-page "On Different Journeys," University of Bridgeport drama students travel to Amsterdam to compete in the Holland Drama and Music Festival with the adaptation of James Joyce's *Finnegans Wake*. Taking this journey "to a nation of strangers," the students were shocked from the collision of cultural values. While Rabe records the clash he also emphasizes the power of art to transcend cultural boundaries. Not really concerned about political issues, the students encountered unsavory views about their country in other competitors' plays and consequently entered a "circle of pressure." In the course of their rehearsals and through the production itself they experienced changing emotions about themselves and their homeland. But most important of all, concludes Rabe, they embarked "on a venture into themselves and the character of their own country they had thought they left behind." They learned that Americans were not just brash and shallow.

"Return to the Orient" is required reading for anyone who wants to understand Rabe's *Sticks and Bones*, first staged as *Bones* at Villanova in February 1969. One of Rabe's most hauntingly beautiful articles for the *Pictorial*, this story recounts the month-long journey of New Haven businessman Harvey Sussman (and his wife) to Asia, especially down "the length of Indonesia." It is a memory trip for Sussman who during World War II was a translator in Burma for the OSS. He returns to make sure the war is over and that it is not going on without him and also because he has not "put his feelings of fascination away." Ever since he was enrolled in the Oriental Studies program at Yale after the war, Sussman wanted to return. "Like a burn, Southeast Asia had marked him." Rabe's poetic description of the Sussman journey—of the people, places, fragrances, and legends— arouses our senses with delight and mystery. On his journey Sussman is often protected in the bubble of luxury hotels or in air-conditioned vehicles. Unfortunately, Rabe notes, Sussman declines a trip on a ship, "black and dirty as if the wood had been burned," which would have shown him "the Asia into which he had not yet gone." The story thus ends with a reference to the secret of the Orient Sussman might have learned but did not and the paradox that accompanies such knowledge in Rabe's rendition of this symbolic journey.

Rabe's story of Craig Aronsen ("A Wanderer Passes Through New Haven") also depends upon symbolic journeys for its effectiveness. Aronsen, who spends his life roaming the globe from the Alps to America and who was then visiting New Haven, is portrayed through Rabe's words as a remarkable traveler, one to be sought out for his wisdom. An artist (he sculpts and paints), Aronsen had the fear "cauterized" out of him; he has inner courage and uncommon vision. Rabe seizes on these virtues to explain why and how Aronsen becomes a part of (or at least unafraid of) the landscapes through which he passes—fields with copperheads, mountains with bobcats, the very seas themselves. Aronsen fills many of the roles that seemed to intrigue Rabe— the artist who is also a loner, the visionary whose mysticism is communicated through nature, and the self-sufficient hero whose fortitude is unshakable. Although unstated, one assumes that, for Rabe, Aronsen is a modern-day Thoreau in love with nature's artwork. In a marvelously lyrical sentence, Rabe observes of Aronsen: "There are spots of trees flowing so furiously he has walked among the topmost branches upon a webwork bridge of limbs, feeling only the exhilaration of height." But the violent and the ugly also enter Rabe's story through his description of Aronsen's journey to calm an artist in jail for having committed a gruesome murder.

Much can be learned about David Rabe from his responses to the books, movies, and plays he reviewed for the "Arts and Leisure" section of the *New Haven Register*. Undeniably the most significant review (at least insofar as offering parallels with Rabe's plays) that Rabe wrote was of Martin Russ's *Happy Hunting Ground* ("The War . . . And What It Does To Men"). Subtitled "An Ex-Marine's Odyssey," Russ's description of the terrible and trivial events of the Vietnam War surely confirmed many of Rabe's own beliefs. Rabe lavishes praise on Russ's book: it is "not the only good or important book to have been published recently about the war, but it is the only one of its kind, filling a gap that the moral and political books have left." That gap is filled, as Rabe points out, by Russ's view of the war as ignoble (unlike World War II), his picture of the carnage and contradictions of the war, and his portrait of soldiers dry of guilt over the "endless array of corpses" they see or produce. Rabe is equally impressed by Russ's style, which he characterizes as "beautiful for the sheer immediacy of its writing."

The other two books Rabe reviewed—both novels—also contained provocative views with which Rabe agreed. "The Unreachable" is Rabe's title for his review of *Victoria*, an early work by Knut Hamsun who was to write *Pan*, which according to Rabe, was "one of the finest novels ever written." *Victoria*, says Rabe, is a "slight small love gesture." The characters learn that human confrontations are dangerous affairs, in part because of the disguises people adopt. If *Victoria* deals with failed love, then *Fat City* (a novel by Leonard Gardner that Rabe reviewed under the title of "Beyond the Power to Redeem") explores failed fighters, washed-up boxers and their shady promoters, men who are lost to themselves and who have no sense of women. Some of the events in *Fat City* that Rabe cites— boxers lace their gloves with razor blades—are sheer horror. (In *Sticks* soldiers stitch razor blades into their hats to use as a kind of lethal salute.) In both *Victoria* and *Fat City* Rabe read and reacted to the crimes of heart that are forcefully present in his own plays, especially *Sticks and Bones* and *In the Boom Boom Room.*

Rabe reviewed six plays for the *Register*. Two of these were performed at campus theatres—a Yale production of Strindberg's *Crimes* and an adaptation of James Joyce's *Finnegans Wake* at the University of Bridgeport. The success of the latter production brought the school into the world of international drama competition Rabe wrote about in his *Pictorial* article "On Different Journeys" (Aug. 24, 1969). Two more of Rabe's reviews surveyed productions of *South Pacific* and Robert Anderson's *I Can't Hear You When the Water's Running* done at a little theatre playhouse, the Westport Summer Theatre. And his other two reviews examined performances given by professional theatre companies—*Whistle in the Dark* at the Long Wharf Theatre and a strenuously avant-garde *Wanton Soup* staged at La Mama. Rabe's reviews of *South Pacific* and *Wanton Soup*— polar opposites as dramatic works—illuminate some representative views that he held about myths in the theatre.

Rabe's review of *South Pacific* (Sept. 2, 1969), signed only with his initials, comprehensively looks at the production of this seminal musical. From the start Rabe announces that viewing *South Pacific* "from any vantage point but nostalgia would be foolish." Of those nostalgic elements Rabe found the music "amazing" (it will outlive the era for which it was composed, he affirms) and the jokes and vaudeville skits comically appropriate. But when Rabe scrutinizes the myths that lie behind *South Pacific* he becomes harshly critical. Where the musical is "wrong and weak" is in the story it tells. *South Pacific* for Rabe presents "World War II as a fairy tale," and while the reality of that tale was legitimate "the myths are not."

As a reviewer and a playwright, Rabe was vitally concerned about the truths that shaped a work of art. In his own plays already in drafts (*Bones* and *Pavlo Hummel*) Rabe sought to debunk the misleading myths that controlled national and domestic policy. For him *South Pacific* distorted the truths of war that his own plays painfully sought to expose. Rabe concludes his review with a bitterly ironic prediction that events in Vietnam would soon bring true. Speaking of the distorted myths of *South Pacific*, Rabe observed that "In just a few more years we will probably get it all again under the title 'Southeast Asia.'" If Bob Hope brought *South Pacific* to the boys in Nam, then Rabe carried *Pavlo* and *Sticks* to the folks back home.

In December 1969 Rabe reviewed Ching Yeh's *Wanton Soup*, then being done at La Mama's Experimental Theatre Club. Intrigued by things Oriental, Rabe found Yeh's play "a work of many wonders and mysteries."

As he describes it, Yeh's play works through transformations. On stage characters undergo strange cultural and psychic shifts. For example, a Santa Claus becomes Buddha, a woman with many diverse ethnic features (Japanese pajamas, New York accent, American hair) reminds Rabe of "Barbara Streisand out of Elaine May," and babies crawl from their dead earth mother. Unlike the dishonest myths shaping *South Pacific*, Rabe approvingly, almost rapturously, testifies that "Myth and fantasy are the realms in which the play lives." His concluding sentence captures the universal truths that Rabe admired in Yeh's play and no doubt hoped to emulate in his own work: " . . . the play seems a rendition of [Yeh's] psyche—his person—a presentation of much humor and gentleness wrought out of struggle of much agony to uncover and know his truest, scientific, sexual, Eastern, Western, transitory and eternal name." These words serve as guideposts to many ideas embedded deep in Rabe's plays.

The Westport Summer Theatre and La Mama's Experimental Theatre Club seem worlds apart, yet Rabe's reviews of productions at both places shed light on his views on myths in drama. Strangely enough, the American jingoistic ethos of *South Pacific* and the mystery of Oriental transformations in *Wanton Soup* had already tragically collided in Rabe's *Bones*, which had been staged months before he reviewed these two productions.

BONES TO *STICKS AND BONES*

In the Rabe canon *Sticks and Bones* is unquestionably the most controversial play; it was controversial in America and behind the Iron Curtain. *Sticks and Bones* began as *Bones*, which Rabe wrote after *Pavlo Hummel*. As we saw, Rabe was helped by a Rockefeller grant in playwrighting and also by an assistantship from Villanova University. The world premiere of *Bones* took place at Vasey Theatre on the Villanova campus on Thursday, February 7, 1969; the play ran that weekend and the next weekend, too—February 14-16. It was directed by Rabe's teacher and friend, James J. Christy, who thought so highly of Rabe's work that he wrote to a number of local drama critics, Ernest Schier from the *Philadelphia Evening Bulletin* among them, urging them to attend a performance of this extraordinary play. The young playwright went by the name of D. William Rabe at this time.

The names of the family were not Ozzie, Harriet, David, and Ricky in the original production. Instead they were Ozzie, Ginger, David, and Richie (and in another draft Ozzie was known as Andy). Speaking of Ginger's performance at Villanova, one critic wondered, "What ever happened to Harriet?" Rabe answered that critic's question three years later in the interview with Jerry Tallmer. Asked why the names of the parents in one version of the play were Andy and Ginger, Rabe replied: "In the very original script they were Ozzie and Harriet. But when it was done at Villanova there was some worry about possible legal things, so they became Andy and Ginger." The question of the names was later hotly debated with Joe Papp and Jeff Bleckner (who directed the play). Rabe noted: "We finally decided to go back to Ozzie and Harriet. I might provide an alternative four names for the parents and the two sons in the printed version . . . but I like Ozzie and Harriet. I think it's right as it is. It's a dimension. It's myth, you know. A whole thing to work against or with. Like Agamemnon." Ironically, in 1971 Richard Watts wondered why Rabe ever chose the Nelson family names since they added, he thought, an "unnecessarily extraneous element" to the play.

Judging from their response, local critics (with one exception noted below) realized they were watching the work of a young man fated to become a major playwright. Beyond doubt, *Bones* launched Rabe's career as Philadelphia's own playwright. The first review of *Bones*—and what might be regarded as Rabe's first major professional review—was written by Samuel Singer and appeared in the *Philadelphia Inquirer* on February 7, 1969. Singer admitted that "Rabe has talent" and characterized *Bones* as "an angry play" that attacked war, racism, hypocrisy, and, most of all, a "lack of human feeling, not just failure to understand but failure to try to understand." Singer found Rabe's use of a "stream of consciousness" technique fascinating and declared that the characters are "so strongly drawn" that one is "ready to jump onto the stage and try and shake some sense or sensitivity" into David's parents and brother. But, as Singer pointed out, the play had faults; the writing "is not always convincing," the characters' insensitivity is "incredible" ("the basic weakness" of *Bones*), and the imagery is sometimes "blurred." Still, Singer applauded Rabe's effort and the Villanova production, especially "the superb split-level setting" by J. James Andrews.

On February 11 Ernest Schier's review appeared in the *Philadelphia Evening Bulletin.* An important figure in Rabe's career, Schier was one of Rabe's earliest and most loyal supporters. Schier prophetically proclaimed: "I believe *Bones* is the best American play to come out of the war in Vietnam and . . . I think its author, 28-year-old D. William Rabe, is a poet-playwright with a future." Schier was full of praise for Rabe's "talent for poetic images," "theatrical images," and "ironic comedy." Such talent notwithstanding, Schier found that *Bones* was in parts "overwritten" and gently rebuked Christy for not having Rabe "edit and refine his play." However, Schier was enthusiastic about Rabe's future and complimentary about Villanova's production, which he believed showed an "act of courage" and "openmindedness." Three years later, on April 27, 1972, Schier was to look back on this auspicious production of *Bones* and write of Christy and Rabe: "Between them they have made an important and valuable contribution to American Theater."

Joshua Ellis, the reviewer for the *Villanovan* (the campus newspaper), also was impressed. He observed: "We have a production on campus that is so menacing—and I mean that in the best possible sense—so well crafted, the Theatre Department is rightly proud." Ellis compared Rabe with Albee and Pinter in using "silence and action" but noted that Rabe "seems to be at odds with himself. He is a poet and a dramatist and these two elements have yet to be coordinated." Ellis characterized *Bones* as "a work of art in the making." Considering the many revisions the play would subsequently go through, Ellis was more prophetic than he may have realized. His conclusion, though, was that *Bones* was a "fine play," even though the "intentionally obscure ending will baffle you." Most critical of the production, Ellis complained that *Bones* deserved "stronger" direction with more "guts and gore." Ellis commented in detail on the acting abilities of the cast—David (David Powers), Ginger (Regina Rappaport), Ozzie (Brian Morgan), and Richie (William Hickey). Of Kaity Tong, who played Zung, Ellis found that her "looks suggest poetry."

The lone torpedo of the first production of *Bones* was fired by Richard Gottlieb in the *Distant Drummer*, a Philadelphia publication founded in 1967, having a circulation of about 8,000, and dedicated to the principles of avant-gardism.[14] Gottlieb was ruthless. Rabe was "no playwright" and his first act crowded in everything imaginable about America. Gottlieb jeered: "I'm still not sure whether Mr. Rabe intended his play to be a comedy . . . ." Of Rabe's speeches on mangled bodies, Gottlieb stated "I assume they were supposed to bring the war right into our living rooms" and further carped that there was "nothing understandably human" about the "ridiculous" family Rabe presented. Gottlieb lectured Rabe that audiences need something "comprehensible about the characters before they can appreciate their stupidity." Gottlieb's barbs would have stung more had he seen the entire play; but, as he himself admitted, he walked out after the first act and apologized for his "bad behavior." For that behavior Gottlieb received a stinging letter from Rabe who mocked his "real true-blue half-assed" review and compared Gottlieb's tactics to a Nixon ploy. A copy of that letter fumes in the Mugar Library at Boston University, where some of Rabe's papers are stored.

As he would do with many of his other plays, Rabe revised *Bones* until it became *Sticks and Bones*. An article in the *Philadelphia Inquirer* for September 30, 1971 reports that Rabe, who had been in New York for the production of *Pavlo*, was back at Villanova "on a lighter teaching schedule" to work on revisions of *Bones*. *Sticks and Bones* opened at Joseph Papp's Public Theatre—at the Anspacher Theatre—on November 7, 1971, while *Pavlo* was still going strong after eight months at the Public's Newman Theatre. When *Sticks and Bones* opened Rabe made theatre history. This was the first time that a dramatist (excluding Shakespeare) had two plays performed at the same time at the New York Shakespeare Festival, a grand Off-Broadway achievement. *Sticks and Bones* ran for 121 performances at the Anspacher until it closed on February 20, 1972.

In the opinion of the New York critics, *Sticks* was a welcome addition to *Pavlo*. T. E. Kalem conjectured that *Sticks* "might be a sequel to *Pavlo Hummel*"; and Irma Pascal Heldman (of the *Wall Street Journal*) said it might "be regarded as a companion piece" to *Pavlo*. Martin Gottfried went even further claiming that *Sticks* was "far more than a worthy successor. It is a striking and original play." *Sticks* "takes up where *Pavlo Hummel* leaves off"; *Pavlo* deals with the battlefield and *Sticks* with the homecoming. In *The Villager* Lillian Africano judged *Sticks* "equally frightening" as *Pavlo*. George Oppenheimer of *Newsday* found that Rabe "blends reality with fantasy" in *Sticks* as he had done in *Pavlo*. A number of reviewers linked the two plays in the brutal ways they dramatized the influence of Vietnam on American culture. And although he had high praise for *Sticks*, Clive Barnes nonetheless felt that *Sticks* was "less confident in its style and texture" than *Pavlo* was.

With his second New York premiere Rabe clearly established his reputation as a significant voice in the American theatre. Gottfried hailed him as an "extraordinary playwright" whose works have "begun a theatre season for the country—a season, a beginning, a sense that the theatre is alive." Barnes celebrated Rabe as "a most gifted playwright," and Richard Watts affirmed that he is an "undeniably arresting playwright." Kevin Sanders compared Rabe with Albee and Miller for his "lean and literate power"; and Heldman discerned O'Neill's "gnashing vitality" in Rabe's work. Honoring Rabe as one of "the more promising young U.S. playwrights," Kalem isolated his special talent for showing "pain distilled into compassion."

The euphoria about Rabe's promise translated into almost overwhelming praise for *Sticks*. Perhaps the most memorable pronouncement came from Barnes: ". . . what is splendid about the play is its dizzy feeling of using the dramatist's medium . . . and producing a play that takes a decently satirical glance at chaos, and a play that has a moral force that neither flinches nor sermonizes." Barnes was not alone in hearing a new, distinctive voice in the theatre, a voice right for the age and society it tried to reach. Writing for the *Saturday Review*, Henry Hewes may have been uncertain about the meaning of *Sticks* but he did recognize that the play was "invading with freshness and honesty some of the most painful ambiguities that afflict contemporary America." Sanders extolled *Sticks* as "the most powerful drama of the season." Leonard Harris called it "vital superior work," and Douglas Watt characterized Rabe's imagination in *Sticks* as "harrowing and powerful."

A number of elements in the play elicited specific interpretations from the reviewers, and these early reactions were expanded by or expended in explication by later critics. The play's message—or theme—was painfully apparent to Rabe's audiences. Complacency about the war, violence in America, national guilt, lack of communication in the family, and hypocrisy were large ideas flowing from the typewriters of many New York critics. The family in *Sticks* commanded much attention. More than one reviewer termed them a "cartoon family"; Barnes warned audiences that they might lose their familial moorings until they realized that Rabe had taken them "inside a political cartoon." Kalem correctly traced their lineage from right "out of an adman's dreams"; they had "boxtop veneers" for Kroll. To Watts they were "the most infuriating family" he had seen. William Glover likened their escapades to an episode in *All in the Family*.

The family—like the other characters in *Sticks*—was identified as a symbol in Rabe's morality play. Although some reviewers found Rabe's symbolism excessive or ponderous, it received a great deal of favorable attention. Watt insightfully pointed out, for example, that David was symbolic of "the entire war experience." Other critics maintained that David's physical blindness contrasted with the moral blindness of his family. Hewes found that the mysterious Hank Grenweller "obviously stands for the values that have led Americans astray." Other key symbolic elements of interest to the critics included the camera Rick flashes, the crass materialism seeping out of Ozzie's inventory of goods, and, of course, the omnipresent television set which, according to Gottfried, "represents the only vision of the family." The highly symbolic ending of *Sticks* baffled some of the critics yet seemed insightful, provocative, and necessarily cathartic for others.

The Public Theatre production drew much praise from the critics. Jeff Bleckner's direction was on target for Hewes, since it avoided the "artificial" on the one hand and the "real" on the other. Gottfried claimed Bleckner had a "thorough understanding" of the play. Kalem announced "the actors are perfect." David Selby's David had a "quiet menace" for Barnes; and the actor "gradually and awesomely let the poison flow" for Watt. Certainly establishing the right amount of distance in the role is essential to accomplish Rabe's dramatic goal. Kalem praised Selby for the "translucent poignancy" he injected into a character "tortured by lost youth, lost potency, lost potential." Seeing the weaker sides of some other characters, Barnes described Ozzie (Tom Aldredge) as "a little Babbitt of a fellow in need of love and a psychiatrist" and Harriet (Elizabeth Wilson) as "a mother who should only have Andy Hardy" as a son. Hewes more correctly, it seems, identified Tom Aldredge's Ozzie as being both "pathetic and insidious." Rick, as played by Cliff De Young, wonderfully exuded "lies and music" for some critics. Asa Gim, the ghostly Zung, was a "pool of silence" for Barnes. Charles Seibert's Father Donald was interestingly typed by Sanders as "a combination of Santa Claus and General Westmoreland."

On March 1, 1972, *Sticks and Bones* opened at New York's John Golden Theater at 252 West 45th Street. This was Rabe's first appearance on Broadway. At first Rabe was angry and apprehensive about the move to Broadway. As he pointed out in his Introduction to *Sticks* and *Pavlo* in the 1973 Viking edition, he feared *Sticks* "would be seriously endangered" in the "circus" world of Broadway, which "was no longer the place where good writing was tested against the best work of others." However, after brutally frank conversations with Joe Papp, Rabe agreed to the move. He liked the benefits of the Golden's proscenium stage where "the play would be at its best" and in the Viking Introduction explains in detail what those advantages were. The Broadway *Sticks* was also directed by Bleckner and used the same cast (with one exception) that performed at the Anspacher. Drew Snyder replaced David Selby as David. Two significant changes in staging occurred, too. David's suicide was now performed with the actor facing the audience instead of having his back to them as at the Public Theatre. And the ghost of Zung was more mercifully strangled behind a couch by Ozzie instead of being covered with a sheet.

The move to Broadway seemed to bode good things for Rabe and for Joseph Papp. It could promise more money (even though orchestra seats on the weekend at the Golden were a low $8.00 as opposed to the generally higher prices a Broadway production commanded). Unfortunately, Papp lost money on the 225 performances, which he subsidized from the profits of other Public Theatre ventures. More promising, however, the move could insure that Rabe's work would reach a larger, more politically powerful audience. Shortly after the play's arrival, a full-page ad appeared in the *New York Times* (Mar. 12, 1972) containing excerpts from glowing reviews penned by 14 extremely influential New York drama critics—representing newpapers and the electronic media—extolling the virtues of the play, the brilliance of the playwright, and the necessity of everyone seeing *Sticks*. The headline for the ad fortuitously offered the following review/command from Clive Barnes: "A Dazzling New Play. Go At Once!"

If the Broadway move was seen as advantageous for Rabe and Papp, *Sticks*'s arrival was presented as valuable, even salutary, for the Great White Way itself by many established critics. Douglas Watt observed: "How strange and how fitting that the New York Shakespeare Festival should be revitalizing Broadway." He hoped that the play and the cast would "all thrive uptown." Jerry Tallmer informed readers at the *New York Post* that "*Sticks* deserves to be there" (on Broadway), although were he choosing a Rabe play for such distinction it would have been *Pavlo Hummel*, Rabe's "far more mature and worked out drama."

The controversial subject matter of the play—and its impact on a Broadway audience—surfaced in a few reviews. Allan Wallach at *Newsday* recognized that *Sticks and Bones* "brings a fresh sense of seriousness and urgency to Broadway" and told his readers that it is "one of the best plays to be seen" there. Writing for the *Morning Telegraph*, Leo Mishkin asserted that while *Sticks* was not for those "Broadway theatre patrons looking primarily for diversion and entertainment," Papp did perform "an inestimable service in bringing it to even wider notice than it may have received before." Leonard Harris at WCBS favorably compared the arrival of *Sticks* on Broadway with the three other Papp productions that preceded it on the journey from the downtown Public Theatre (*Hair*, *Two Gentlemen of Verona*, and *No Place to Be Somebody*). Attacking the Broadway theatregoers' preference for happy, escapist entertainment, Harris concluded his review with a stinging indictment, doubtless very pleasing to playwright Rabe: "If you stay away because I say *Sticks and Bones* is serious, that's your loss. The state of mind it finds something rotten in is ours." Mutual Broadcasting's reviewer Virginia Woodruff might also have had the vulnerable targets of Rabe's satire in mind when she pronounced that "*Sticks and Bones* portrays the very heart of the middle class . . . ."

Sticks and Bones won a number of very prestigious awards. Beating out Neil Simon's *Prisoner of Second Avenue*, it captured the Tony Award for the Best Play of the 1971-1972 season. Rabe expressed amazement at having won the award; he has said: "I have almost no memory of the moment." Reflecting on the award, Rabe later observed: "If you win, you don't really beat anyone else. What happens is you become a part of the company of those men. And that in itself is more impressive."[15] Rabe should have also won the Pulitzer Prize, but for no announced reason the jurors refused to make an award in drama for the year. Edward Albee ten years earlier felt the same arrows of outrageous fortune when *Who's Afraid of Virginia Woolf?* was denied the Pulitzer. In addition to the Tony for *Sticks,* Rabe won a New York Drama Critics Circle Special Citation and the John Gassner Medallion for playwrighting from the Outer Drama Circle, although there was some confusion as a result of incorrect tallying. A poll of New York drama critics conducted by *Variety* found Rabe to be the most promising playwright of the year. Rabe was also the first recipient of the Elizabeth Hull-Kate Warriner Award, presented by the Dramatists Guild for his *Pavlo* and *Sticks.* The Hull-Warriner Award was begun to honor the playwright whose work most significantly dealt with highly controversial issues involving contemporary political, religious, or social issues.

Finally, in 1974 the American Academy and Institute of Arts and Letters gave Rabe an award ($3,000) for his outstanding plays, including *Sticks.* The following citation accompanying the award was written by Kurt Vonnegut who also was a member of the committee that chose Rabe and others for awards:

> To DAVID RABE, born in Dubuque, Iowa, in 1940, a veteran of Viet Nam: for his angry and handsome plays, and for finding words and feelings for the most deplorable and deadly war in our history. If we are ever to heal even a little bit, it will be with his plays that the healing began.[16]

As we saw, *Sticks and Bones* earned rave reviews on Broadway. A much more troublesome reception awaited Rabe's Tony Award-winning play when it was transformed into a teleplay. In 1972 Joe Papp signed an eight million dollar contract with CBS to produce 13 dramatic and cultural productions over four years. Rabe's *Sticks and Bones* was the second production under the terms of this contract. At first CBS thought *Sticks* was a wise, relevant choice for its viewers; then the network backed down and out. This story forms one of the most controversial chapters in the history of Rabe's play and in the history of American broadcasting. Stuart Little's book *Enter Joseph Papp* explores every detail of Papp's involvement in the CBS fray; and articles in newspapers across the nation, especially the *New York Times* and the *Philadelphia Inquirer*, reported almost every word exchanged between the feuding parties. Students of Rabe should read and savor these accounts. All that I propose to do below is offer highlights of the battle.

Under contract to CBS, Papp worked with director Robert Downey and Rabe on the television script of *Sticks.* The result was radically different from Rabe's play. Rabe had a stormy relationship with Downey, writing and rewriting his Broadway success many times. Downey himself made a good number of changes in the teleplay *Sticks*, changes in tone and texture, and reworked the text a great deal to accommodate his own polemical views. Zung, who was strangled under a sheet at the Public Theatre and behind a couch on Broadway, was stuffed into a garbage bag by the xenophobic family. Downey's camera work further transformed Rabe's drama. CBS also required changes, which included dropping the Nelson family names; they became Andy and Ginger for the parents and Daniel and Bucky for the boys. The cast for the CBS *Sticks* included Anne Jackson as Ginger the mother; Tom Aldredge played Andy the father (as he had done on Broadway); Alan Cauldwell was the guitar-strumming Bucky; and Cliff De Young, who had played Rick on Broadway, was now the blind veteran Daniel. Asa Gim still played the ghostly Vietnamese Zung as she had on Broadway. And Brad Sullivan chewed a cigar in his role as Father Donald while Joe Fields (of *Pavlo* fame as we shall see) played the Sergeant Major. Downey shot the film in January 1973 in a New England country house in Bronxville, New York. The cost of the production was $500,000. Executives at CBS saw the teleplay, liked it at first, wanted to schedule it in February, but finally decided to air *Sticks and Bones* in March.

The big day was Friday, March 9 and the time was 10:00 p.m. EST. But on March 6, three days before airing the play, CBS cancelled it, said *Sticks* was to be postponed indefinitely, and ran the *Cincinnati Kid* instead. Seventy-one of CBS's 184 affiliates refused to carry Rabe's play; they had seen it in a closed-circuit screening and backed out. Even two of the five stations that CBS owned itself refused to run *Sticks*. The course of the war had changed from 1972 to 1973. In March a large group of P.O.W.'s was scheduled to come home, and the climate of opinion in America was, these affiliates feared, downright hostile to Rabe's drama of a returning veteran.

Offering CBS's official explanation, the president of the network Robert Wood was quoted as saying that showing *Sticks* "at this time might be unnecessarily abrasive to the feelings of millions of Americans whose lives or attention are at the moment emotionally dominated by the returning P.O.W.'s and other veterans who have suffered the ravages of war." Wood then added: " . . . the play deals in compelling allegorical terms with the callous reception of an American veteran returning blinded from the war. Most of us agree that the production is a serious, concerned, and powerful tragedy of some of the uglier aspects of human nature . . . ." The decision to veto *Sticks* came even higher up than from Wood. William S. Paley, Chairman of the Board at CBS, saw a screening of *Sticks* and nixed the play. On March 19, some ten days after *Sticks* was to have been aired, Paley admitted: "Someone finally had to bite the bullet, and although this decision, like all important ones, had to a degree to be arrived at collectively, the decision properly went out over my name, and I stand by it."

Words—like halberds—flew from Papp and Rabe toward CBS. Papp accused the network of "a cowardly cop-out, a rotten affront to freedom of speech and a whittling away at the First Amendment." He thought CBS's decision was "frightening," since "They're accepting control by their affiliates, denying millions the right to see an important work of art. This is a First Amendment issue." Papp accused CBS of being pressured by the Nixon administration, which tried to influence programming done by the affiliates to create a politically balanced schedule. What infuriated Rabe was CBS's confusing, contradictory behavior. In a March 7, 1973 interview, parts of which appear in a story by Dubuque *Telegraph Herald*'s Mike Tighe ("CBS Puts Off 'Untimely' Rabe Play"), Rabe said he was initially surprised that CBS had even agreed to do the play. When they decided to do it, "They seemed to be functioning out of an ambivalence of wanting to do something they thought would be good, make some sort of serious statement, then when it got down to the wire, they hesitated." Rabe recognized that the play was controversial but noted in that important interview with Mike Tighe of the Dubuque *Telegraph Herald*: "I think that to be afraid to put it on the air is not a good thing. I don't know that it's good to take away the opportunity to see it when people could just turn the channel if they don't like it."

The broadcast war having been announced, sides were drawn on the battlefield. The pro-CBS forces included the *Chicago Tribune*, Newton Minow (the former Chairman of the Federal Communications Commission), and a few other groups. On the Papp-Rabe side were numerous newspapers and the A.C.L.U. which sent a strong telegram to Wood saying: "This explanation cannot disguise the fact that the postponement was based on the controversial political content of the production. The CBS decision offends the First Amendment. It interferes with both the rights of the creative artist involved and the public's right to view a dramatic production dealing with an important social issue" (quoted in "A.C.L.U. Decries C.B.S. Over Play," Albin Krebs, *New York Times*, Mar. 9, 1973). A large number of theatre critics also cried foul. Among them was Rabe's ardent supporter Ernest Schier. In his column for the March 8, 1973 *Bulletin*, Schier conjectured in anger: "CBS may be the first institution anywhere to attempt to sweep a war under the rug." Similarly, in Rabe's hometown of Dubuque, a columnist for the *Herald,* Mike Tighe, ironically claimed "CBS was right for the wrong reason." Rabe's "masterful work" was "a moody production that should be viewed intact," free from foolish commercial interruptions. Tighe took CBS to task for pandering to America's wishes to forget Vietnam.

As Rabe, Papp, and others were aware, CBS's postponement might have been two decades long. According to the contract the network signed with Papp, though, they owned the rights to the teleplay through the current season, which would come to an end in September of 1973. Deciding to reschedule *Sticks*, CBS finally aired the teleplay on Friday, August 17, from 9 through 11 p.m. EST. This time, 94 of the 184 affiliates refused to carry the play, including CBS stations in Providence, Houston, Salt Lake City, and Cincinnati. *TV Guide* reported these broadcast facts, and also noted that some independent stations, on the other hand, even asked for *Sticks*, including PBS stations in Seattle and Schenectady. Papp's response to the new CBS decision was that "CBS is getting an albatross off its back." Ultimately Papp and CBS parted ways about his producing any further cultural programs for the network. Viewer response to the rescheduled *Sticks* was not as vocal and angry as the affiliates earlier had anticipated. A headline in the August 18, 1973 issue of the *Philadelphia Evening Bulletin,* for example, read "Sticks and Bones Stirs Little Local Comment." Of course, some angry letters were written to CBS and to newspapers.

The television critics were not nearly as effusive in their praise of the teleplay as the Broadway reviewers had been of the play. For example, Rex Polier, who admitted that he did not see the play, found the television adaptation "repetitious" and "vexing" and "hardly rated all that fuss." But Harry Harris (from the *Philadelphia Inquirer*) began his review with the following warning: "This program may be dangerous to your mental health" and concluded "it's 'must' viewing for anyone who welcomes an occasional living room jolt." Harris pointed out that "Downey's own caustic point of view penetrates *Sticks* to such a degree that he may deserve co-author credit." Downey's hand was seen as responsible for placing greater emphasis on the father than on the son.

Looking back after 15 years, we might say that the furor over the televised *Sticks* seems overblown. Today we are accustomed to seeing the graphic violence and cruel stupidity of the war depicted in such films as *Apocalypse Now, The Killing Fields,* or *Platoon.* But, as Rabe himself noted, when he was preparing *Sticks* for television, the only movie about the war Americans had seen up to that point was *Green Berets.* And John Wayne was not Daniel, alias David. Again, David Rabe must be credited with an important contribution to our understanding the war and its effects on the national psyche.

Another chapter in the controversial history of Rabe's play might be entitled "*Sticks and Bones* Behind the Iron Curtain." From November 1972 to April 1973 a pirated version of Rabe's play (*Brat Bratu—As Brother is to Brother*) was staged at Moscow's Sovremennik Theatre. It was directed by

Andrzej Wajda, the famous Polish director, and starred Igor Kvasha, a 40-year-old actor playing the young veteran David. This Soviet version distorted the text, the characterization, and the meaning of Rabe's *Sticks and Bones*. According to an article in the *New York Times*, by Theodore Shabad, to whom I am indebted for much of my information, "American plays on the Soviet stage, with a few exceptions, are so directed as to stress any grotesque qualities that may be found in either the play's characters or structure" ("*Sticks and Bones* Wins Favor in Soviet," Mar. 12, 1973). *Sticks and Bones* (or *Brat Bratu*, rather) was no exception; it was nothing short of Russian propaganda directed against a warmongering United States. Of Ricky, one Soviet critic wrote: "He snaps pictures of his blind brother as he might have snapped pictures of those who were shot at Song My. He in fact personifies Song My" (quoted in Shabad). Another Soviet reviewer after seeing *Brat Bratu* warned the Russian youth to beware of such American diseases. Of course, the Russians pleaded the truthfulness of their ways. In an article for *Pravda* (Jan. 1974), vitriolic actor and director Viktor Komissarzhevsky professed that *Brat Bratu* "accurately portrays the deep spiritual crisis of a sick society" (quoted in Shabad).

Papp legitimately cried foul. On January 10, 1973 he sent a formal letter of protest to the Soviet embassy in Washington. And on March 18, Rabe was sufficiently angered to write a letter to the Soviets which was printed in the *New York Times*. Rabe expressed his "disgust" with the pirated Soviet production which distorted the purpose and design of the play. Attacking the Russians for using a 40-year-old actor to play 20-year-old David, Rabe denied that there was "art or seriousness" in their effort. The Russians turned Rabe's play into propaganda by not seeing the universal application of its message. Professing that *Sticks* was "about sophisticated tribalism" everywhere, Rabe demanded that the Russians see themselves in his play and that they desist from performing it at once. Or, if they refused, they should include his letter in their program or post it outside their theatre.

On April 12 the Russians replied—incompletely and unsatisfactorily—to Rabe's charges. An article in *Literaturnaya Gazeta* (*The Weekly of the Writers' Union*) charged that the decision by CBS to cancel a showing of *Sticks and Bones* proved that censorship existed in America and that freedom in Rabe's homeland was a fiction. Moreover, the Russian retort mocked Rabe for not addressing his letter to the right and current director of the Sovremennik Theatre—Oleg Tabakov. Oleg Yefremov, to whom Rabe addressed his letter, had stepped down from that post two years earlier. Tabakov himself got into the fray by denouncing Rabe's claim that changes were made in the play and chided him for judging a production he had never seen.[17]

Moscow was not the only communist country to stage *Sticks and Bones*. On May 6, 1973, *Jak Brat Bratu* [*Like Brother to Brother*] opened at Theatre Stary in Krakow, Poland. The director of the theatre, Jan Pawel Gawlik, one of Poland's leading directors, wrote a three-page analysis of the play in the program. According to Gawlik, Rabe's play had a deeply moral message. Except for some comments on the shallowness of the middle class and the mechanization of the individual, Gawlick really did not turn *Sticks* into a piece of anti-American propaganda. Instead he focused on the aesthetics of the play. Interestingly enough, the cast of characters at the Theatre Stary is listed as David, Rick, Matka (Mother), and Ojciec (Father), and Hua-Lan (not Zung) who was played by Jadwiga Lesniak-Jankowsha. Evidently, Polish television did not show reruns of *The Adventures of Ozzie and Harriet*.

In February 1974 *Sticks and Bones* came to Budapest at the Pesti Szinhazban. The Hungarian title of the play was *Bot es gitar*, which in English means *Stick and a Guitar*, a translation done by Bakti Mihaly. Obviously, Rick's decadent music played a significant role in the Hungarian production. In the Hungarian reviews Rabe did not fare terribly well. Although he was compared with such absurdists as Pinter and Albee, Rabe was not given credit for writing a major piece of work.

In addition to these productions in Russia and the Soviet block, *Sticks* has had an interesting history in other parts of the world. It was staged in Madrid in September 1973, but few records exist for this performance. A Greek production took place at the Papamichael-Voyouklai Theatre in Athens from approximately November 14 to December 17, 1972. The Melbourne Theatre Company, on Russell Street, performed the play from September 26 through October 10, 1972. Directed by John Summer, it starred Edwin Hodgeman as Ozzie, Irene Inescourt as Harriet, Tony Llewellen-Jones played Rick, Sean Scully was David, and Dimon Chilvers took the role of Father Donald. An Australian interest in Rabe's work at this time must partly be attributed to our ally's concern about the war that had been raging so long and also so close to their homeland. Overall, the Summer's production was well received. One reviewer in particular, Geoffrey Hutton for *The Age*, appreciated the way the Melbourne Theatre Company emphasized the black comedy in *Sticks*. The opening sentence of Hutton's review reveals that for Australians *Sticks* was best seen as a political allegory: "In a sense this play is a manifesto, a biting attack on the results of American policy in Vietnam, not only on the soldiers who were there, but on the public which closed its mind to truth."

The first and only (up to late 1986, that is) German-speaking production of *Sticks* was at the Schauspielhaus in Zurich, where Rabe's play was performed under the ironic title of *Willkommen* (*Welcome*). The German translation the Schauspielhaus used was done by Joachim Brinkmann who entitled his work *Knuppel und Knochen* (*Stick and Bone*). This production was directed by Tom Toelle, and starred Peter Arens as Ozzie and Margaret Ensinger as Harriet; Christopher Reiner was Rick and David was played by Ulrich Kuhlmann. Unfortunately, *Willkommen* did not win high marks from either the Zurich or the German critics and folded after only 15 performances. The reviewers pointed to the political message of Rabe's play and compared it with the post-World War II Heimkehier (or returning veteran) plays. Although the production was not successful, a very interesting document came out of it. The Schauspielhaus Zurich issued a 27-page program which could easily serve as a Vietnam casebook; it contains comments on the war (including some from Lt. Calley), photographs, and excerpts from German critics.

Sticks was staged in Toronto in November 1973 and in London in 1978. The London production received more attention from reviewers. It was done at the Theatre at New End from January 27 to February 25 and was directed by Lawrence Taubman. Ozzie and Harriet were played by Don Fellows and Pat Starr; their boys were played by Michael Tarn (Rick) and Peter Weller (David). The first Rabe play exported to Britian was *In the Boom Boom Room*, so *Sticks* gave the U.K. its first taste of Rabe's Vietnam trilogy. Irving Wardle admitted that it might be unfair to Rabe that the British were seeing his work "so late and out of sequence," but overall Wardle's assessment of the play and the production were highly favorable. He agreed that *Sticks* presented an "authentic American experience" and that while the play is "about experience good old American innocence keeps showing through." Seeing the play some seven years after its Public Theatre debut, Wardle was concerned about it being old fashioned. And while he found that the "pain and anger of the play have not dated," he did conclude that since "its public pretext has subsided into history, it does emerge as more old fashioned" than it did in 1971. Wardle used the phrase "old fashioned" to mean typically American in the treatment of the father, love, and the "ambiguously American attitude to violence." In his review for *Plays and Players*, Peter Stothard also liked the Theatre at New End production ("a subtle and powerful interpretation by an ad hoc American cast") and the play ("a near-masterpiece of moral theatre"). He readily conceded, though, that *Sticks* is "not an easy play to make work on stage" and that Rabe's "singular vision has to be mined and extracted rather than simply laid bare."

Under the title of *Bokire To Hone*, *Sticks and Bones* was performed in Tokyo in October 1981 by the Mingei Theatre Company using Marie Kai's translation. According to the Mingei program notes, David was a man blinded in Vietnam who returns to a home which was peaceful before the war. This production, judging by the attention it received in both the daily press and the monthly reviews, was very popular.

American productions of *Sticks* since its New York premiere have taken place all over the country. Two were done in Los Angeles, one in January 1976 and another in 1985. A major production of *Sticks* was staged by the Academy Theatre in Atlanta from March 12 through April 10, 1976. Directed by Frank Wittow, this *Sticks* cast John Stephens as Ozzie and Yvonne Tenney as Harriet; Larry Larson as Rick and Chris Curran as David. Director Wittow told audiences in their program guide that "*Sticks and Bones* is a truthful response to contemporary American mores by a courageous playwright. It is disturbing in the best meaning of the word." Reviewers agreed; they emphasized the terror and the agony captured in the Academy's production. *Sticks* has also been staged on campuses at Indiana University in November 1975 and at the University of Texas in December 1975.

THE BASIC TRAINING OF PAVLO HUMMEL

Bones (revised to *Sticks and Bones*) may have been performed before *The Basic Training of Pavlo Hummel*, but the latter play launched Rabe's career on the New York stage. *Pavlo Hummel* was the first Rabe play to be professionally produced, preceding *Sticks and Bones* at the New York Shakespeare Festival/Public Theatre by some seven months. *Pavlo Hummel* was also written before *Bones*; Rabe started the play about *Pavlo* in about June 1967, six months after returning from Vietnam. As Rabe noted in commenting on the early process of composition, in the Viking Introduction to the two plays, "In actuality *Pavlo* was under way long before *Sticks and Bones*. With a full draft of *Pavlo* completed, I began *Sticks and Bones*" (p. xix). He confirmed this order of composition in a later interview given jointly with Neil Simon and published in the *New York Times* on May 16, 1985: "In the beginning—with *Pavlo Hummel*—I wrote until I had a draft, and I didn't go to anything else. Once I had a draft, I started writing *Sticks and Bones*. When I had a draft of that, I went back to the other one."

The story behind Rabe's first major success reads like a fairy tale every aspiring playwright wishes would come true for him or her. For two years or more, Rabe tried to get *Pavlo* performed. As he told Jody Brockway in the *After Dark* interview, it was "rejected by almost all of America's regional and experimental theatres—including Long Wharf, the American Place, Chelsea, Yale, the O'Neill, Lincoln Center, and the Arena Stage." Rabe also sent a script of *Pavlo Hummel* in the mail to Joseph Papp, the impresario of the Public Theatre. At first Papp put the script aside but then one of his directors, Mel Shapiro, who had also received a copy from the hopeful Rabe, enthusiastically reminded Papp about it. Finding it fresh and provocative, Papp originally scheduled *Pavlo Hummel* as a workshop production in the relatively small Open Stage (seating 108) at the Public Theatre. But to Rabe's good fortune, Papp became very excited about the play and its expansiveness and decided to move it—even before it was to premiere at the Open Stage—to the larger Estelle R. Newman Theatre (seating 299) at the Public Theatre, making it a showcase performance. And so on May 20, 1970 the *Basic Training of Pavlo Hummel* had its world premiere, running for 363 New York performances before moving—with a few changes in cast—to Philadelphia's Locust Theatre for two weeks.

In the opinion of Ernest Schier, in his "Proving of Mr. Rabe" in the May 21, 1971 *Philadelphia Evening Bulletin*, the Public Theatre at this time was beyond doubt "the busiest, most progressive and most exciting theatre in America." Rabe's association and friendship with Papp proved beneficial for both men and will certainly go down in theatre history as a powerful alliance of promotion and talent. Unquestionably, Rabe was fortunate to have the opportunities provided by Joe Papp who, according to Leonard Probst in his review of *Pavlo* for NBC TV, was "to be congratulated for taking a chance on an unknown playwright." Papp hailed Rabe as "the most important writer we've ever had" and has compared him to Eugene O'Neill.[18] Beyond doubt, Rabe benefited from suggestions from Papp and others at the Public Theatre as he revised the original script of *Pavlo Hummel* during production. Rabe acknowledges in detail his debt to Papp in his *New York Times* article ("So We Got Papp in to See a Runthrough") and in the Introduction to *Pavlo* and *Sticks* (pp. xii-xv). Moreover, Rabe realized that his work was right for Papp, too. In a March 1972 interview with Ellen Kaye, he agreed: "I think my plays are strangely appropriate for Joseph Papp. We seem to agree about a lot of things, both theatrically and philosophically."

Like many other American playwrights whose first plays were smiled upon by the critic-gods of Gotham, Rabe skyrocketed to immediate fame, launched by the reviewers' superlatives. Clive Barnes of the *New York Times* hailed Rabe as "a new and authentic voice" in the theatre. In *Women's Wear Daily* Martin Gottfried euphorically announced that "David Rabe is someone to celebrate, anticipate and welcome." The "most important thing,"

George Oppenheimer of *Newsday* pointed out, was that "Mr. Rabe reveals a new and striking talent." John Lahr of the *Village Voice* called Rabe "the best talent the Public Theatre has discovered." In his wrap-up review in *Saturday Review* Henry Hewes maintained that Rabe was "possibly the most promising playwright" of the 1971 New York season. Numerous critics observed that as a veteran himself Rabe captured the language and rituals of military life perfectly; his "voice" and approach were unnervingly "real." Perhaps most gratifying to Villanova's Rabe was the review written by his early supporter, Ernest Schier of the *Philadelphia Evening Bulletin*. With a clear sense of vindication and pride in the local dramatist, Schier wrote that *The Basic Training of Pavlo Hummel* at the New York Shakespeare Festival Theatre "confirmed what is already known in local circles, that Rabe at 31 is a dramatist of considerable force and vision with a major career ahead of him."

The critics were nearly as generous with their applause for the play as they were for the playwright, although a few naysayers expressed reservations. It was inevitable that Rabe's treatment of the war would be contrasted with other plays on the same topic. And in virtually every instance Rabe's work was judged far superior to such plays as George Tabori's *Pinkville* or Megan Terry's *Viet Rock*. In her *New Yorker* review Edith Oliver unabashedly said about *Pavlo*: "It makes everything else I've seen on the subject seem skimpy and slightly false." Jack Kroll believed *Pavlo* "is the first play to deal successfully with the Vietnam War and the contemporary American army," a sentiment shared by Leonard Probst of NBC TV and John Simon in *New York*. Gottfried called the play "extraordinary," and John Schubeck in his review for ABC TV admitted *Pavlo* was "one of the most moving pieces of theatre I have seen in some time." In his *Village Voice* review, Dick Brukenfeld spoke for many in the audience when he observed that the play "rings with documentary truth." Rabe's strident brand of truth was not for the timid, the escapist audience nurtured on Broadway musical comedy. As George Oppenheimer warned, "*Pavlo Hummel* is not for weak stomachs." In his review for the *New Jersey Journal*, William A. Raidy somewhat comically linked Rabe's play with another war: "in many ways [*Pavlo*] might be considered the contemporary answer to *From Here to Eternity*."

The figure of Pavlo himself aroused both admiration for and a little disappointment in Rabe. Gottfried saw universal truths embodied in Rabe's gung-ho recruit: *Pavlo Hummel* "represents all of us in a single exercise of that ritual—an exercise that, when complete, concludes in a pointless death in a useless war." When he saw the play later in Philadelphia, William Collins observed that there is "something of Everyman and something of Kilroy" in Pavlo (*Philadelphia Inquirer* [April 6, 1972]). Most reviewers, however, refused to see themselves in Pavlo and instead chose to widen the distance between Pavlo and the audience. With characteristic understatement Barnes began his review noting that Pavlo has a "slight mental disturbance" and maintained that what makes Rabe interesting is "his obvious feel for the dynamics of character confrontation." Lahr in the *Village Voice* called Pavlo a "buffoon . . . so lonely and so lost that a set of shades and his green dress uniform can give him a new identity." Seeing Pavlo as "an eternal patsy in a phony world," Richard Watts of the *New York Post* found him a "ridiculous" creation and remarked that "I felt Pavlo never really developed as a character."

Candid disapproval came from other critics who objected to a lack of connection between Pavlo's basic training and his brutality on the battlefield and his meaningless death in a Saigon whorehouse. Most harsh of all was John Beaufort of the *Christian Science Monitor* who bluntly concluded that "*Pavlo Hummel* fails as drama because its characters—instead of rousing interest—are tiresome and depressing." Pavlo's unwinning ways have caused a number of critics to attack Rabe repeatedly instead of the system which creates and manipulates such a forlorn dogface. Focusing on Pavlo's ambiguity, Clare Woock of *Drummer* seemed to speak the wisest words of all when she directed attention to Pavlo's "dangerous innocence."

As the comments by Beaufort and Watts above demonstrate, Rabe's first New York attempt did not escape censure. While the critical reception was largely and enthusiastically positive, a few grumblings were heard. Interestingly enough, the types of objections Rabe's first reviewers raised still linger in the ongoing critical reaction to *Pavlo* and to Rabe's other works. Among problems some critics recorded were Rabe's diffuse, confusing plot and his inability to integrate various parts of the play. Lee Silver of the *Daily News*, for example, judged the play "somewhat uneven and a bit hazy in its development" and complained (mistakenly, I believe) that Pavlo's death at the beginning "dissipates the dramatic tension." Brukenfeld objected that the "irony" of the tragic ending "doesn't come off" and that the play has a "curious buckshot quality . . . as if Rabe has imposed a panoramic structure on his material . . . chopping rather than shaping it." Oppenheimer, who also found the plot "fragmentary," expressed mild dissatisfaction with what was to be a controversial element for many Rabe critics; Rabe "has dealt with symbols and subtleties, sometimes too subtle for complete understanding."

But if some of Rabe's early reviewers introduced caveats, many times unfoundedly, then at least one early critic called attention to a Rabe technique that would elicit recurrent praise for *Pavlo* and later Rabe plays. Kroll insightfully observed: "Young playwright David Rabe treats the Army as a microcosm of the ironies and personalities at large in society itself."

Rabe's first Off-Broadway play benefited from what the critics regarded as an exemplary production. Director Jeff Bleckner, a Vietnam veteran himself who was later to direct *Sticks* and *Orphan*, was singled out for special tribute by many reviewers who labeled his work "impressive," "superb," and "excellent." Lahr probably paid Bleckner the highest compliment: "There are some outstanding accomplishments in this play and the most significant is the fluid, carefully paced direction of Jeff Bleckner." Kroll cited examples of Bleckner's art which created a powerful syncopated choreographic rhythm that churns up "riptides of dramatic action, black humor, and vivid character." No doubt Bleckner, who also worked very closely with Rabe revising the script, understood that the playwright's meaning was most forcefully expressed through the series of rituals found in the play. Bleckner was quoted as saying that *Pavlo Hummel* was "about a young soldier seeking self identification in the Army system." Along with Bleckner's direction, David Mitchell's sparse, abstract setting captured the spirit of the play for the critics. For example, Gottfried acknowledged that Mitchell's set "is mostly space and light [and] . . . is perfectly adaptable to the play's cinematic style, with its interweaving and overlapping times and places."

William Atherton who played Pavlo also won applause from critics who saw his Pavlo accurately true to Rabe's intention, variously defined of course. In the Introduction to the Viking edition Rabe said of Atherton: "He had a Huck Finn mix of innocence, toughness, and mischievousness." To Gottfried, Atherton played Pavlo "with such compassion" that he greatly contributed to Rabe's "tragedy in the Greek sense." Similarly, Schubeck in his review for ABC TV believed that the actor's performance of Pavlo "draws deep sympathy for Pavlo when the heroics end at the end of the play." As far as Barnes was concerned, Atherton merited high praise: "Rawboned and awkward, good-natured but stupid," Atherton's Pavlo "goes through the play like a stifled cry of pain, going to his death like a slaughtered lamb." Commenting directly on Atherton's physical features and delivery, Lahr praised the actor's "angular gestures, his understated wit and tall tales, [which] contain a universe of anger and self-loathing." Lahr further noted that Atherton brought the right "stumbling gullibility" to the role. For John Simon, too, Atherton was "the perfectly befuddled Pavlo." Finally, William A. Raidy observed that Atherton "plays the comic-grotesque Pavlo in an incredibly believable manner."

Others in the cast of 25 received commendation for their fidelity to the roles Rabe created. Not surprisingly, the black actors were given special attention for their extraordinary performances. Joe Fields, who played First Sergeant Tower, won the critics' hearts (as he did Rabe's when the playwright first heard him at an audition), in part for his acting and in part for the literally central position Tower occupies in the play. Brukenfeld exulted over Fields's making Tower "the show's delight," correctly emphasizing the humor as well as the fright Rabe built in the role; Oppenheimer saluted Fields's Tower for "being a rabble-rousing revivalist whose religion is war." Simon also singled out Fields's "hilarious" portrayal with his "succulent cadences," and noted that the audience "laughed with pleasure each time Fields appeared." Both Gottfried and Kroll stressed the accuracy of Rabe's ear and eye in creating the drill instructor ably played by Fields; Kroll claimed that Fields was the "apotheosis of all first sergeants." Fields's portrayal of Tower according to Raidy was a fine example of "minor brass going through the motions of war." Ardell, played by Albert Hall, also captured critics' attention for his influence on Pavlo; Silver of the *Daily News*, perhaps ironically, calls Ardell "a model G.I."

Rabe was showered with awards for *Pavlo Hummel*. He won the *Village Voice*'s Obie Award for the Best Off-Broadway production. (Bleckner, too, won an Obie for his directing.) Rabe also earned a Drama Desk Award as well as the Elizabeth Hull-Kate Warriner Award ($3,000) of the Dramatists Guild Council for writing the 1970-1971 season's best plays (with *Sticks*) on a controversial subject. And he won the enviable support of one of the most powerful theatre producers in America—Joseph Papp— who promised to stage Rabe's future work, a promise wisely kept as we saw from the brief look at the history of *Sticks and Bones*.

The Theatre Company of Boston (TCB), directed by David Wheeler, staged a revival of the *Basic Training of Pavlo Hummel*, opening on April 24, 1977 at Broadway's Longacre Theatre. The TCB had done a very successful *Pavlo* in 1972 and decided to stage a new version of a past success in New York. The critics inevitably seized upon the changing political climate between Papp's 1971 Off-Broadway production and TCB's revival. With a sigh of disgust, T.E. Kalem noted in *Time* (May 9, 1977): "Now that the Viet Nam War is over and shamelessly and shamefully forgotten, the stress of the play has been shifted from outrage to pathos." For Kalem Rabe appropriately used a whorehouse as a "metaphor for U.S. involvement in Southeast Asia." Less willing to grant the continuing political importance of Rabe's play, Beaufort, in his review for the *Christian Science Monitor* (May 5, 1977), claimed: "Detached from the immediacy of the Vietnam conflict, the drama has lost something of its original urgency, if not concern."

Even so, critics and—more importantly—audiences found the story of Pavlo moving. Gottfried sustained his high praise of the play from his 1971 review, judging that "it is an emotional and accessible play but it is also a poetic and multi-layered one. Thematically rich and structurally complex. . ."

(*New York Post*, Apr. 25, 1977). In his review for *Newsweek* (May 9, 1977), Kroll believed that *Pavlo*'s "raw meat and its anguished sincerity has a jackhammer force." Writing for the *Detroit Press*, Jay Carr unhesitatingly affirmed that Rabe created "a fiercely moral play." And Edwin Wilson (*Wall Street Journal*, May 9, 1977) concurred that the "play generates tremendous power," although he found the domestic scenes "irrelevant" and cut-worthy.

Pavlo 1977-style also elicited widely differing interpretations, as did his 1971 prototype. For Gottfried, Pavlo was elevated to mythic levels becoming an archetype: "He is all of life's unnoticed young men." Equally archetypical in his interpretation, Howard Kissel bubbled that "the Tyll Eulenspiegel-like central character is wonderful." Carr labeled him "a Wozzeck, a born loser, a scapegoat"; similarly, Kroll admitted that Rabe made Hummel "into all the losers who were dispatched into the heart of darkness that was Vietnam."

Unquestionably the most significant element of the 1977 revival for the critics was that Al Pacino played Pavlo, as he had done in the first TCB production in 1972. By the way, it was this 1972 performance that helped launch Pacino's career. Kissel brazenly asserted "Pacino is the main reason for seeing the revival." Pacino in many ways unintentionally upstaged Rabe and even the character that the playwright created. Heaping kudos on Pacino, Gottfried honored the actor for "using his box office clout for the highest of theater purposes"—to spread the cause of serious theatre. Leonard Probst claimed that Pacino played the role better than it had been done in 1971. As far as many reviewers were concerned, the reason for Pacino's success lay in his mannerisms. Kalem explained: "If Al Pacino was not born for this role, no one will ever know it. He shuffles about the stage liked a neophyte boxer unable to target his opponent." Kroll dubbed him "an athlete of the inarticulate" whose "jittery motions" made the role. Pacino's stage movements and sounds were not universally respected. Gottfried especially disliked the "slouching, manic physicality and the slurred reading of Brando's Kowalski" that Pacino brought to the part from his film roles. But perhaps the most significant observation of Pacino's acting as it affected an interpretation of the play came from Kissel who went so far as to say that "in the way he always seems to be testing the other characters with his lies, [Pacino] has a way of making the nervousness outweigh the dishonesty—so we care about Hummel, almost against our better judgment."

Another actor in the TCB cast received rave reviews. Joe Fields repeated his original role as First Sergeant Tower once again earning him critical respect. Carr saw his performance as a "benevolent brown moon of a master sergeant" while Kroll found that Fields gave "a bloodcurdling enactment of a strong man tragically perverting his own strength." Gottfried may be closer to the truth by combining the extremes Carr and Kroll found in the role as played by Fields who was both "brutish" and "funny." Other members of the cast were honored for their performances, too, although Kalem thought they "are too deferential to Pacino and spotty in ensemble strength for the play's good." Perhaps a strong Pavlo is not in keeping with Rabe's intention. Overall, then, the TCB production was judged valuable if not powerful ("conceptually" large in Gottfried's words) enough to carry the play and Pacino's presence in it.

Besides the Pacino revival, two other productions deserve comment for the light they shed on the reception of Rabe's play in the 1970s and 1980s. In March of 1979 the Gladsaxe Teatre in Copenhagen staged a powerful *Pavlo*, which in Jan Maagaard's Danish translation became *Soldat Hummel*, starring Christofer Bro in the title role. Widely reviewed in Denmark, the Gladsaxe production was described as terrifyingly brutal. The Danes were intent on capturing the absurdity of the war and the horrors of death. Rabe's reputation was clearly as bound up with the Vietnam War for the Danes as it was for Americans.

In January 1984 Famous Rider and We're Entertainment staged a joint production of *Pavlo* at the Famous Rider Cultural Center in Pittsburgh, the first Rabe play to be performed in that city. Jonathan Kunkel in the *Pitt News* was one of the few reviewers to point out that Famous Rider was taking a chance on doing the play "because of its difficult nature and its large cast." Overall, the production was praised, with Philip John Winters as Pavlo and David Early (a Lou Gossett look-alike) as Tower. The camouflage set by William Mitas featured a ramp that led down to the audience for greater realism. Director Fred Donatelli strove for complete fidelity to army customs. Actors (barely five or six years old when the Vietnam war was raging) were required to get crew cuts and to follow the instructions of "two military advisers from the Special Forces who . . . came on board to teach the men maneuvers, marching, rifle training," according to Marylynn Uricchio of the *Pittsburgh Post-Gazette* for December 31, 1983.

Explanations about Pavlo's continuing popularity are diverse. As long as the specter of Vietnam haunts us so will *Pavlo*. As the reviewer of the We're Entertainment *Pavlo* for *Market Square* noted, the play "does not seem to age" because there is still disagreement about the war. For some the play is a tribute. When asked why he chose to stage *Pavlo*, Donatelli told Uricchio that "It's my way of paying homage to the men who served in Vietnam." For others *Pavlo* has great significance as a warning against future political entrapment. As Chris Rawson of the *Post-Gazette* put it, "In fact, exposure to Rabe's play might well be salutary for those faced with possible service in Lebanon or Central America or even more for those of us whose policies or acquiescence might send them there."

THE ORPHAN

As with many other Rabe plays, *The Orphan* reveals a complicated textual history. At least six or more drafts stand behind the final version of the play which was presented at the Manning Street Theatre in Philadelphia in 1974. Originally, Rabe started with a one-act play entitled *The Bones of Birds* (alternately titled *Nor the Bones of Birds*) which he had written after seeing Euripides's *Iphigenia at Aulis* Off-Broadway in 1967. Rabe's dramatic curiosity was sparked as he wondered why no one had questioned the priest's interpretation of the entrails (or bones) of the bird, an interpretation that led Agamemnon to murder his own daughter to release the Greek fleet at Aulis for Trojan battle. *The Bones of Birds* was performed at Villanova's Vasey Theatre in 1968 when Rabe was a post-graduate student. Barnet Kellman—who later directed *The Orphan* in 1974—helpfully points out that this one-act play "had most of the themes and imagery of *The Orphan*'s first act." *The Bones of Birds* was, according to Kellman, a "play of sounds," Agamemnon's, Clytemnestra's, and of course, Iphigenia's.

While *Sticks and Bones* was in production in 1970, Rabe rewrote and considerably expanded *The Bones of Birds* which resulted in *The Orphan, or Orestes and the E=MC²*. Like its one-act predecessor, Rabe's new two-act *Orphan* was again produced at Villanova's Vasey Theatre, performed by the Villanova Theatre Company, and directed by Rabe's colleague and the first director of *Boom Boom Room* Robert Hedley. *The Orphan, or Orestes and the E=MC²* played at Villanova on October 14-18 and 21-25, 1970, with a revival on November 18-22. Rabe was then playwright-in-residence at Villanova. In a November 15, 1971 interview with Sidney Fields of the *New York Daily News* Rabe recalled: "*The Orphan* was only half done when the Villanova drama department decided to stage it. I had to work on it 10 hours a day for three weeks to finish it." Previewing the play for the *Villanovan* (Oct. 14, 1970), Joshua Ellis pointed out that this was "the first public performance of David Rabe's original work."

Ellis's article is important for a number of reasons, chief of which is that he gives valuable background information about the production, Rabe's view of it, and two contemporary works that influenced Rabe. Ellis indicates that *The Orphan* was being produced by a company and director that followed a performance theatre style; this physical (non-verbal) theatre was not to be liked or disliked but "felt and experienced." Consequently, Ellis advised his student readers—future members of the audience—to "get involved, and for this reason, it is suggested that you wear casual clothing to Vasey Theatre." He further noted that it was a "bold step to bring avant-garde theatre" to Villanova. According to Ellis, at first Rabe was suspicious of avant-garde techniques, having a "strong hostility towards the non-verbal theatre." But after seeing Jean-Claude Van Itallie's *The Serpent* at the Open Theatre Rabe had changed his mind. (Some five years later, Bernard Weiner of the *San Francisco Chronicle* remarked pejoratively that *Sticks* was "virtually [a] straight imitation of the style of Jean-Claude Van Itallie's earlier *America Hurrah!*") In writing his original work, Rabe "made his mind a passive receptor of the thoughts of the play." Ellis helpfully added that Rabe "communicates in this play without literal representations" and that "the lyrics of Bob Dylan greatly influenced" him.

The first published review of *The Orphan* was by Joshua Ellis for the *Villanovan* on October 21, 1970. Ellis was lukewarm about the play but decidedly cool about the production. He believed that Rabe "has stripped the melodrama from Euripides' plays and has replaced it with cloudy scientific and psychological references." Rabe lacked the "penetrating insight into his subject and characters" that led to *Bones*. But Ellis did praise the avant-garde center from which Rabe's work supposedly sprung; "only in the scenes of physical violence does the validity of non-verbal theatre come through." But no thanks to the production. Ellis feared that "Rabe's experiment in form" was "not entirely well served by Villanova's Theatre Company"; however, he conceded that some of the performances were good (as a result of the "vocal and physical exercises" the actors had to endure).

Reviewing the production for the *New Haven Register* (Oct. 25, 1970), James Childs liked the play, the playwright, and the directing. Childs believed that *The Orphan* "provides the audience with much intellectual and emotional pleasure" and that the "reality" of the "intricacies of relativity" is significant. Childs's article is important for more than his critical assessment, however. It contains a number of quotations from Rabe whom Childs had interviewed. Two of these quotations shed considerable light on Rabe's intentions. Orestes for the playwright represents "the youth of today." Speaking of the play as a whole, Rabe observed: "It's an interesting play . . . I'm attempting to present a remembrance of things in the mythological past through the eyes of memory and the presence of today's reality and relativity."

Ernest Schier also wrote a review of the Villanova *Orphan* for the *Philadelphia Evening Bulletin*, and although he liked Rabe's other work he declared that this play was "uneven" and "probably too long." Still, Schier recognized Rabe's ability in *The Orphan* (as in *Bones*) to "handle many complex deeply interwoven characters and situations." Impressed by the staging, Schier complimented Hedley's ingenuity in having the audience sit on bleachers directly on the stage and in using the curtain to cut off the auditorium from the stage. Schier's opening sentence left no doubt in anyone's mind that he still had the highest regard for Rabe: "There may be no other playwright in America writing against violence with as much passion and sense of commitment as David W. Rabe."

Revising the play once more and coming to terms with Papp on production details, Rabe had a new *Orphan* open at the Anspacher Theatre of the New York Shakespeare Festival on April 18, 1973, but it closed in less than a month after some 50 performances. Jeff Bleckner, who had successfully directed *Pavlo Hummel* and *Sticks*, also directed *The Orphan*; and Santo Loquasto, who likewise worked on *Pavlo* and *Sticks*, designed the set for Rabe's new play. Critical response to *The Orphan* was largely negative, although positive comments were voiced about Rabe's dramatic power and his continuing promise as a writer. Regardless of the degree of their hostility to *The Orphan*, the critics concurred that Rabe had written the most ambitious play of his career. A number of them conceded Rabe's larger purpose and broader scope in *The Orphan*. He's "after bigger game," said Clive Barnes; and Douglas Watt admitted that Rabe was attempting to "find a unified design in man's history of slaughter." But the complicated threads in that design worried the reviewers. Rabe intermixed events from the high tragedy of the *Orestia* (taking liberties with the sacred Aeschylean script) with contemporary deeds of horror from the Manson murders to show tragic parallels. On top of this Rabe injected poetic explanations about the limits of relativity. Recall that the original title contained the famous Einstein equation.

Critics who were kind called *The Orphan* "provocative" or "difficult"; those less so branded the play as "bewildering," "perplexing," or "irritating." Given these charges against Rabe, *The Orphan* became his *Tiny Alice*. The conflation of stories in the play was assailed as "totally unreasonable" and "heavy handed" by Lillian Africano who further showed disdain by refusing to describe a single event from *The Orphan*. Kroll complained that although Rabe made an "admirable attempt" the play was "a callow excuse for thought." Catharine Hughes saw it as "intellectual clutter"; Watt as "overelaborate," and "confusing and static"; and Novick called it a "phantasmagoria full of sudden shifts in time and space and sudden changes of subject." In his short (one-minute) review for NBC TV, Leonard Probst used a shotgun to blow the play up and apart—"it is pretentious, over-blown, over-written and over-long."

Two critics, however, singled out *The Orphan* for loving praise. James Childs of the *New Haven Register* called it "superlative theatre . . . demanding much from its audience and giving much in return." And Albert Bermel (for the *New Leader*) claimed that "this is a good play, pretentious in the best sense (having big pretensions), and crowded with exciting scenes and some of the most entertaining soliloquies."

A number of reviewers were angry with Rabe for tampering with Aeschylus's "simple" story in the first place and then for transforming it into a diffuse narrative. Most distasteful to them, it seems, was the liberty Rabe took with the Greek characters, their times and cultural ethos. Most criticism seemed to center on Rabe adding two Clytemnestras and minimizing Electra's role (or, worse yet, having her use a telephone).

The critics had a field day at Rabe's expense in explaining the contemporary significance of Rabe's Greeks being dressed in modern costumes. Agamemnon was outfitted like a general and waved a whiskey bottle, a true embodiment of a warmonger, but for the critics this modern transformation of the tragic king was a sign of poor or confused taste. Aegisthus was described as "another old Greek who looks like a modern shoe salesman"; he was a "caricature of President Nixon" for Glover. Wearing a T-shirt and singing rock music, Orestes was "the modern hip" for Barnes. Watt disliked Apollo portrayed as a "rock idol" dressed like Charles Manson trying to sway Orestes with mind-boggling drugs. For Kroll the deceitful, entrails-reading Calchas "wears a modern suit with an attaché case manacled to his wrist like a CIA man carrying top secret materials." Pylades, Orestes's friend, looked like a drug pusher to Bermel.

The critics, of course, compared *The Orphan* with Rabe's two earlier plays on Vietnam—*Pavlo* and *Sticks*—and Clive Barnes concluded that *The Orphan* was the last play in Rabe's "Vietnam trilogy." However, Rabe himself admitted that although he saw parallels among the characters of these three plays his original intention was not to write a unified trilogy. Moreover, in a 1972 interview with Jerry Tallmer of the *New York Post*, Rabe denied that *The Orphan* was about Vietnam: "There's no reference to Vietnam in the play, not specifically. There may be one. But if I hadn't been there I wouldn't have written it." And in a March 5, 1974 interview with Joe Adcock for the *Philadelphia Evening Bulletin*, Rabe elaborated: "I just used the myth [of Agamemnon] . . . but what concerned me was certain things about generations, about idealism and the lack of it, about the betrayal of the young by the old, and then the vengeance of the young on the old. It's basic to all families."

Nevertheless, the presence of Vietnam haunted reviewers of *The Orphan*. Kroll announced that with this play Rabe "continues to explore the moral morass of Vietnam." And while a number of reviewers agreed that the violence of Vietnam was a symptom of American violence in general, they proceeded to attack *The Orphan* for not being like Rabe's two earlier plays. Even though it exploded with the savagery of war as did *Sticks* and *Pavlo*, *The Orphan* for Gottfried was "a lesser work"; the "horizontal time" sequence that worked so well in *Pavlo* failed in *The Orphan*. Rabe's language—crisp, real, poignant in the earlier plays—became inflated, declamatory, or stale in his latest work for many reviewers. According to Africano, *The Orphan*, unlike *Pavlo* or *Sticks*, had "no real characters." Perhaps the most rewarding way to link these three plays was to identify the themes they had in common, as Barnes attempted to do in his review. All three plays, Barnes maintained, emphasized the "essential violence" of the American character and "the living death of conformity" individuals are "destined" to suffer.

Although the critics were less than enthusiastic about *The Orphan*, many of them confirmed their faith in Rabe's promise and their respect for his awesome and forceful style. Sampling a few of their remarks we can appreciate the state and power of Rabe's reputation in 1973. Watt praised the New York Shakespeare Festival for producing "even the less satisfying works of a young playwright of Rabe's stature." Kalem voiced a widely accepted sentiment about Rabe's integrity: "Often as silly and awkward as [*The Orphan*] is ambitious, the play nonetheless bears the mark of a dramatist who dares and cares." Barnes hailed Rabe as a "playwright of shining promise and talent, but I think at times his dramatic ideas outrun his dramatic language." In a darkly pensive vein Catharine Hughes agreed with many critics that *The Orphan* was a failure but asserted that its failure "is the consequence of aspirations on a scale so much broader and deeper than those of virtually any other American playwright writing today that the American theatre and anyone interested in its future has a considerable stake in Mr. Rabe's discovering *why* it does not succeed."

Barnet Kellman was one of those very interested in why *The Orphan* did not succeed, and his interest in Rabe and the play begins another chapter in the history of *The Orphan*. Having heard that Rabe was revising the play after its New York struggles, Kellman wanted to stage it at the North Carolina School of the Arts in Winston-Salem. He had been asked by Ron Pollack, the dean of the drama school there, to direct an innovative, experimental play as part of a grant that the North Carolina School of the Arts received from the League of Professional Theatre Training Programs of the NEH. *The Orphan* struck Kellman as a wise choice, although he thought that the second act was too long and hence not as effective as it could be. Kellman and Rabe had met in the summer of 1970 when Rabe interviewed Kellman who was then the co-director of the New American Theatre Ensemble in New Haven. (Rabe's article appeared in the *Register* on July 12, 1970.) Rabe agreed to revise the play while he was working on *Boom Boom Room* in New York. (Ironically enough, Kellman would be directing *The Boom Boom Room* in Williamstown, Massachusetts, in 1974.) So while Kellman worked with the students at the North Carolina School of the Arts Rabe revised *The Orphan* and conducted discussions with Kellman about the play over the telephone. On November 12, 1973, when the play opened in Winston-Salem, Rabe was in the audience and approved of the production.

The story of the Kellman-Rabe *Orphan* has been told by Kellman in great and valuable detail in his 1977 article for *Theatre Quarterly*, so there is no need to repeat the numerous details of collaboration between director and playwright. The North Carolina production offered a revised and structurally tightened play; and it featured a young actor with a bright career ahead of him—Thomas Hulce of *Amadeus* fame—in the role of Orestes. Kellman is quoted as saying: "I hope this [production] will encourage David not to pass off *The Orphan*."[19]

Rabe did not pass it off. So enthusiastic was he about Kellman's work and the momentum of the revised *Orphan* that Rabe helped to bring the play back to Philadelphia where it began. On March 15, 1974, a new *Orphan*, revitalized in the hills of North Carolina, opened at the small, experimental Manning Street Actors Theater on Lombard Street. Manning's artistic director, Joe Stinson, saw many good things in store for his theatre by staging Rabe's play. This production was in part sponsored by Joe Papp, who contributed $1,000 toward it, and was again directed by Kellman and starred once more Hulce as Orestes. Some reviewers grew more approving; others did not change their minds about the play. Schier appreciated the play "in its rewritten form, a considerable achievement" and praised the "performances which shine with professionalism and an overall effort that almost matches the demand" of Rabe's play. He did wonder whether *The Orphan* was a "philosophical play or a religious one" and answered that it was "perhaps both." Offering a less sanguine view of the revised *Orphan* was William Collins who concluded that the play "succeeds as statement but fails as drama. It is too much of an exercise to be gripping." Collins did, however, commend Rabe's "bold" attempt to "revise tragedy" and pointed out that *The Orphan* does "amplify" Papp and Rabe's "underlying concern with violence in modern man."

(IN) THE BOOM BOOM ROOM

Boom Boom Room, Rabe's fourth play to be professionally produced, has a varied history theatrically and textually. In its multiple versions the play has been staged in almost every conceivable theatrical environment. It was first performed at Villanova University in 1972 while Rabe was teaching in the theatre department. Then, much expanded, the play opened at Lincoln Center in November 1973. The next year in December it was back at the Anspacher at the Public Theatre. A number of campus productions flourished in the 1970s and 1980s at universities in Indiana, Hawaii, Kansas, North Carolina and New Jersey. Most recently, the play has experienced an Off-Broadway revival (in January of 1986) by the Orange Theatre Company at the South Street Theatre. There has also been continuing talk of making Rabe's screenplay of *(In) The Boom Boom Room* into a movie. About this screenplay Rabe said in a 1977 interview with Bob Prochaska of *Dramatics*: "Yes, I've written a screenplay of my play *The Boom Boom Room*. The script has been mailed to 12 directors, Arthur Penn, Bob Fosse, Hal Ashby among them. I found that if you bounce between writing for stage and film your work benefits . . . ." By the early 1980s Rabe would change his mind about such benefits.

Bibliographically speaking, the scripts of the play also have a dynamic history behind them. The original Villanova production was based upon a two-act play. When working on the Lincoln Center debut, Rabe expanded the play—"a scene, some speeches and amplifications of moments, all of which occurred in the first act (of the two-act version), with the result that the first act became excessively long for the format" (see "Author's Note" to Grove Press revised version, 1986). The result was a three-act play that neither Rabe nor the critics thought was the ideal length. Rabe characterized the three-act construction as "a forced solution," "a change of pace rather than a real solution" ("Author's Note"). Some critics complained that the play was excessively long (three hours). Watt labeled it "a long and tedious expressionistic play" in his *New York Daily News* review. Otherwise complimentary about Rabe's work, Kroll proclaimed that one is "angry" at Rabe because his play which is "so strong, so affecting" suffers from being "too long, repetitious." Before the play moved to the Public Theatre the following year, Rabe again worked on the script, and this version appeared as *In the Boom Boom Room* and supplied the text when the play was first published in 1975.

A few critics commented on the dramatic effect of the changes Rabe made. Clive Barnes pointed out: "The play has been considerably rewritten—something like 25 percent is new." Specifically he noted that in "this new and better focused version of the script" Rabe presents "the portrait of the woman" (*New York Times*, Dec. 5, 1974). Ernest Albrecht observed that "Rabe has been revising the work. It seems now to be even more specific about imprisonment . . . [he] has deleted most of the references to ambition, giving and fulfillment." In *Michael's Thing*, a New York little magazine, Herman Alex Joyce claimed that "the play seems in the process of becoming a completed work, more of a whole." However, some reviewers, like Harold Clurman, confessed that they could "not discern the extent or the exact nature of the revision."

And the story of revisions continues. Having worked on an Off-Broadway revival of the play by the Orange Theatre Company, and being given an "invitation to republish" the play by Grove Press, Rabe decided to "try once more to resolve the difficulties of the text" ("Author's Note"). The result was the publication of *In the Boom Boom Room, Revised to the original two acts*, in 1986. In this latest (and last?) version of the play Rabe returned to his earlier intentions. He affirmed that "the organic nature of the play demanded a return to the two-act construction." To accomplish this required no "amputation" of entire scenes but only "minor snips" which would "return to the play the original balance which had been thrown off by those first additions for the Lincoln Center production."

However unbalanced the script was for that production, the performance made New York theatre history. In 1973 Joseph Papp took over the ailing Lincoln Center, which, in the words of Julius Novick, became "the newest outpost of the Shakespeare Festival." David Rabe's *Boom Boom Room* was the first play to be staged there under Papp's tenure (at the Vivian Beaumont Theatre), and became the exemplar of Papp's "new play policy" at Lincoln Center, outlined in his manifesto "New Plays for Old" included in the program notes for *Boom Boom Room*. According to this controversial change in direction at Lincoln Center, the "production of new works by living writers must take priority over revivals." Papp emphasized that the American theatre needs to reflect "the national character of our people and their relationship to society." Acknowledging what everyone knew, Papp said: "I am a working producer of plays, in a commanding position to exert an influence on the course of American Theater." In that capacity he further

added: "We will take chances with new plays; we will gamble with new ideas
. . . ." He concluded by affirming that "the living playwright therefore is a
resource we must treasure, nourish and protect." David Rabe (with his *Boom
Boom Room*) was Papp's treasure, his "ace" (Gottfried's phrase), his
favorite playwright. Needless to say, the critics heaped coals of wrath on
Papp for his "new play policy," variously branded as anti-intellectual and
egotistical. Controversy haunted Papp, "probably the most powerful single
figure in the American theatre" at this time, according to Novick.

Controversy stalked the production of Rabe's *Boom Boom Room*,
too. Shortly before the play was scheduled to open on November 8, Papp
fired director Julie Bovasso and replaced her with himself. Critics seized on
this change to pound Papp further; even friendly Gottfried wondered why
Jeff Bleckner, who had brought such talent to Rabe's earlier plays, had not
been assigned to *The Boom Boom Room*. Papp also had difficulty with the
set for the play, and a $60,000 set had to be scrapped (according to Gary Jay
Williams in his review for *National Review*). In the eyes of some critics, the
house itself was not suited for Rabe's play. It was too large (cavernous) for
the intimate effect *Boom Boom Room* demanded. Sarcastically, William
Glover, the AP drama critic, remarked that the play at the Beaumont "certainly
fulfills producer Joseph Papp's pledge to be different." No stranger to
controversy, Papp also had trouble with the critics before and during the
opening of the play. A story in *Variety* for November 14 described the "run-
ins" he had with William Raidy, whom he refused to admit to the preview of
the play after a reception given by Mrs. Mitzi Newhouse, and with Clive
Barnes whom he called at home to lambast for writing a bad review.

These difficulties aside, *Boom Boom Room* itself received some
highly favorable attention from critics who had been closely following Rabe's
career as Papp's featured dramatist. Despite his trouble with Papp, William
Raidy greeted the play as a "bold beginning" for Papp at Lincoln Center,
adding that it was "unforgettable and powerful" (*Star-Ledger,* Nov. 10,
1973). As he had been in the past, Gottfried was highly complimentary:
"*Boom Boom Room* is one hell of a play . . . It is a near masterpiece,
theatrically thrilling, awesome in its humanity, technically and poetically
proficient beyond ordinary expectations." Emory Lewis of the *Record*
proclaimed *Boom Boom Room* "The Best Play of 1973." In the *Philadelphia
Bulletin* Ernest Schier acknowledged that "David Rabe is one of the best
playwrights on the American scene. *Boom Boom Room* is his finest play."
For his WINS audience Virgil Scudder announced "*Boom Boom Room* is a
superior play. Perhaps a masterpiece." Kroll labeled it a "modern encounter
drama"; and Clurman found it "funny and probing within the ghostliness" of
the sordid world Rabe portrayed. And Kevin Sanders noted in his review for

WABC TV what was one of Rabe's continuing strengths—*Boom Boom Room* "was intensely symbolic."

Less enthusiastic was the response from critics who quarreled with or mocked Rabe's latest attempt to dramatize a suffering America. Barnes quipped that *Boom Boom Room* was "full of chic filth and a desperate Archie Bunker style of racism" and pinpointed what he thought was the major trouble—"we really know no more about her [Chrissy] at the end than we did at the beginning." Marilyn Stasio of *Cue Magazine* branded the play as "a structurally chaotic work." And Douglas Watt disparaged the presence of "musical comedy in its nightclub scenes."

The go-go dancers in those scenes elicited a spirited response from reviewers. A vital part of Rabe's play, the six gilded cages housing the animated dancers came in for a fair share of instant interpretations. On the super-serious side, Kroll philosophized that the dancers (and cages) represented "the eternal feminine lobotomized to an apoplectic travesty of its femininity." Psychoanalytically, Leonard Harris told WCBS TV viewers that "the quintet of dancing girls served as a brassy counterpoint to the Freudian agonies of Chrissy." The girls reminded Gerald Karey of "a kinky Greek chorus." For Watt and Sanders (and perhaps to anyone with ogling eyes) Rabe's go-go girls were pleasantly distracting. Gottfried found that they were "insufficiently" integrated into the play. The gilded cages suggested imprisonment, sensuality, or even a lack of integrated staging to some critics. Finally, to complete this survey of the diverse range of opinion about this element of *Boom Boom Room*, we need to record William Glover's assessment—the girls "enact tawdry showbiz with deadly over-accuracy."

Boom Boom Room automatically triggered comparisons with Rabe's three earlier plays, all of them dealing with the Vietnam War. Critical opinion was almost evenly divided about the benefits of the Vietnam influence. Sanders at WABC TV maintained that *Boom Boom Room* was not a bit like Rabe's Vietnam plays while Gottfried emphasized that Rabe's story of a Philadelphia girl was "written with the elliptical, awesomely orchestrated structure that made *Pavlo Hummel* so technically impressive." Barnes questioned whether Vietnam "drew things out of him that the urban blight of proletarian womanhood fails to do?" Yet Clurman pointed out that *Boom Boom Room*, like the Vietnam plays, shows the "little men and women . . . in whom beneath the filth of stupid habit, grinding mechanization, tumultuous insanity, mindless verbiage and ugly frivolity" lie "human desire and aspiration." Wilson thought that *Boom Boom Room* lacked the "inclusiveness," the vision, that held *Pavlo Hummel* together. For Karey Rabe "seems to have lost his way" in leaving Vietnam whereas Gottfried rejoiced that Rabe "finally abandoned the subject of Vietnam." Novick expressed what was to be an oft-repeated critical assessment of Rabe's heroine; Chrissy is in "some ways a female equivalent" of Pavlo. Beyond doubt, Chrissy and Pavlo are not that far apart. Chrissy describes dating a young soldier, arousing him by sticking her tongue in his mouth and then rushing away after saying goodnight; Pavlo recounts a young girl doing the same thing to him when he was home on leave. Doubtless Pavlo and Chrissy met on their journeys of despair.

The switch in location—if not theme—led many critics to use the occasion of a new Rabe play to assess his current reputation in the theatre and to predict his fate there. Rabe was only 33 when *Boom Boom Room* came to Lincoln Center, a fit age for such assessment, or a convenient time for crucifixion. A common question, as suggested above, was where does Rabe go from here now that he has left the subject of Vietnam? Gottfried believed Rabe had established himself and should "rank with the theatre's finest." Kroll, too, was complimentary, calling Rabe "a developing writer." Less certain, Edwin Wilson announced that "the final verdict is not in." Watt saw *Boom Boom Room* in a peculiar biographical light. He suggested that "Rabe may have been trying to exorcise some personal demons." What was most useful, critically speaking, at this juncture in Rabe's career were the overall assessments of his themes and techniques by critics like Barnes and Kalem.

Generally speaking, the Lincoln Center production won the critics' approval. Not unexpectedly, a great deal of attention was given to Madeline Kahn who played Chrissy, "an exhausting role" as Kroll pointed out. It was so fatiguing that Ellen Greene, a later Chrissy, remarked that "The part was longer than Hamlet."[20] Overall, Kahn received exceptionally high marks for her performance. Gottfried exclaimed that she gave the "performance of a career"; Wilson said the role was "expertly played"; and Kalem concluded that she deserved a Tony. In dissecting her performance, critics of course judged her work against how well she fulfilled Rabe's intentions, or at least how well the critics perceived those intentions. Among those praising Kahn a consensus of sorts maintained that Chrissy was best played as having a "fighting vulnerability," in the words of Kroll. While there was no doubt that Kahn was right in presenting Chrissy as a "real, sad troubled human being," in the words of William Raidy's *Star-Ledger* review, Stasio insightfully observed that Kahn deserved praise for her "sensitive (but never sentimental) portrayal." Although Novick thought Kahn was "doubly miscast" because she "looks wrong" and lessens the pity we have for Chrissy, he did isolate some vital elements in the part with these memorably relevant words: Chrissy is "convincingly crass, uncouth, nasty and yet innocent at the same time." Kahn's comic renditions were alternately pleasing and discomforting to the critics. Watt appreciated Kahn as a "spunky" comedienne while Barnes complained that she "mugs" the part in ways more appropriate for a television sketch. Like Pavlo, Chrissy is not an easy character to categorize or to play on stage; humor, pathos, inarticulateness, and dignity—all are crucial ingredients the actor must mix in equal measure when playing these roles. Edwin Wilson appropriately noticed that at times Kahn walked the thin line that separated her performance from caricature but in the end she was able to blend "humor" and "truth."

Other members of the Lincoln Center cast also were applauded. Kalem professed "everyone is splendid." Receiving universal acclaim was Charles Durning as Chrissy's father; his portrayal of Harold was judged realistic, especially in the way Durning emphasized the character's urological difficulties. Mary Woronov as Susan, the butch leader of the go-go's, received above average grades for a role that Gottfried described as "awkward." Woronov's beauty, a requisite for the part, appealed to Barnes who found her "slinkily attractive." The toughs—Al and Ralphie—also impressed the critics; Stasio memoraby characterized Robert Loggia's Al as "properly swinish."

Offering a tighter, more focused script and a new cast, the revised *In the Boom Boom Room* opened Rabe's second New York premiere of the play on November 20, 1974 at Papp's home-base, the New York Shakespeare Festival Public Theatre on Lafayette Street. In the summer between the time the play closed at Lincoln Center and the time it opened at the Public Theatre, it had been staged and tested by the Williamstown Theatre Festival's Second Company directed by Barnet Kellman, who had already directed *The Orphan* and whom Rabe had interviewed in 1970 for the *New Haven Register*. Young Tom Hulce (who would later star in *Amadeus*) played Guy. Brought back changed, *In the Boom Boom Room* ran for 31 performances at the smaller Anspacher Theatre at the Public Theatre. This revised version of the play was directed by Robert Hedley, a long-time friend of Rabe's who taught at Villanova with him and who also directed the original production of the play at Villanova's Vasey Theatre in 1972.

Like its predecessor, *In the Boom Boom Room* received predictably mixed reviews from the critics. Those who liked it or disliked it in 1973 generally held their ground in 1974. However, a few shifts of opinion occurred, and in some cases old faults were emphasized in the new production. Raidy continued to like the play but loathed the Anspacher production. Barnes praised Rabe for getting "into the feminine mind" but thought the playwright would have been better advised to write a new play rather than revise an old one with a character who "never develops." Clurman liked the smaller theatre for its intimacy, so necessary to Rabe's play, but concluded that "the faults of the script and staging are more glaring" at the Anspacher.

Believing that Rabe had the "power to become a great playwright" and that some of his scenes and speeches were unquestionably strong, Michael Feingold in the *Village Voice* nonetheless faulted the play for its lack of a clear moral intent; the audience lost sympathy for Chrissy when it should have most comfortably sided with her. Henry Popkin arrived at pretty much the same conclusion—Rabe's play was powerful and really came to life but it wrongly received "laughs at the expense of this poor girl." Regardless of these caveats, many who saw the 1974 production agreed with Jean Ogden in her review for WBRW radio—Rabe wrote a "devastating character study that goes to the heart of alienation." A particularly sensitive review of *In the Boom Boom Room* by Ernest Albrecht called attention to the audience's difficulty in facing the "ugly and violent truths" of the play; the go-go cages symbolized the "captivity" we all fear.

As the observation by Clurman above points out, the new production both hindered and helped Rabe in the eyes of the critics. Ellen Greene, a well-known nightclub performer and jazz singer, replaced Madeline Kahn as Chrissy. Herman Alex Joyce greeted Greene on her "unofficial theatrical debut." Her interpretation of the role was considerably different from Kahn's. Where Kahn was judged more earthy and forceful, Greene was seen as less assertive and street smart. Feingold applauded Greene for her "vulnerability" and "fervor." Similarly, Ogden found Greene's Chrissy "so vulnerable and emotionally virginal" that the audience would be "as shattered" as Chrissy was at "her sleazy end." Greene won praise from Barnes, too, who thought Kahn was miscast but that Greene was "brilliant" for her portrayal of Chrissy as a "failure in life," not just in the world of show business. Barnes, too, commented on Greene's "vulnerable" Chrissy and characterized her mannerisms, including a "clumsy grace" as a dancer. But respect for Greene's Chrissy was not as "solid" as one critic reported. Albrecht and Raidy were disappointed by the humor they saw Greene pump into the part. A horrified Albrecht warned that Greene "places the performance in constant jeopardy of becoming camp."

Others in the cast were praised, though none was regarded as better than the actors in the Lincoln Center production. Tom Quinn as Chrissy's father was judged good but not the equal of Charles Durning. According to Feingold, Philip Polito performed the "play's most impossible role," the sperm-selling homosexual Guy.

The way Hedley approached the play solved or created problems for many reviewers. Barnes complimented the director for his realism consistent with what the reviewer perceived to be the anatomy of a lost soul Rabe was presenting to his audiences. Raidy faulted Hedley for wrongly going for the laughs; Joyce maintained Hedley "flounders" in the face of the "complex nature of the material" in Rabe's play. And Albrecht was concerned that Hedley "keeps the performances perpetually sexual." Hedley's own sense of direction, of course, was influenced by the resources of the smaller Anspacher. Lacking the gaudy, technological trappings of Lincoln Center, the Anspacher offered a simpler stage. It was the "splash" of the Lincoln Center production which Raidy thought captured the intention of Rabe's script. Doubtless, too, Hedley had a different perspective of the play than did Joe Papp.

In the Boom Boom Room was the first Rabe play to be imported to England. It was done in December 1976 by the American Repertory Company (directed by Stuart Orme) at the Square One in London. Odelle Mireaux designed a set of black backdrops and glitter, the latter picked up in the girls' go-go costumes. Jane Hallaren played a spirited Chrissy; and Robyn Goodman was a Susan who bragged about her sexual and sordid experiences. The British critics conceded the sympathy that Rabe felt for his heroine and thought that his writing was sharp and fresh but overall found the play too long and convoluted. Anne Morley-Priestman—for *The Stage and Television Today*—remarked: "One cannot help but feel, however, that the apparent American obsession with psychiatric detail is perhaps beginning to negate true dramatic fulfillment; this seemed one of those plays which has turned in on itself too deeply and too quickly."

Judging from the number of times it has been staged in this country, *In the Boom Boom Room* is one of Rabe's more popular works. In the last ten years the play has been done at least three times by California acting troupes, perhaps a comment on California tastes and talents as much as on Rabe's play. In 1977, the Group Repertory Theater, directed by Ernest Martin, staged a highly successful production. Reviewing it for the *Los Angeles Times*, Sylvie Drake compared Rabe with Arthur Miller in dramatizing the dissolution of the family, further observing that *In the Boom Boom Room* is like a Greek tragedy and Chrissy can be likened to a determined survivor. In 1977, the Quantum Leap Company performed *In the Boom Boom Room* at the Venetian Bakery Theater in San Francisco, a production that did justice to the "wiry street dialogue" and some of Rabe's "most brilliant word imagery" according to critic Glenn Lovell. Although Lovell termed the first act "fast paced," he was disappointed with the long two acts that followed. Lovell determined that in trying to present a female character Rabe "feverishly covered all fronts" by including too many neuroses in the role. Overall, the Quantum Leap production was judged compelling. The 1979 production at Long Beach, directed by Peter Flood, starred actress

Jill Clayburgh, Rabe's wife. Ironically, Clayburgh first met David Rabe when she unsuccessfully auditioned for the role in New York in 1973. In a production that received high marks, Clayburgh was praised for playing a "pliant" Chrissy against the discomfortingly forceful Al played by John Aquino, one of Rabe's best Philadelphia friends. Clayburgh's Chrissy was characterized by Drake as "a lost girl, victimized by men she gives in to mostly out of a sense of obligation. Love is a word without definition. Her world jeers at her."

A December 1983 production of *In the Boom Boom Room* at West Chester State University brought demonstrations against the play and school administration by black students angered by "racial epithets." The director, Jay Berkowitz, refused to "edit" the script of the play. A 1986 revival of the play Off-Broadway by the Orange Theatre Company at the South Street Theatre deserves special merit, as we saw, since this production led to the revised published text of the play.

STREAMERS

In his review of *Streamers*, Douglas Watt referred to Rabe's fifth professionally performed play as a "'trunk' play" because "it stems from the author's early and, so far, most productive period," the time of *Pavlo* and *Sticks* (*New York Daily News*, Feb. 9, 1976). Watt was partially correct. The genesis of *Streamers* may go back even farther than the first drafts of *Pavlo*. Rabe recalls that very soon after his return from Vietnam he worked on a one-act play he then entitled *Knives*; this brief work contained the seeds for the later *Streamers*. In a 1976 interview ("How Nichols and Rabe Shaped *Streamers*," *New York Times*, Apr. 25), Rabe revealed that portions of *Streamers* date back "at least four or five years—fragments of speeches, characters. That's the way I work; I pick things up and put them down. The work I did after New Haven [1969-1970] was mostly an attempt to focus the play more clearly." Rabe supplied the following information in a 1983 interview with Clarke Taylor of the *Los Angeles Times*: "It eventually took over seven years to write what turned out to be the full-length play . . . although actually it probably took about 10 full days of writing time." And in a 1977 interview with Kevin Kelly of the *Boston Globe* Rabe set the record straight about *Streamers* and the other plays in his Vietnam trilogy: "*Streamers* is not the conclusion of a trilogy that began with *Pavlo Hummel* and continued with *Sticks and Bones.* The conclusion was, whatever one thought of it, *The Orphan. Streamers* may be interrelated to these plays, but *The Orphan* caps the trilogy. I just wish critics would get that straight."

Beyond doubt *Streamers* reflects Rabe's own experience in the military. Perhaps coincidentally, the play is set in 1965, the year Rabe himself was drafted, although he was never stationed at a post near Washington, D.C. But Rabe must have felt the tension of barracks life and the apprehension of being given a death ticket to Vietnam.

An important part of the history of *Streamers* is tied to Rabe's relationship with Mike Nichols who directed the play. In 1974 Rabe had sent Nichols a copy of *In the Boom Boom Room* to see if he would like to direct the play. He did not like *In the Boom Boom Room* but did like *Pavlo* and *Sticks* and had a number of pleasant conversations with Rabe. In 1975, after the pressure of having four of his plays done in five years, Rabe was once again in Hollywood eager to do a screenplay and in September he met Nichols. Here is the rest of the story in Rabe's words: ". . . and while I was talking to him about getting into films he was talking to me about doing some theatre. He asked me if I'd written a new play. I said I had, but that I wasn't sure if I wanted it produced just yet. He asked if he could read it, and the following Monday he told me he wanted to direct it."[21]

As with Joe Papp, Rabe was fortunate to be working with Nichols who had received five Tonys in the last five years, including one for directing *Prisoner of Second Avenue*, the play that Rabe's *Sticks* beat out for a Tony in 1972. Moreover, Nichols also directed the film version of another American classic—*Who's Afraid of Virginia Woolf?*. With his background in comedy as well as in serious theatre, Nichols brought multiple and valuable perspectives to bear on Rabe's work. Clearly Nichols understood the text and the texture of *Streamers.* As Robert Leeney, who reviewed the play for the *New Haven Register*, correctly observed: "Mike Nichols evokes laughter and tender comradeship as a background for carnage." These are the very qualities Rabe stressed in the play. Nichols wanted *Streamers* to be done at the Long Wharf Theatre in New Haven. And on his farm near Bridgeport, Connecticut, he and Rabe worked together on the script of the play. Again, as he had with Papp, Rabe formed a strong alliance with one of the most important figures in the American theatre.

And what became of Papp? In the Rabe constellation of the four previous plays, Papp was the primum mobile. None of Rabe's plays (except for non-professional productions at Villanova) was done away from the auspices of the New York Shakespeare Festival. Nichols is quoted as saying that he and Rabe spoke about Papp and, according to Nichols, "Joe said, 'If that's the theatre you feel most comfortable in, then go and do it there.' So we did. We were all agreed that Papp would have first call on it after that. I must say he's [Papp] been totally supportive from the first moment" ("How Nichols and Rabe Shaped *Streamers*," *New York Times*). Rabe's version confirms Nichols's, but Rabe added that he had "involved meetings" with Papp.

At any rate, *Streamers* had its world premiere at the Long Wharf Theatre on January 30, 1976, and stayed in New Haven until February 27. Nichols was a good friend of Arvin Brown, the artistic director of the Long Wharf. And certainly Rabe had close ties with New Haven, having been a feature writer for the *Register* for 16 months back in 1969-1970. Long Wharf was a propitious place to open Rabe's masterpiece. It posed none of the financial or psychic threats of Broadway. Moreover, its location offered a kind of subtle irony. As Jack Kroll interestingly noted, Long Wharf is "a comfortable theatre tucked away in a meat-packing yard." How grotesquely appropriate—to have the blood and gore in *Streamers* spilled on a stage in the middle of a meat-packing yard! Among other things the violence and gore made *Streamers* the most controversial play of the Long Wharf's season. The fourth play done in that season, *Streamers* may have been the "most professionally burnished production ever done at Long Wharf," according to *New Haven Register* critic Markland Taylor (Feb. 15, 1976).

The play opened to rave reviews from the New York critics who traveled out of town to see it. The headline of Douglas Watt's *Daily News* review left no doubt about his enthusiasm for Rabe's work—"*Streamers* is Worth a Trip to New Haven." Watt called *Streamers* "the most powerful piece of theatre we've had all season," far superior to any other American play of 1976; he further characterized Rabe's new work as "a kind of psychological mystery play." Less effusive but still praiseworthy, Clive Barnes's review honored Rabe for writing a "straightforward play," one in which Rabe is telling "a plain tale plainly—and yet very effectively." Allan Wallach found *Streamers* "unsettlingly real and terribly sad." For Kroll *Streamers* was "tough," "unflinching," and "explosive."

Rabe received mixed reviews from the Philadelphia critics who came to New Haven. Schier informed readers at the *Evening Bulletin* that *Streamers* is "lean, eloquent, moral" and that it is "the simplest of Rabe's plays to absorb, and simultaneously, the drama that explodes and fills the stage . . . with interesting ambiguities." William Collins faulted Rabe for some of his writing and found that a few of the actions were irrelevant but overall praised the dramatist for the shock value of the play and for continuing to expose the causes and results of violence of America. In his review for the

Philadelphia Gay News, Marion De Frie concluded that *Streamers* "delivers tense, invigorating drama without coming close to any political or social issues at all." He offered the following analogy for his readers to ponder: "Imagine Kafka's *The Trial* rewritten by Agatha Christie and you'll have an idea of how close *Streamers* comes, but how far off target it is."

A number of the Connecticut critics saw the same merits in *Streamers* that their New York brethren did. Markland Taylor, for example, told readers of the *New Haven Register* (some of whom no doubt remembered Rabe from his *Sunday Pictorial* days) that *Streamers* was "his most daring" work, his "most mature and compassionate play." Writing for the *Bridgeport Post*, Richard Day believed that "while it is possible that Mr. Rabe has indulged somewhat in self-indulging overkill, there can be no denying the sure, craftsmanship manifest in his latest opus." But a few local reviewers gave Rabe the unkindest cuts of all. Robert Leeney (for the *Register* on Feb. 3) complained about the "uncontrollable emotion" in the play and feared that it "shifts almost without warning from nuance to nightmare." The critic for the *New Haven Advocate* conceded that he saw "an intelligent portrait of violence" on stage but objected to its being there at all since it was not justified. Informing readers of the *New Haven Register/Journal-Courier* that "barracks humor gives way to uncontrollable bestial emotions," Florence Johnson labeled *Streamers* (with no pun intended, I am sure) "a sorry affair."

A number of critics—local as well as out of town—offered comparisons with Rabe's earlier work. The time and setting of *Streamers* reminded reviewers of Rabe's two other plays about soldiers—*Pavlo* and *Sticks*. The Vietnam connection was strong for Kroll who said that *Streamers* forms a trilogy with *Sticks* and *Pavlo*, a label to be applied by many other critics over the years. According to Wallach, Billy was the "Pavlo Hummel of *Streamers*." For many critics *Streamers* raised Rabe to new heights; they saw significant changes from his previous plays and a promise of a new direction for future ones. Taylor believed that with *Streamers* Rabe was no longer an angry young man; his anger "is more in perspective" now that his work has escaped from the "polemical and propagandistic" *Sticks* and *Pavlo*. Watt claimed that *Streamers* showed Rabe's writing at its best. Tracing Rabe's development over the last seven years, Schier compared him with O'Neill, noting that Rabe was "more economical now and in finding it easier to say more with less he is approaching an unstudied eloquence." Judging *Streamers* to be a "well-made play," many critics applauded Rabe's masterful, new dramatic approach.

While the critics may have disagreed about the merits of *Streamers*, they held firm in expressing what they regarded as the theme of Rabe's play. Violence, in its many shapes, was Rabe's target and technique. The ways that violence was manifested took some interesting turns, however, in the reviewers' notices. For Collins the "model for the violence" Rabe was writing about was found in "the American character." It was not Vietnam slaughter that occupied Rabe but the violence at home. To Rabe, according to Collins, "Bill Westmoreland's America was of less interest than Charlie Manson's." Similarly, De Frie claimed that it was "Charles Manson, not Richard Nixon, who fascinated Rabe." Richard Day saw *Streamers* as a "protest against violence . . . far from the designated enemy" on the battlefield. Domestic violence in *Streamers* was inextricably caught up with sexual images and assault for a number of critics. As Malcolm Johnson pointed out, Rabe uses homosexuality "as a catalyst to violence" and claimed that the play "cuts more deeply into the national male psyche to show the violence that can happen unexpectedly." Homosexual rape led Bone in *Variety* to abhor the play, claiming that Rabe "explores the subject [of homosexuality] to its lowest depths." Writing for the gay press, De Frie rather strongly suggested that *Streamers* is likely to bring out a "love-hate reaction in most gays who see it."

Seeing violence not in domestic and sexual but in philosophical terms, critics like Barnes, Schier, Taylor, and Kroll examined the moral underpinnings of Rabe's message. For Barnes the violence shows "death as an accidental joke"; similarly, Taylor found that Rabe was stressing that "most violent deaths are arbitrary and meaningless." For Kroll the real violence was "the moral and psychic savagery" released in the play. Finally, Schier believed that *Streamers* was about "life and suddenness of death" and offered "a stronger moral tone" than any play that Rabe had attempted before.

The New Haven cast won high marks for its performances. Some representative reactions were "the cast is, to a man, to be treasured" (Markland Taylor); the "acting exquisitely fitted the play" (Clive Barnes); the production "could scarcely be improved upon" (Douglas Watt). Joe Fields, who distinguished himself in other Rabe roles (Sergeant Tower in *Pavlo*, the Sergeant Major in the TV *Sticks*), played a truly menacing Carlyle. Some critics stressed the sympathy hidden in the role that Fields brought out to perfection. Taylor, for example, recognized that "Fields covered the emotional spectrum . . . One feels for this ill-at-ease fearful, lonely, eager, suspicious child-man." And Malcolm Johnson also stressed that Fields's Carlyle "is detestable, yet pitiable and finally [a] sympathetic creature, who is played with almost virtuosic jiviness." Emphasizing the dark, messianic side of the role, De Frie depicted Fields's Carlyle as "a Malcolm X with a switchblade." And admitting that the part was "difficult," William Collins pointed out that Fields has a "menacing kind of bonhomie which can turn to anguish without warning."

Dolph Sweet (Cokes) and Kenneth McMillan (Rooney) were also well suited for their parts. They were "drunkenly touching" for Barnes; combined comedy and "tenderness" for Taylor; and were similarly "funny and pathetic" for Collins. Again, Rabe created characters who commanded sympathy through their excesses, their vices. Roger (played by Herbert Jefferson, Jr.) escaped any charges of being a military Uncle Tom; quite to the contrary, Bone praised "this level-headed black" character, and Barnes commended the "Rousseau-like noble savagery" built into the role. John Heard's Billy was seen as a victim, a clean-cut young man, and a pseudo (and false) intellectual. Finally, Richie (played by Peter Evans) received the most contradictory assessments. Taylor praised Rabe for avoiding stereotypes in creating the role, yet De Frie accused Rabe of bringing nothing but stereotypical thinking to the role. Evans's Richie is like "other gay stick-figures" that audiences have seen. Wallach accurately summarized the change the actor playing Richie must undergo from "swish and scornful at first [to] hysterical and shaken at the end."

Evidently some in the Long Wharf audience found the violence too powerful to bear. Doubtless they should have read Bone's comment in *Variety*: "*Streamers* is a theatrical presentation for people with steel stomachs." A handful of people did walk out of the play because of its horrific violence, especially in the climactic knifing scene. A few reviewers assailed the production by describing the revulsion of those around them. The reviewer for UPI stated: "During the performance I attended one woman fainted . . . Others, male and female, had their hands over their mouths, quelling nausea or fright, or both." William B. Wickwire of the *Clinton Recorder* confessed that the play "sickened me physically." A few letters of protest also appeared in the *Register* about Rabe and Long Wharf. The writer of one letter ("Rabe's 'Bloodbath,'" Feb. 12) objected that he never imagined "we would be driven from our seats in disgust and terror" and concluded that "fortunately" he saw no children at the theatre, although he did see "a couple of pregnant mothers." The writer of another letter ("Unholy Mess," Feb. 22) blamed Long Wharf for not giving the audience advance notice about the graphic violence. (Rabe himself refused to have any previews of the play, believing that they would ruin the effect he wanted to create.) The letter writer went on to attack *Streamers* because it "spews a kind of bitter hatred towards our military men" and falsely accused the army of being "responsible" for the "dilemma of homosexuality." In arousing such vitriolic responses from some members of the audience, Rabe's play joins ranks with many other controversial (and classic) works, e.g., *Playboy of the Western World, Who's Afraid of Virginia Woolf?*.

In his review of the Long Wharf production Douglas Watt had hoped that *Streamers* might be brought to New York at some point. His wish came true on April 21 when *Streamers* opened at the Mitzi Newhouse Theatre (formerly The Forum) at Lincoln Center. Papp now came into the *Streamers* picture as the show's new producer. The Lincoln Center *Streamers* was directed by Mike Nichols again and kept the two sergeants—Dolph Sweet and Kenneth McMillan—in grade; but three new recruits joined the cast—Paul Rudd as Billy, Terry Alexander as Roger, and Dorian Harewood as Carlyle. The switch from Joe Fields to Harewood occasioned disbelief from Gottfried who fumed that there was "no sense" in the replacement. Watt said he "missed the almost jolly menace" of Joe Fields. Overall, though, the new production was greeted with great expectations. Clive Barnes even noted that Mike Nichols, "in this transfer to the New York Shakespeare Festival, has tautened the production slightly . . . ." *Streamers* was taut and resilient enough to run for over 400 performances at the Newhouse.

According to many critics, *Streamers* came to New York at just the right time. In an effusive review, Rex Reed joyfully proclaimed in the pages of the *New York Daily News* that *Streamers* broke the grip of a "peculiar lethargy" that held New York captive that summer, and he hailed Rabe's work as "quite the most accomplished new American play in years." In his review for *Women's Wear Daily*, Christopher Sharp pointed out that *Streamers* arrived at a time when the New York stage had "been softened by revivals" and praised the play for being "hard-hitting" as well as "solid and intelligent." Gottfried announced that New Yorkers would see "no finer play presented this season." And Edwin Wilson jabbed away in his review at anyone who might think *Streamers* was light comedy; it was "strong stuff—a body blow to the gut . . . [that] would also make you think."

Several critics, like Gottfried above, repeated their New Haven assessments. Watt again found *Streamers* masterful and now lauded the "inevitability" with which it moved to conclusion. Comparing *Streamers* with *Sticks* and *Pavlo*, Barnes declared it to be "the best play of the trio—although . . . it is the most controversial, the least adventurous." Kalem saw *Streamers* operating in "no man's territory" of the psyche. A lone dissenter among the influential New York critics was John Beaufort of the *Christian Science Monitor* who, in a review scarcely 180 words long, branded *Streamers* as "crude sensationalism," devoid of "any fresh insights."

The critics paid a great deal of attention to the metaphor in Rabe's title. Gottfried astutely pointed out that this metaphor "has several meanings": it could stand for the "arbitrary lunacy of death" as well as the "lunacy of the army." John Simon identified the streamer as one "master image" of two in the play, the Viet Cong trapped in the spider hole being the other one.

Emphasizing how people are cut off from each other in the play, Wilson saw in the streamer Rabe's suggestion that "many people today are hurtling toward destruction, cut off from those things which might sustain or save them." For Reed the streamer represented the characters' lives that are "threatened and altered by forces beyond their control"; they are "struggling with rip cords that will not open." Discussing the meaninglessness of death in the play, Barnes reminded readers that "We are all, Mr. Rabe is suggesting, subject to streamers, as people and . . . as a nation." Beaufort simply noted that the streamer was a "parody of a paratrooper song."

In an interview given in 1983, and used as part of the press leaflet for the movie *Streamers*, Rabe carefully provided his own interpretation of this hauntingly provocative metaphor:

> It's . . . everybody. Everybody is a streamer. Your
> life is a streamer. Ultimately, the chute doesn't open because
> we all die. And one's reaction to that fact, whether we know
> it or not, largely forms the way we shape our personalities,
> how we live, what panics us, what attracts us, or what kind
> of compassion we have or don't have. Ultimately, the play is
> saying that everybody is in that situation and that it should be
> possible *not* to get caught up in the struggles that are in the
> play, the judgments of one another, the treacheries and lies,
> however harmless. It's that very small, subtle fabric of
> misunderstandings and betrayals that makes the final thing
> happen in the play.[22]

Important features of Rabe's play—in its message and its tone—were effectively realized through the settings designed by Tony Walton for both the Long Wharf and the Newhouse productions. Walton was praised at Long Wharf for his use of footlockers, iron beds, and clapboard for a look of "functional starkness" (to quote Richard Day). On the larger stage at Long Wharf, Walton suggested an entire army base by "running wire fencing off on either side of the stage," which offered the "distillation of realism" according to Markland Taylor. On the smaller Newhouse stage Walton had to adapt the setting (beds and footlockers were once again present but not wire fences) and achieved remarkable success in conveying savagery in a little room, the quintessence of Rabe's dramatic approach. As Gottfried alerted his readers, "Enclosed within the snug confines of the Newhouse, [the play's] tension fills the place as tight as a pressure cooker."

The "pressure cooker" simile is exactly on target. Rabe is using a single room—an army barracks—to portray the expanding suffering inherent in "the human condition" according to Watt. The claustrophobic quality of the play (achieved admirably through the dimensions of the Newhouse stage) moved a number of reviewers. Because of the "suffocating proximity" in which they live, Rex Reed, for example, felt as if he knew each of the men in *Streamers* personally. As others would also point out, Reed saw shocking parallels between prisons and the barracks—the closed world where violence inevitably erupts. For a later critic like Carol Rosen (see #381), this condition becomes the world of impasse. Perhaps Walter Kerr expressed the *Streamers* message of doomed claustrophobia best when he said "We are all—black, white, straight, queer, parents, children, friends, foes, stable, unstable—living together in the same 'house.' And we cannot do it."

The "actors are exemplary" (Wilson of the *Wall Street Journal*); it has a "cast that has no flaws" (Barnes of the *New York Times*). These words of praise reflect many (though not all) critics' views of the Newhouse production. As might be expected, most attention was directed to the sergeants and to Carlyle. What the sergeants represented (and how well they did it) produced some interesting variations of opinion. To the skeptical John Simon the sergeants "are a ludicrous and frightening pair of fatsos, a gross Tweedledee and Tweedledum . . . . " Watt found them "hilarious." A little disappointed in McMillan and Sweet's naturalistic acting, Gottfried protested that Rabe had intended the two older men to be "mythic figures, played in a stylized vaudevillian style." Carlyle, their most dangerous recruit, was described as an outcast looking for a home, a representative ghetto black trading one prison for another. Barnes, who regarded Harewood's Carlyle as "brilliant," nonetheless admitted that he gave the play "a different dimension" from Joe Fields's performance in New Haven. As other Rabe characters do, Carlyle blends jokes with lethal jabs. Critics were quick to point out these diverse elements in the role. Kalem, for example, stressed that Harewood's character "was equally intense in its falsely gibing nonchalance and in its true sorrow." On the one hand, Carlyle is (as Gottfried summarized) "obsessed with victimization" while on the other he slides into bonhomie with comic comfort. Reed graphically identified another set of contradictions through the following simile: Carlyle is "like a scorpion searching for a flower, poisoning everything with his tail to hide his inner sensitivity." As he had been in New Haven, Mike Nichols was also highly praised for his directing.

Streamers won a number of impressive awards. The New York Drama Critics voted it the Best American Play for 1976. The play also won a Drama Desk Award and the Los Angeles Drama Critics' Circle Award in 1977. Coincidentally in 1976 Rabe was given a Guggenheim Fellowship, too. Putting things in perspective, Rabe remarked in a 1976 interview with Ira Summers of the *Louisville Times*: "It's not my favorite play, although I do like it . . . It's a more traditional play than some of my others, more realistic in form and more accessible. The production [in New York] is also excellent, probably the best actors and direction a play of mine has ever had."

Streamers is beyond doubt Rabe's most frequently performed play. In the last ten years it has seen more than twenty productions, by large and small professional companies and at universities in Wisconsin, Kansas, Pennsylvania, Montreal, and elsewhere. *Streamers* has been acted by some of this country's most talented companies. In 1977, just a year after the play's Lincoln Center debut, it was performed in Seattle by A Contemporary Theatre, in Chicago at the Goodman Theatre, in Washington, D.C. at the Arena Stage, and in Detroit at the Attic Theatre. Lively and important productions of *Streamers* also took place at the Academy Theatre in Atlanta in March of 1979 and in Portsmouth, New Hampshire, at the Theatre by the Sea. The Hunger Artists Metro Theatre in Denver staged the play in 1985 as did Chicago's famed Steppenwolf Theatre Company, which brought *Streamers* to the Kennedy Center that same year. Unquestionably, the Best American Play for 1976 will continue to fascinate, shock, and educate audiences across the country.

A sampling of some reactions to Rabe's play at regional theatres demonstrates its continuing dramatic intensity as well as its persistently controversial reception. Reviewing the Arena production, James Risser asserted: "Never in the quarter-century history of Washington's bold and innovative Arena Stage has a production generated such controversy and intense audience reaction as the powerful play by Dubuque, Ia., native Rabe." Risser recorded that "more than 30 faintings, and at least two epileptic seizures" occurred in the theatre during *Streamers*'s six-week run. Also reviewing the Arena production, David Richards focused on the perennial issues raised by Rabe's play: "He is, I think, asking basic questions that long predate the war and, unanswered, will continue to fuel horrors as ghastly as Vietnam." Offering his view of the streamers symbolism, Richards claimed that "It embraces all the human identities that fail to flower—dashing some men to a quick end, others to a death that takes a lifetime."

Streamers made its Midwest premiere at Chicago's Goodman Theatre in a highly charged 1977 production directed by Gregory Mosher. Richard Christiansen acknowledged that *Streamers* was an "important production for the Goodman" eager to change its image; Linda Winer likewise noted it "was a strong, courageous selection for the Goodman." For Christiansen, as for many other critics, *Streamers* was a "profoundly disturbing and deeply moving play"; he saw Richie (W. H. Macy) having the "key role" and found Robert Christian's Carlyle "inspired, gut-wrenching." Winer called *Streamers* Rabe's "most economical" play so far, and concluded that *Streamers* at the

Goodman "was more profound to me than when I saw Mike Nichols's more consistent New York production last year." Glenna Syse, however, declared that the Goodman *Streamers* was neither profound nor important. She was angry at the violence that offended her intellectually and emotionally and wondered how the critics who gave *Streamers* the best play award could sleep at nights. In her review for WFMT, Claudia Cassidy, like a number of the New York critics, emphasized the cloying, claustrophobic effect of the play: "*Streamers* soon made me feel that I was trapped in my own no-exit, smack in the middle of the handsome theater with no lateral aisles."

Two Los Angeles productions of *Streamers* also merit attention. In February of 1978 the Westwood Playhouse staged Rabe's play under the direction of Milton Katselas. The cast was stellar. Richard Thomas—of the *Waltons*—played an innocent yet gung-ho Billy; and Bruce Davison (Richie) won praise from critic Jules Aaron for his "campy singing of *He's Just My Bill* to Billy's empty bed." Ralph Meeker as Rooney and Charles Durning as Cokes were both comic and extremely moving. Durning was no stranger to a Rabe role having played Chrissy's father Harold in the Lincoln Center production of *Boom Boom Room.* When *Streamers* moved to San Francisco's Cannery Theatre it opened to rave reviews, too. Discussing Warner Shook's Richie, James Armstrong—in *After Dark*—exclaimed, "Richie is something new on the boards, for in Richie we have our first depiction of one of the less attractive human types"—the emotional, childish and selfish "nascent queen." In *B.A.R.*, a San Francisco publication, Bob McCarthy pointed out that "Rabe's Marxist characterization of the useless homosexual is not for those with short tempers." The *Streamers* done by City Lights Theatre in Los Angeles in January of 1986 earned a place in the stage history of the play. This production was directed by a gay director who, it was thought, could bring unique and valuable insights to Rabe's play.

Streamers was not performed as widely or as frequently abroad as *Sticks and Bones* was, although, as we shall see, the film version of *Streamers* made Rabe's script famous all over the world. The play was done in Canada, England, and Japan. *Streamers* was also performed at the Eblana Theatre in Dublin in 1978 as part of that year's Dublin Theatre Festival. The Irish *Streamers* was directed by Sean Tracy and starred Guy Gregory as Carlyle, Liam Neson as Billy, James Brackington as Roger, Malcolm Douglas as Richie, and Ronan Wilmot and Frank McDonald as the sergeants. Overall, the Irish critics were not kind. They objected to the "barracks room obscenities," the violence, and the length of the play. While Desmonde Rushe did concede that *Streamers* was a very good example of its type ("a depiction with photographic realism of a slice of brutalised life"), he found the play "infinitely depressing, an experience of almost unrelieved ugliness."

Emanuel Kehoe complained that the little American writing produced by the war was disappointing, including *Streamers*. A number of reviewers did admit that *Streamers* was not specifically about Vietnam, though, since it attacks the brutality of any military system. In this light Gus Smith of the *Sunday Independent* interestingly observed: "The work will hardly appeal to women, though young men who want to learn about the absurdities of war might find it rewarding."

In February 1978 *Streamers* made its British premiere at the Round House Playhouse in Liverpool. It was produced by Leslie Lawton; and James Aubrey, who played Carlyle, garnered much praise from British reviewers. Their response to the play was quite another matter. Reviews by Randall Craig in *Drama* and John Peter in the *London Sunday Times* reflect the conflicting British opinions of Rabe's work. Craig saw *Streamers* as a typically but disappointingly American play in which "unwilling conscripts" are assailed by "a negro with obvious psychotic tendencies and a pronounced attack of erotomania." The message of *Streamers*, maintained Craig, was that "a society as individually violent as America must result in the institutionalised violence of an unjustified war. But then of course the reverse could well be true." Examining the same cultural phenomena, John Peter arrived at an entirely different assessment of *Streamers* and its author. Like Rabe's earlier work, *Streamers* for Peter captured the pain of Vietnam; "it is a harrowing and tormented play, bursting with passion, indignation and guilt and clearly written by a man who wants to get something out of his system." As a successor to Edward Albee, Rabe meets the "challenge of the American experience." In short, Peter concluded: "I must salute an American who can confront the traumatic experience of his nation with so much integrity and feeling."

A Japanese production of *Streamers* took place from May 31 through June 8, 1979 at the Kinokuniya Hall in Tokyo. The play was performed by the Gekidan Seihai Company which was founded in 1954 but dissolved soon after the *Streamers* production. This production was directed by Shinpei Fujiwara and starred Sumio Takatsu as Cokes, Minoru Hodaka as Rooney, Masao Tamura as Carlyle, Seiji Mora-oka as Billy, Kenji Mitamura as Roger, and Yutake Yakoi as Richie. The Japanese title of this *Streamers* became *O Uruwashi No Rakkasan Hiraiteokure*, or *Oh, Beautiful Parachute, Open!* The play was translated by Professor Marie Kai, who also wrote an extensive and valuable interpretation of it. The original title of her translation was *Sutorimazu (Streamers)* which was used only as a subtitle by the Seihai Company. The Japanese *Streamers* was widely reviewed with, as might be expected, a heavy emphasis on the political and social implications in the play. In many Japanese reviews and critical studies *Streamers* was referred to as a Vietnam play that attempted to reexamine the meaning of the war. In *Teatro*, a Tokyo magazine, the reviewer characterized *Streamers* as a scalpel into the American conscience; and the reviewer for the *Tokyo Shinbun* praised *Streamers* for its earnest portrayal of an American problem but wondered if it was possible to revive the deep emotion felt by an American audience on the Japanese stage. Did not a racial gap exist?

A French production of *Streamers* is scheduled to premiere in the spring of 1988 in Paris. The translation has been prepared by Henri Behar who rendered Rabe's title as *Chutes Libre*, deliberately and delightfully punning in French and English. Given the heated reception of Robert Altman's film *Streamers* in France, it will be interesting to follow the course of Rabe's work in that country.

In 1983 *Streamers* was made into a movie directed and produced by internationally famous filmmaker Robert Altman. The film was a Jack Mileti presentation of Streamers, International and released by Rank Film Distributors. It ran 118 minutes, which was obviously shorter than the stage play on which the film was based. The film *Streamers* was shot in 21 days in August at Studios at Las Colinas in Dallas, and when the film was released it carried an R rating for its language and violence since there was no nudity in the film. No one in the cast had appeared in the stage version of the play. Matthew Modine played Billy, Michael Wright was Carlyle, Mitchell Lichtenstein was Richie, and Roger was played by David Alan Grier. The parts of the two sergeants were taken by Guy Boyd (Rooney) and George Dzundza (Cokes). *Streamers* premiered at the Venice Film Festival in September and was immediately acclaimed. The nine jurors, all of whom were highly respected directors, were so impressed by the acting that they were unable to award the best actor designation to a single member of the cast and instead gave it to the six actors named above. Rabe himself was exceptionally pleased with the actors chosen for the parts, and in a November 6, 1983 interview with Jay Newquist observed that "It's easier to get actors who look the right age for movies . . . For the stage you can't get near the age." *Streamers* was also shown on the closing night of the New York Film Festival on October 9 at Avery Fisher Hall to an audience that cheered as the spotlight fell on Rabe who was present in the audience and who had remarked to Clarke Taylor of the *Los Angeles Times:* "I liked the film a lot, and I'm sure it's as good or better than the stage version, but I'm still very much haunted by the play."

As with his alliances with Joe Papp and Mike Nichols, Rabe's artistic collaboration with Robert Altman continued a tradition of working with impresarios. *Streamers* was Altman's nineteenth film, and he had a remarkable string of successes to his credit. He directed such works as *Come*

Back to the Five and Dime, Jimmy Dean, Jimmy Dean, Nashville, and *M*A*S*H* (done in 1969). Dan Fainaru of the *Jerusalem Post Magazine* quipped that *Streamers* was a "sardonic version" of *M*A*S*H*, and Altman himself said of the two films: "I am telling the same story but it just isn't funny any more."[23] Deciding to make a movie of Rabe's play, Altman was once again demonstrating his interest in the theatre. Ironically, though, Altman admitted that he never saw *Streamers* on stage. In making *Streamers*, Altman was also venting his own political views. In an interview included in a press leaflet distributed by the Rank organization, Altman confessed: "I don't think I would have made this film had the African and Central American situation not been what it is." This comment reveals that *Streamers*, first produced in 1976 as the Vietnam War was brutally fresh in memory, transcends one political moment or one controversial war.

The press leaflet from which Altman's interview comes is an important document for understanding the film. In addition to the Altman interview and one with Rabe, the kit contains a short preface by Altman giving his interpretations of the play turned film. In Altman's view, "Times of war" become "a time for bravery and even laughter," but "in times of impending war, bravery is not commendable and it is certainly no time for laughter. *Streamers* is about men in such circumstances. Men who don't know when to be brave or not to laugh." Altman staunchly maintained that "there should be no leading character. That each of the four boys was as important as the other."

Altman was aware that changes would have to be made between Rabe's play and the film version of it. He recognized that "in *Streamers*, the actors used the playwright's words, although we did make improvisational changes and did a lot of cutting from the stage version." Fortunately, Rabe played a vital role in editing the film. He was able to negotiate with Altman and others involved in producing the film so that he could assist in the cutting. "We edited the final film slowly," remarked Rabe who was pleased with the way the shooting went.[24]

If Altman and Rabe cut, Altman also added. The film *Streamers* contains action not found in the play *Streamers*. Rabe's play opens with Martin dashing in panic after he has slashed his wrist. The movie starts with the two sergeants lighting a fuse to some explosives. Later in the film, these two sergeants imitate a paratrooper falling through air, his ripcord pulling nothing but air, a scene not included in the play. A crack marching squad (Maj. Jim Brackenridge and the Sam Houston Rifles are given special thanks in the film credits) and five songs (*Boy from New York City, What A Guy, Let's Go Together, The Kind of Boy You Can't Forget*, and *I'm Gonna Make You Mine*) not found in the play are crucial parts of the film. Finally,

Altman added a silent soldier who peers from his bunk throughout the film, an enigmatic character who both fascinated and angered the critics.

Critical opinion about the film varied greatly. Vincent Canby in the *New York Times* (Oct. 9, 1983) panned it, attacking Altman's stylized methods of using an "endless succession" of close-ups, which distorted reality and "upstaged" the actors. Equally displeased, Elliot Stein of *Film Comment* branded *Streamers* "an inert film which fatally exposes the artifice of the play." Kell of *Variety* called it an "overlong, overemphatic film." Yet Judith Crist (in *Saturday Review*) called *Streamers* "an engrossing and harrowing film," and a "literally stunning adaptation" of David Rabe's play. For Jack Kroll Rabe's play "was chillingly filmed" by Altman. Writing for *What's On* [London], Phillip Bergson praised *Streamers* for being "a strong, moving and brilliantly acted" piece of work "full of humour and flashes of insight, with a sexual charge rarely felt in American films." Michael Feingold of the *Village Voice* was lukewarm ("you'll have a tolerable evening's entertainment").

The relationship of Rabe's play to Altman's film was perhaps the most crucial issue. Translating an artistic creation from one medium to another is no easy task. Working on *Streamers*, Altman did not "try to open it up or make it any different. I wanted to really make it a film" (see press leaflet interview, #165). Emphasizing one major difference between the stage and the film, Altman zeroed in on faces in his screen adaptation of the play. His camera persistently, penetratingly followed the actors' facial movements in close-ups, frame after frame. Faithful to Rabe's sense of claustrophobic space, Altman's camera never left the barracks room. The Altman film remained faithful to Rabe's dialogue, too, since Rabe had written the screenplay.

Not surprisingly, the critics zoomed in on Altman's attempt. They debated whether he made a satisfying film or a poor version of a filmed stage play or whether he did neither well. Judith Crist and Jack Kroll praised the Altman film. Admitting that "the stage roots are evident," Crist commended Altman for using Rabe's speeches and location to the best cinematic advantages. Kroll likened Altman's camera to "an invisible eavesdropper, appalled at what he sees but insisting on seeing it with punishing clarity." In contrast, Feingold denied *Streamers* the status of a film and claimed it looked more "like a decent PBS rendering of a better-quality regional theater performance." As indicated above, Canby found that "the highly literary quality of the script" and the close-ups destroyed the cinematic effect of *Streamers* and the sense of reality audiences demand from a film. Canby concluded that Altman's *Streamers* was neither a film nor a play: "It's something less than either one." Elliot Stein, too, believed Altman was held captive by Rabe's words: "Hermetically enclosed as Altman's film is, you're always aware of how schematic Rabe's script is." Perhaps the most satisfying response to the play/film controversy came from Dan Fainaru of the *Jerusalem Post Magazine*: "Who cares, as long as it grips you from beginning to end. And anyway, why not accept Altman's explanation that, unlike theatre, he brings the spectator right onto the stage, tells him what to look for, and eliminates the distance created by the proscenium?"

The film has been shown around the world. Zurich, Paris, Milan, London, Barcelona, Madrid, Berlin, Copenhagen, New York, New Orleans, and Jerusalem are only a few of the places where *Streamers* has been reviewed by film critics. One interesting interpretation, among many that could be cited, is found in the Spanish rendition of the word *streamers*—"desechos," or residue, remnants, leftovers, garbage, nothing worth saving. Octavi Marti in *El Pais* from Madrid offered a unique reading of Rabe's metaphoric streamer: "Robert Altman himself is a streamer, engaged as he is in continuing to leap in spite of the fact that each time his parachute is smaller and his rate of fall faster . . . his method of the depiction of artistry is now a modest realization (or sell-out to) television pictures."

RABE'S SCREENPLAYS

In addition to *Streamers*, Rabe has done a number of other screenplays. A story by Aljean Harmetz in the *New York Times* for July 13, 1978 reported that Rabe was scheduled to write the Hollywood screenplay *Prince of the City*, a film to be directed by Brian De Palma. Based upon the work of Los Angeles Deputy Police Commissioner Robert Daley, *Prince of the City* would dramatize the undercover activities of Detective Robert Leuci in bringing members of the Special Investigation Unit to justice for their graft and corruption. Crime, betrayals, urban terror—all familiar Rabe themes—would have been important elements of *The Prince of the City,* which Harmetz noted would be "Mr. Rabe's first screenplay." Alas, Rabe's *Prince of the City* was never filmed. Nor were Rabe's adaptations of the book *First Blood*, the autobiography *It Gave Everybody Something To Do*, or his screenplay *Just Married* ever released.

Rabe's screenplay *I'm Dancing as Fast as I Can*, however, was released in March of 1982 by Paramount Pictures. The screenplay was based upon the autobiography of Barbara Gordon, an Emmy Award-winning producer of television soap operas and documentaries. Gordon's painful biography describes in harrowing detail her addiction to Valium (she took 60 milligrams a day), her victimization by her own doctor, and her imprisonment in her apartment for 57 days by her mad lover-lawyer. Gordon's autobiography was a best seller; it offered readers honest sensationalism and a timely warning about the dangers of drug addiction. Rabe's screenplay made a number of changes in Gordon's memoirs. He turned a minor character—Jean Martin, a cancer victim whom Gordon had interviewed and been deeply influenced by—into a major one, played by Geraldine Page. And according to *Vogue*'s Molly Haskell, Rabe (and the other filmmakers) "lightened the tone and shifted the emphasis from the heroine's Freudian past to her workaholic present." No doubt Rabe's one hour and 45-minute screenplay condensed and rearranged a number of events in Gordon's autobiography. The film was rated R, but subsequently appeared on television in the summer of 1986.

In many ways, *I'm Dancing as Fast as I Can* was a Rabe family project. Not only did Rabe write the screenplay but he also was the executive producer for the film. Starring as Barbara Gordon was Jill Clayburgh, Rabe's actress-wife. She told Glenn Collins in his March 7, 1982 *New York Times* article: "A lot of the lines are so much me—only David could have written them." It was Clayburgh, in fact, who was responsible for her husband-playwright becoming involved in the project. Michael Eisner at Paramount Studios had sent Clayburgh a copy of Gordon's book in galleys suggesting to her that "There's something going on here we really haven't fully explored," referring to the line about valium in one of Clayburgh's previous movies, *Starting Over*. Clayburgh recounts Rabe's encounter with the Gordon book: "Finally one day David took the galleys and he just started writing. He wrote 60 pages of a script, we took it to Paramount and Michael said 'go with it'" (quoted in Collins). David Rabe's sister, Marsha, was also indirectly involved in the film. One of her arresting poems, "Dinner Conversations," was used by the Jean Martin character (Geraldine Page) in the film. Making his debut as a film director was Jack Hofsiss, who, like Rabe, had been associated with Joe Papp's New York Shakespeare Festival and had won much deserved praise for his direction of *The Elephant Man*. Another Rabe connection might be found in Ellen Greene's playing a role in *I'm Dancing as Fast as I Can*. Eight years earlier, she had played Chrissy in Rabe's *In the Boom Boom Room*. Hollywood and New York—small worlds!

Gordon's autobiography had much in it to interest Rabe. Its themes and characters would naturally appeal to the playwright. Interpreting the meaning of the film, director Hofsiss described it in characteristically Rabean terms to Chris Chase of the *New York Times*: "*I'm Dancing as Fast as I Can* is about a woman seemingly having achieved the life she'd always hoped to live, yet finding this emptiness at the center and using Valium to avoid it." Pavlo, Chrissy, the lost souls in *Hurlyburly* all search for the dream that will bring happiness but leads to emptiness instead. Rabe knew a great deal about Gordon's particular brand of escape—drugs. He had seen the ravages of drug addiction and the painful process of recovery in his visits to Daytop and described both in his stories for the *Sunday Pictorial*. The drug-infested world of creative producers (such as Gordon's), always looking for the right image, supplied the setting for Rabe's next major play, *Hurlyburly*. But perhaps the most horrific element of Gordon's book that gnawed at Rabe was the portrait of a vulnerable woman, caught in a twisted world of bondage (to drugs and to her lover), reeling from psychic and physical torture. Chrissy of *In the Boom Boom Room* was held captive by the men who would control and eventually destroy her; and the women in *Hurlyburly* likewise would be abused by their men and by the entire Hollywood mystique.

Many critics showered Clayburgh with praise for her characterization of Gordon. As in her previous films (*An Unmarried Woman*, *First Monday in October*), Clayburgh had established a reputation for playing roles of women confronting a series of contemporary problems about love, work, and life. With the Gordon role Clayburgh had a new and more serious challenge to meet. Rabe's script no doubt played a major role in the change. As Scott Haller of *Saturday Review* observed, "As played by Clayburgh, Barbara Gordon is not the book's whining princess preyed upon by psychiatrist and lover. Instead she's a self-made woman with self-inflicted wounds." In her movie review for the *Los Angeles Times*, Shelia Benson applauded the "lean, unsparing no-tricks" performance Clayburgh gave and concluded that "Hofsiss and Clayburgh and, one suspects, Rabe . . . have collaborated to create a compelling portrait of a not-uncommon modern woman." Commenting on Clayburgh's previous roles and what the new one would do for her, playwright-husband Rabe pointed out to Glenn Collins: "Her characters have always expressed vulnerability, among many other things. In the movie I let the vulnerability go to a level that hasn't been seen before, so it's not cute, but raw."

I'm Dancing as Fast as I Can did not fare well with the critics or at the box office and so was withdrawn by Paramount earlier than Rabe had expected. Generally speaking, he is sour about his Hollywood experience and does not plan to write further screenplays. In the October 12, 1983, interview with Clarke Taylor, Rabe acknowledged: "I think I've been naive about the film industry and what kinds of films get made."

GOOSE AND TOMTOM

Goose and Tomtom, Rabe's two-act comedy, offers perhaps the most controversial stage history in the Rabe canon. Written in 1978, this play dramatizes the mishaps of two small-time jewel thieves whose own pirated loot is stolen by a rival gang. Rabe initially brought the play to the small Off-Off-Broadway Cubicolo Theater in early 1982 to work on it and mounted two closed productions at his own expense. Reviving his relationship with Joe Papp, Rabe showed the theatre mogul *Goose*, and at once Papp wanted to work on it with Rabe. The playwright agreed but did not want the play to open officially. He is quoted in an article by Dena Kleiman as saying, "I wrote it without understanding it," and he believed the play was not yet ready for the bitter scrutiny of the New York critics. At Papp's Public Theatre, the launching pad for other Rabe productions, *Goose* closed twice, once in rehearsals and another time in the previews. Rabe thought he had an agreement with Papp that the play would not open at all. Rabe wanted Papp to close it, have time to work on it further, and then have Papp himself direct it. Much had to be done before the play would be ready for a public showing.

When the play did open publicly on Thursday, May 6, Rabe was furious. "If I hadn't looked at the newspaper . . . I wouldn't have known that my own play was opening." At once the playwright sent telegrams to the critics disavowing the production. Rabe's reasons for denying the production were clear: "I felt the play was overproduced, too much paraphernalia . . . It obscured what the play was about." That production was fatal for the Rabe-Papp friendship. According to Rabe, "this is the final chapter. I doubt very much that he'll do my next play."[25] Perhaps Rabe compared this production to the Soviet production of *Sticks* in 1972—thinking both were pirated and untruthful to his intentions. Papp evidently harbored no ill will toward Rabe whom he still called "the most powerful new playwright we've ever produced."

At any rate, the Public Theatre *Goose* ran for 59 performances, from the previews beginning on April 13 through the last night on May 16. It was directed by John Pynchon Holms and starred Jerry Mayer as Tomtom, Frederick Neumann as Goose, Gale Garnett as Lorraine, and Will Patton as Bingo. Rabe's fears about unfavorable reviews came true. Mel Gussow, for example, attacked the play, Rabe's language, and "animated cartoon" characters. "It is difficult to believe that the author of the searing *Basic Training of Pavlo Hummel* and *Streamers* could have created such an impecunious caper comedy."

As he had done with his other plays, Rabe continued to work on *Goose and Tomtom.* In 1986, four years after the Public Theatre debacle, he was directing the play in a closed production at the Mitzi Newhouse Theatre at Lincoln Center, the scene of other Rabe triumphs. (Earlier Rabe had tried to use the Williamstown Festival theatre in Massachusetts but arrangements could not be worked out.) Bernard Gerston, the Executive Producer of the Lincoln Center Theater, agreed to let Rabe use the Newhouse for a closed showing of the play. And in late August of 1986 *Goose and Tomtom* had a brief closed run at Lincoln Center. Unquestionably, one of the most newsworthy features of this closed production was the cast. Sean Penn and his famous wife Madonna took the parts of Tomtom and Lorraine after Rabe's producer friend Frederick M. Zollo sent Penn the script of the play. Harvey Keitel, who was to play Phil in *Hurlyburly*, was Bingo, Barry Miller was Goose, and Lorraine Bracco took the part of Lulu. Rabe said that he would invite a few special guests to a performance or two but would not go public with the Newhouse *Goose.* There was talk that Mr. and Mrs. Penn might give a public performance of *Goose and Tomtom* either in Massachusetts or in New York, but such an eagerly awaited production never materialized. And so the David Rabe publicly sanctioned *Goose and Tomtom* remains unproduced. Rabe scholars might be temporarily satisfied, though, by the publication of the play in early 1987 by Grove Press.

HURLYBURLY

Hurlyburly was one of Rabe's most recent plays to be professionally produced. Set in Hollywood, this grim comedy explores the lives of creative types addicted to booze, drugs (especially cocaine), free sex, and self-destruction. Critics have searched for autobiographical roots in *Hurlyburly*, and no doubt the seeds for the play were sown in Rabe's psyche during the time he spent in Hollywood in 1975. In the process of getting a divorce from his first wife, Elizabeth Pan (with whom Rabe had a son Jason), Rabe tried to get work as a screenwriter in Hollywood and had difficulty adjusting to both his new single status and the bizarre world of Hollywood, sometimes more accurately known as "Hollyweed." While there, Rabe thought of some ideas for a play which he tentatively titled *The Guys*, which of course he later expanded into *Hurlyburly*. In invaluable interviews with Leslie Bennetts (*New York Times*, May 11, 1984), Helen Dudar (*New York Times*, June 17, 1984) and Samuel G. Freedman (*New York Times*, June 29, 1984), Rabe spoke about his life in Hollywood and the biographical elements in *Hurlyburly*.

When Freedman asked how much of Rabe there is in Eddie, *Hurlyburly*'s key character (a disillusioned idealist caught in the hurlyburly of meaninglessness), Rabe replied: "To the extent that Eddie is the hub of that group of men, there's none of him in me . . . . To the extent that he has a fascination with self-destruction and an anger with it, there is some of me. I was very alienated from where I came and from most of the people in Hollywood. I had an insane terror of the place." But, as Rabe pointed out to Bennetts, the action in *Hurlyburly* could have happened anywhere; it was not exclusively about California. That location was appropriate for the theme—which affected Rabe personally—weaved throughout the play. "I set it there because that was my last spasm in the bachelor world . . . I was separated then and in the process of divorce and I felt there was no verbal articulation going on of the prices men were paying in this sort of social upheaval." *Hurlyburly*, as Rabe has said, is about men forced back into a second adolescence. Another biographical link might be made between Phil, Eddie's violent actor friend who commits suicide, and Rabe's close friend, actor John Aquino who died from "heavy drinking and an undiagnosed alcohol intolerance," in Freedman's words. Of Aquino Rabe said in an interview with Helen Dudar: "He died of an inability to live with masculinity. He just couldn't hold it together. It really is true that he opened my heart in a certain way to whatever this play is about." Still one more biographical fact enters the play. Rabe's daughter Lily was born in 1982, and this event possibly triggered the scene in Act Two of *Hurlyburly* where the men pass around Phil's baby daughter woefully predicting that in time she'll grow up to be just another broad.

The history of *Hurlyburly* on stage reflects Rabe's continuing association with Mike Nichols. Rabe at first showed a copy of *Hurlyburly* to

Fredrick Zollo who recommended that Rabe get Nichols to direct it. Eight years earlier Rabe had worked with Nichols on *Streamers* and respected Nichols's talent. Nichols readily agreed to direct Rabe's new play and at his urging Rabe sent a copy of *Hurlyburly* (as yet not bearing this title) in April 1983 to Gregory Mosher, the artistic director of Chicago's Goodman Theatre. Eager to do any work by Nichols and moved by Rabe's script, Mosher quickly agreed to have the play come to the Goodman. By January of 1984 Nichols had cast the play and begun rehearsals in New York. The seven-member cast was spectacular and included some of the most gifted and well-known people in the business: Eddie (William Hurt), Mickey (Christopher Walken), Phil (Harvey Keitel), Artie (Jerry Stiller), Darlene (Sigourney Weaver), Donna (Cynthia Nixon), and Bonnie (Judith Ivey). In March the cast, set designer, playwright, and director moved to Chicago for the Goodman opening.

　　Hurlyburly made its world premiere at the Goodman where it ran from March 23 through April 22. The official opening of the play was on April 2, after going through nine previews. From April 2 until it closed *Hurlyburly* was performed 21 times. The play was performed in the Goodman's intimate 135-seat Studio Theatre. Ironically, only a few individuals were able to see the premiere of Rabe's new play. All performances were sold out before the play ever opened. Limited numbers of tickets (from cancellations, etc.) were available at the box office each night, and pleas for them were published in the Chicago newspapers. The Goodman was no stranger to Rabe's work, having done a controversial *Streamers* in 1977, as was noted above.

　　Nichols handpicked the Goodman. He had begun his career in Chicago with the Compass Players and Second City Company in the early 1960s, and he knew Mosher well. When asked by Richard Christiansen of the *Chicago Tribune* (May 6, 1984) why *Hurlyburly* made its world debut at the Goodman, Nichols replied: "I looked for a small place in a loving atmosphere to explore the play." For Nichols *Hurlyburly* was a play in progress. It was not ready for "the usual pre-Broadway route" and so needed, as Nichols explained to Christiansen, "a good womb to begin with." Clearly Nichols had intended to take *Hurlyburly* to New York after Chicago and needed the time to work on the play. Chicago audiences benefited by seeing a major production with a major cast. According to Nichols in another interview with Glenna Syse of the *Chicago Sun-Times* on April 24, 1984, this all-star cast would also profit from the Goodman environment which assured that "other issues" would not get in the way. Those "other issues" meant the disturbing and intruding publicity the cast of *Hurlyburly* would have surely triggered in New York.

In that interview with Glenna Syse of the *Chicago Sun-Times* Nichols discussed the technique, theme, and place of *Hurlyburly* in his own work. For Nichols *Hurlyburly* "was an extraordinary play . . . the most difficult I've worked on, but in some ways the most rewarding." Nichols maintained that *Hurlyburly* was not "realistic," and that "the whole thing is a metaphor." The theme of the play for Nichols was "an explanation and criticism of the macho ethic of men as macho buddies who use women as interchangeable commodities . . . ." The director's words deserve comparison with the playwright's.

The Chicago reviews of Rabe's new play were mixed. While most reviewers saw *Hurlyburly* as a dark comedy, or a tragicomedy, they disagreed about Rabe's mastery of the form. A critic like Richard Christiansen fell in love with Rabe's virtues and what he regarded as his vices: "Wildly hysterical and beautifully lyrical, grossly misshapen and precisely formed, sloppily expressed and keenly observed, *Hurlyburly* is David Rabe at his most brilliant and his most excessive." For a number of reviewers Rabe's language was unredeemingly excessive. In his *Variety* review Mor found the play at first "exhilarating" but then saw it deteriorate because of "excessive oratory"; the characters are "killing themselves and others with words" that exist only so they can "admire" themselves. Similarly, Glenna Syse attacked the play for being "garrulous to the extreme." One wonders if such reviews would have been substantially modified had the critics seen the play again at the end of its run after it was considerably shortened. Themes the critics consistently identified included the failed dreams and empty world of Hollywood, the destructive existence of a society addicted to drugs, and the plastic world of television banalties in which Rabe's characters live. Syse admitted that Rabe's play revealed that the "whole American dream is exploding to oblivion."

The production received rave notices. The cast was judged "superb," and Nichols's direction was heralded as a plus for the playwright. William Hurt's Eddie reminded Christiansen of a "failed Dostoyevsky hero"; Hurt was "handsome and physically perfect for the fiendishly difficult role." A number of reviewers found Walken suitably "flip" as Mickey, and provided "some much needed irony" for Mor at *Variety*. Keitel's Phil captivated reviewers with his "frighteningly acute portrayal of the neo-primitive" in Christiansen's words. Sigourney Weaver's Darlene (who briefly goes topless), Judith Ivey's easily seduced Bonnie, and Cynthia Nixon's "innocence and corruption" (Mor) were also favorably reviewed.

When *Hurlyburly* moved from Chicago to New York, it "made theatrical history of a sort," according to Jack Kroll. Rabe had everything going for him. *Hurlyburly* opened on June 21 at the relatively small 380-seat

Promenade Theater Off Broadway and "had a production of any playwright's dreams" according to Frank Rich. As in the Goodman production, *Hurlyburly* was directed by "superstar director" (Beaufort's phrase) Mike Nichols and boasted the same all-star cast. Most critics agreed with Edwin Wilson that the "production was flawless." As in Chicago, too, the play was sold out even before it opened. According to Enid Nemy (*New York Times*, May 25, 1984), *Hurlyburly* "set what is believed to be an opening day box-office record for an Off Broadway production last Sunday. Some 800 tickets were sold—for $23,000—at the Promenade Theater in six hours." When asked why he did not take *Hurlyburly* directly to Broadway from Chicago, Mike Nichols was quoted by Jack Kroll ("Hollywood Wasteland," *Time*) as saying: "I wanted a safe house for this play. On Broadway you have to deliver in one night. This play is best served where it can breathe. If it turns out it should go to Broadway then it can go."

And go to Broadway it did. *Hurlyburly* opened in early August at the Shubert's Ethel Barrymore Theatre and ran for 343 Broadway performances. It arrived on Broadway with only one initial change in cast—Ron Silver replaced Christopher Walken's Mickey. Into production, though, there were further changes. Alison Bartlett played Cynthia Nixon's Donna and Sigourney Weaver's Darlene was at first taken over by Candace Bergen and then by Susan Anton.

While not all the reviews were rave, overall they were strong. As *Sticks* and *Streamers* had also done, *Hurlyburly* won superlatives from the critics. Kroll celebrated Rabe's new play as "a powerful and permanent contribution to American drama" that "deserves as wide an audience as possible." Robert Brustein predicted that *Hurlyburly* "may well go down in theatre history as a watershed of American playwrighting." Gerald Weales proclaimed that *Hurlyburly* deserved a Tony, awarded that year to *Biloxi Blues* instead. Rabe was nominated for the Tony, though. Admitting that it was an "important" play, Barnes further added that "I was entertained, horrified, and intrigued by *Hurlyburly*." Perhaps Barnes arrived at that conclusion because, in the words of Frank Rich, *Hurlyburly* "offers some of Mr. Rabe's most inventive and disturbing writing."

Rabe's detractors were angry about *Hurlyburly*'s length—three hours and 15 minutes with not one but two intermissions—and troubled by shifts in tone and texture. Some reviewers maintained that *Hurlyburly* worked well as satire but failed as serious commentary. Watt complained that *Hurlyburly* was a "play that seems about to lift us with every line but lets us down instead," signifying only "the author's hurt." For Wilson *Hurlyburly* was "not a play but a series of incidents and vignettes that could go on forever." Collins of the *Philadelphia Inquirer* held that there "is no depth to the play";

and Humm of *Variety* labeled it "mediocre," yet he admitted it succeeded only because of superior acting. Kissel of *Women's Wear Daily* and Beaufort of the *Christian Science Monitor* (hardly Rabe supporters) were brutal, giving Rabe a one-two punch throughout their reviews. "David Rabe's plays purvey a dumb misanthropy," asserted Kissel; and Beaufort found *Hurlyburly* "disappointing" because it lacked "some clarity."

What is *Hurlyburly* all about? As we saw, the play has strong biographical implications for Rabe, who suggested that it explores the vicissitudes of men entering a second adolescence. Further probing into the meaning of the play, Rabe told Helen Dudar: "It's about the price some guys pay to be men . . . I guess the theme of the play is this guy and his effort to control his life and everybody around him. And his feelings—you have to control them or you cannot control everybody else." In his "Afterword" to the play published by Grove Press, Rabe elaborates about the meaning of the *Hurlyburly* in an attempt to understand "the completed play's subterranean nature and needs." Among the numerous controlling themes of the play that Rabe explores are "the union of opposites" (embodied in Phil and Eddie), the place of destiny (especially manifested in Phil's suicide note), friendship, "conflicting personal conceptions," and accidents. The core theme of the play, Rabe believes, was most poignantly expressed in a statement he had made during a rehearsal: "Eddie, through the death of Phil, was saved form being Mickey" (page 168).

Many of the critics entered Rabe's Hollywood setting to find the meaning of the play. The show business world of Mickey and Eddie gave reviewers many possibilities for making thematic statements. In Rabe's Hollywood reviewers saw the death of spirituality in America, the treachery of alliances and friendships, and "shattered beliefs" of all sorts. In this world of "pharmaceutical experiments" drugs of all types are everywhere, leading critics to comment on the vices of the doped-up inhabitants. Another major theme for critics concerned the characters' use (or misuse) of language. The *Hurlyburly* world was "full of mist and words, a wasteland of lost meanings and psychological probings" for Barnes who ironically claimed it was "the first play to make a dictionary its hero," referring to Eddie's use of a dictionary to decipher Phil's suicide note. A number of critics commented on the meaninglessness of language in *Hurlyburly* (giving much attention to "blah, blah, blah" words and thoughts), or its debasement by characters who have adopted the empty slogans and cliches of advertising and television. Kroll lamented the "wasted intelligence" of individuals who were won over by despair. Milan Stitt in *Horizon* voiced another idea frequently discussed by reviewers; *Hurlyburly* issues "war zone reports from the battlefield of the sexes." Critics emphasized that the three women in the play were the victims, pawns, or temporary playmates of the men. Their portrayal as sex objects caused some to question Rabe's own view of women, falsely concluding that he disliked them. Rabe vehemently denied this charge in the Dudar interview, and when the issue arose in Chicago during the Goodman production, Mike Nichols tried to set the record straight in his interview with Glenna Syse of the *Chicago Sun-Times*: "Rabe loves women. It's his characters who hate women. Rabe thinks of women as smarter, more resourceful, resilient, forgiving and flexible, vastly more connected with life than men."

The Hollywood setting played both a functional and symbolic role in *Hurlyburly*. In both the Chicago and New York productions it was designed by Tony Walton who had worked with Rabe and Nichols before on *Streamers* and had a firm grasp of the kinds of stage images both men wanted to project. Walton's set presented a messy Hollywood Hills house with liquor bottles, newspapers and magazines, and garbage scattered among the plastic plants of Eddie and Mickey's living room and kitchen. Outside the windows Walton showed a jungle virtually ready to engulf the house and its residents.

Walton was praised for his accurate—and symbolic—set even by critics who failed to appreciate the other elements of the play. For Glenna Syse in the Goodman production Tony Walton's "shrewd, tacky Hollywood apartment reeks with paranoia, jealousy, selfishness, duplicity, and indolence" (*Chicago Sun-Times*, April 4, 1984). Kroll believed that it was an "unerringly designed Hollywood house" and added that "Junk looms over the play like a Moloch of the technipop age." According to Rich, the "tropical villa designed with seedy elan" was not that far removed thematically from the *Streamers*'s barracks where other men played dangerous games. Emphasizing the visual, Barnes claimed that *Hurlyburly* was "more a picture than a story" and so found the characters floating around Rabe's language and Walton's "decorative coral paraphernalia." The Hollywood setting and Hollywood props are key ingredients of Rabe's parable about the loss of faith and meaning in the new cocaine culture of the 1980s.

Perhaps because of its Hollywood setting, critics were not prompted to draw comparisons between *Hurlyburly* and previous Rabe plays; or perhaps his earlier Vietnam-linked successes were too far removed from the 1984 production to draw sustained comment. But what few comparisons critics did make were generally useful. Seeing a parallel between Carlyle and Phil, Frank Rich pointed out that "as in *Streamers* one man is a psychotic waiting to detonate" and that in many of his plays Rabe chronicles "the brutal games that eternally adolescent American men can play." The issue of manhood forged some links for a few critics. Samuel G. Freedman indicated that while the "subjects" of Rabe's plays "may appear wildly different, they share one of his common concerns: the difficulty of manhood." This view, as well as the one advanced by William B. Collins, is consistent with Rabe's own remarks about the play. According to Collins, Rabe "is comfortable in male society"; his *Pavlo Hummel* "reflected the same kind of milieu" found in *Hurlyburly* which "is rich in male bonding . . . ." Kissel unflatteringly noted that *Hurlyburly* "doesn't arouse as much passion on Rabe's part" as his Vietnam "agitprop" plays.

Unquestionably, on the basis of subject matter, *Hurlyburly* demands comparison with Rabe's *In the Boom Boom Room* and his screenplay *I'm Dancing as Fast as I Can.* These three works suggest to me a domestic trilogy which is the counterpart to Rabe's Vietnam trilogy. Not exploring the connection far enough, Rich noted only in passing that Judith Ivey, who played the balloon-peeling stripper Bonnie, is "surely born to rehabilitate Mr. Rabe's *Boom Boom Room* someday." Bonnie in fact is a more insightful, mature Chrissy; both women nonetheless are victimized by a cruel, savage society. *Boom Boom Room*'s Philadelphia or New York are not essentially different from *Hurlyburly*'s Hollywood. Similarly, *I'm Dancing as Fast as I Can* reveals the horrors of drug addiction and human bondage that Rabe more fully painted two years later in *Hurlyburly.* Rabe himself offered one way of looking at all his plays that he had not articulated before the 1984 interview with Helen Dudar: "There's always somebody in my plays who's trying to get into some closed society."

Hurlyburly was staged in Australia from August 20 through September 20, 1986 at the Melbourne Theatre Company on Russell Street. This theatre company has been hospitable to contemporary American plays; just the year before they had imported David Mamet's *Glengarry Glen Ross* with admirable success. *Hurlyburly* was directed by Gary Downs and starred Shane Bourne (Eddie), Gary Files (Mickey), Terrence Donvan (Phil), Robert Essex (Artie), Fiona Spence (Bonnie), Ailsa Piper (Darlene), and Sally Cooper (Donna). The production was roundly cheered, with special attention going to Bourne's Eddie, the central role. Downs's direction, too, was acclaimed, with a notable exception coming from Jennifer Ellison of *The Bulletin* who believed that "There's little evidence that he has fully explored the potential of the play."

By Australian standards, *Hurlyburly* was a highly charged play. Brochures warned theatregoers that *Hurlyburly* carried an R rating for its strong, sometimes vulgar language. As Naomi Vallins, the reviewer for the *Jewish News*, pointed out: "*Hurly-burly* will not be everyone's cup of tea." Don Dunlop of the *Herald* cautioned readers in the first sentence of his review: "Don't go to *Hurlyburly* if you want a nice night's entertainment," and then conceded it was "powerful" theatre. It was so powerful, in fact, that some members of the audience walked out during performances of *Hurlyburly*. But a good number of Australian critics discovered more than the sensational in Rabe's play. Sally Heath of *The Melbourne Times* declared it was a "thoughtful, witty and brutal play" that "looks at the mess men and women are in." In the *Knox Sherbrooke News*, Jo Healy-North concluded that "the central concern of the play is the men's self-loathing, manifest in their inability to treat women as more than dismissible objects." As their American counterparts had done, the Australian critics identified a host of other themes in addition to the men's abuse of and alienation from women. They focused on the drugs, booze, and the despair of Rabe's characters who live, in the words of influential theatre critic John Larkin, "in this ice-cold hothouse of despair." Vallins laconically stated that *Hurlyburly* was "a play of disillusion."

Many of the critics expectedly turned to Rabe's view of America presented in *Hurlyburly* and added a few of their own perceptions (or prejudices), too. The reviewer for the *Geelong News* pointed out that "the author insists it [*Hurlyburly*] reflects life in certain circles in America today." Dunlop deduced that the play "could only be American in its subject and verbosity." And most critical of all, Dennis Davison observed: "Catholics confess in private, but certain Americans love to confess in public and at length. It is irritating rather than moving, and when he [Phil] appears, clutching his baby . . . our credulity is strained."

Much was made of Hollywood—as a place and as a symbol—in the land down under. Leonard Rudic of *The Age* told his readers that "this is not a glamorised treatment of life on Sunset Boulevard. Nor is it a story of success." He found that "life in the film capital is a fairly sordid business." A. C. of *Scene* said of the Hollywood as Rabe sees it: "if it's really like that, remind me not to go there." Larkin offered the most graphic view of Rabe's Hollywood when he described it as "the playground of the mind, the San Andreas of the psyche, where the shifting plates of consciousness slide and bump around together, ready to erupt at any moment into a chasm of eternal aloneness."

Almost every reviewer remarked about what might be the hallmark of this Australian production—the incredibly fast-paced delivery of the lines. The Australian *Hurlyburly* must have been speeded up in its journey from New York. The reviewer for the *Herald Times* claimed that the "play lasts nearly 2 1/2 hours," and Bob Crimeen of *The Sun* commented on the "2 1/2 hours of verbal bazookering" in which "the words are spat out at such an intense velocity and for so long that the brain is in danger of being numbed." Although generally in keeping with Rabe's overall purpose, this fast, frenetic delivery was variously interpreted. For some reviewers the delivery was a detriment. But for Sally Heath "the play is saved from being simply a heavy dose of social and self analysis by Rabe's tight and fast script." Admitting that the dialogue is quick, Jo Healy-North believed it was also "full and at times very funny." And Vallins perceptively pointed out the characters "talk at a frenetic pace to conceal their inner chaos."

The Melbourne Theatre Company was not the only troupe to stage *Hurlyburly* in 1986. At least four other important productions can be recorded for this year: (a) the Actors Theatre of Tulsa directed by Clifton Justice at the Phoenix Theatre; (b) the Station Theatre in Champaign, Illinois; (c) the New Jersey Shakespeare Festival; and (d) the Trinity Repertory Company in Providence, Rhode Island.

Hurlyburly made its New Jersey premiere when it was staged from November 25 through December 14, 1986 at the New Jersey Shakespeare Festival at Drew University in Madison. This *Hurlyburly* was directed by Paul Barry and presented a cast that was generally praised for its efforts. Ed Dennehy (Eddie) was clearly the star, although John Hertzler (Phil), David Cecsarini (Mickey), and Albert Sinkys (Artie) also were singled out for their work. The men, one critic noted, all went "largely sockless." Steven Solomon in his review for the *Ridgewood News* claimed, though, that "it is the performances of the women who really make this production one" of which the director can be proud. Talented black actress Elizabeth Van Dyke played Bonnie. The reviewer for the *Daily Record* noted Van Dyke "couldn't have looked hungrier as an exotic dancer whose oral aptitudes are not limited to words." Suzanne Samson, however, in her review for *Time Out*, worried that "the trouble is that Van Dyke does not look like someone degraded." Sherry Skinker as Darlene, "the media woman," and Raye Lankford as waifish Donna were regarded as highly appealing.

The New Jersey Shakespeare Festival production attracted a fair amount of criticism. It was advertised as "not for children." In a letter to me, Ellen Barry, the producing director, claimed "our recent production of *Hurlyburly* was both praised and scorned." Justifying their production of such an electrifying play, Paul and Ellen Barry wrote a 2-page explanation included in the program notes. They pointed out that the play even received advance protest: "*Hurlyburly* is one of the few plays in the past fifteen years to have aroused indignation even before it opened." Yet even in the wake of receiving "a fistful of tickets" back, the Barrys persisted. For them the play was "ugly, profane" but for a key reason: "Only by presenting the decadence can Rabe protest it." They claimed that *Hurlyburly* is "a play about what happens to artists when they abandon integrity and consequently lose pride in their art; when, by working in a valueless milieu for an extended period of time they become moral representatives of that milieu." Rabe's "spiritually bankrupt" characters have sold out to the world of advertising, and thus the play "hits very close to home" for the Barrys since so many actors are forced to take jobs in advertising while waiting for their big break. Such was the director's theme of this *Hurlyburly*.

Many reviewers applauded the Barrys' decision to stage the play. The reviewer for the *Daily Record of Northwest New Jersey* acknowledged that "The festival must be lauded for not only producing one of the most important American plays of the '80s but, under Paul Barry's direction, for staging it uncut, uncompromisingly, and indeed well." (The uncut version of *Hurlyburly* for some New Jersey critics lasted four hours!) Suzanne Samson compared *Hurlyburly* with *Who's Afraid of Virginia Woolf?* because of its "verbal brilliance." Similarly complimentary, Robert Daniels of *Good Times* held that "Director Barry has managed to pace the long play with fiercely solid punches which one can't help feeling in the gut." Diane Reidenberg was less sure of the merits of staging the play: "I don't know if the N. J. Shakespeare Festival should be praised or condemned for selecting the play and including it in their subscription series . . . ." Speaking of the dissipation of Rabe's characters, Daniels made one of the most provocative comments about the production: "Only the plants in Mark Evancho's handsome set seem to be alive."

The Trinity Rep *Hurlyburly* in Providence, Rhode Island from December 12, 1986 through January 25, 1987 may be the most important production of the play to date. According to Frank Dolan in his review for WEKK Newsradio in Boston, Rabe believed that Trinity gave the "definitive" production of his play. The reason for Rabe's dissatisfaction with the earlier *Hurlyburly*s can be found in an interview given to William Gale ("This *Hurlyburly* is the Real One" in the *Providence Sunday Journal*). For the first time in public Rabe revealed that director "Mike Nichols and I were at such odds over the New York production that only a facsimile went to Broadway." According to Rabe, this facsimile wrongly emphasized "the California-movie business aspects of the play and was overly satirical toward the men in it." Rabe again stressed that the play does not have to be set in California to work and that Nichols went astray in pushing the "neat and amusing" over the "unwieldy, thrashing, alive and passionate" world of *Hurlyburly*. Rabe further maintained that "I think it's more about older guys . . . divorced, who have been thrown out and are pursuing an adolescent way of life." Also upset with the cuts Nichols made, Rabe eagerly restored Act 1, scene 3 in the Trinity Rep production and in the published text of the play released by Grove Press.

Rabe had high regard for Trinity Rep. In December he spent four days working with director David Wheeler and the cast. Wheeler, who directed Al Pacino in the 1977 Broadway revival of *Pavlo Hummel,* has been heralded as "the invisible director" by John Engstrom of the *Boston Globe.* The Trinity *Hurlyburly* differed in a number of significant ways from the New York Nichols-directed version. As we just saw, it preserved Rabe's even more detailed and descriptive script. For example, the scene dropped from the New York production was added to make *Hurlyburly* longer and Rabe believed more cohesive. Such changes were not universally appreciated by the critics. Acknowledging Rabe's hand in the production to restore the play to his original intentions, Carolyn Cary called it "an exhaustive (and exhausting) production." Another major change made Phil into a much more sympathetic character. Judging from the review written by Don Fowler for the *Cranston Herald* Rabe was successful: "You won't forget Peter Gerety's portrayal of Phil, a violent little man who knows he had a serious problem and can't stop himself. You will not like him, but by the end of the play you will at least have some compassion for him."

These changes notwithstanding, *Hurlyburly* remained a controversial play; a few critics observed that Trinity Rep was taking a risk in presenting it. Publicity announcements warned potential theatregoers that the play was intended for mature audiences. The drugs, sex, booze, and vulgar language received their fair share of notoriety. Fowler, with tongue in cheek, cautioned his readers that Rabe's characters "are not your typical Rhode Islanders." The liquor consumption in particular led a few critics to draw some highly favorable comparisons between O'Neill's *Iceman Cometh* and *Hurlyburly.* Engstrom noticed that *Hurlyburly* was "written in the barroom-marathon tradition of *The Iceman Cometh* and *Who's Afraid of Virginia Woolf?*" And Carolyn Clay, who ranked *Hurlyburly* seventh in her list of "10 best plays" (*Alcestis* was first; *Glengarry Glen Ross* was third), found that the characters "were spending endless, telescoped hours in the thrall of alcohol and incoherence—much as the men do in that other far-from-neat great American drama, *The Iceman Cometh.*" Less inclined to concede parallels with other great American tragedies, Kevin P. O'Connor claimed that *Hurlyburly* was plotless and that the men were "jerks and brats, selfish babies who won't grow up" and of the three women "two are floozies who are drawn more shallow than comic book characters and the third is a bit of a twit."

Many reviewers avoided O'Connor's censorious caveats and instead focused on a number of serious, painfully contemporary messages embedded in the Trinity production. For Arthur Friedman of the *Boston Herald* Rabe's characters are "hollow men . . . so alienated they're incapable of feeling." Fowler pointed out that "There are many implications in *Hurlyburly.* The play says a lot about our violent society and what makes it that way." In his review for *Studies in American Drama, 1945-Present*, Sam Coale took a very broad, historical view noting that Rabe offers a "splendidly searing vision of what he sees as the degeneration of language, love, consciousness, and ourselves in these burnt-out dead-end days of the 'Me Generation' of the Eighties, of the drugged Sixties, of the splintered souls of the hungover Seventies." Engstrom characterized the play as "bleakly impressive," a reaction that summarized much of what emerged from the Trinity production. As Rabe remarked, in the Gale interview, about the confused men of *Hurlyburly*: they "think they are being smart about their lives but you can see that they are lost."

Overall, the Trinity production received applause from the critics. Friedman crowned the actors' performance by referring to them as "a cluster of jewels." Even those who disliked the play's length praised the actors for their endurance. William Damkoehler's Eddie "mixes tears, sneers, and vitriol into a real Molotov cocktail" for Clay who also noted that "his Eddie is fighting tooth and nail the temptation to become Mickey," a view advanced by Rabe himself in his "Afterword" to the play. Peter Gerety's Phil for Gale was a "perfect parody of Miami Vice cool" in a costume designed by William Lane. Gale further claimed that Gerety "gives Phil a wacked out, scary edge that makes us cringe." Engstrom, too, labeled Phil a "sputtering firebomb" and interestingly observed that Eddie and Phil "interact like two halves of the same divided personality." Keith Jochim's Artie was suitably burly and dense. According to Fowler, he perfectly "captured" Artie's "Jewish guilt" and feelings of "being rejected." Daniel Von Bargen played Mickey as "coolly distasteful" (Friedman) as he went about "sarcastically jabbing away at life" (Fowler).

Becca Lish's Donna had an attractive Midwestern accent in a depressing role—the most bruised victim of the brutal men. Norma Bailey of *Newport This Week* informed readers that after receiving numerous beatings Donna "leaves the stage to the weak, scattered applause of some women in the audience." Bonnie as played by Anne Scurria is, if we listen to Coale, "all discombobulated, drugged out, heartfelt caring, a spaced-out trick with a heart of gold, the bruised creature of fantasyland and adolescent wet dreams come to disconcerting life." Lish and Scurria suggested "dignity in degradation without stooping to sentimentality" according to Friedman. Margot Dionne played a worldly Darlene and received kind words from Engstrom for "expressly [using] gesture and glance to convey the subtext of her dialogue."

The set for the Trinity *Hurlyburly* was designed by Robert Soule, and, according to a number of reviewers, effectively mirrored Rabe's themes. Coale found that it "is as California anonymous as these creatures with its pale orange stucco, acres of windows with palm trees and cactus outside." Norma Bailey perceptively wrote: "Green plants, so nervous and spiky, loom beyond the windows. They might be symbolic of the lives of the characters within." The television set was an "intruding metaphor" for Gale who insightfully concluded: "It represents a desperate search for some reality. These guys know they won't get it from the tube, but they can't think of anything else to try."

Three *Hurlyburly*s were produced in May 1987, perhaps a world record. Rabe's play was done in Stockholm, by Berkeley Rep in California, and by the Dartmouth Players in New Hampshire. This book went to press before I could receive reviews of the first two productions, but I was able to talk with Mara Sabinson who directed the Dartmouth production, May 13-16 and then again from May 20-23. She informed me that among the reviews was one which falsely accused her of having her actors smoke actual marijuana cigarettes during the performances. Quite to the contrary, she had her players smoke jinseng cigarettes for their olefactory similarity to the dope Mickey, Phil and their friends use. I would like to conclude this section on *Hurlyburly* with Sabinson's interpretation of Rabe's widely performed play:

> *Hurlyburly* is the chronicle of a spiritual malaise and demise of moral consequence born to a world where arbitrary brutality and instant gratification have become an anthem. Set in a dark landscape of anxiety, greed, despair and destruction, this play parallels the degeneration of language and heroism as they consume and are consumed by television imagery, drug culture, psycho-babble, and faddist mysticism. In short, it is the extension of popular culture and the spectre of contemporary violence come home to roost.

CONCLUSION

What can be said of Rabe's achievements thus far? In asking this leading (or concluding really) question, I know it is dangerous to speculate on the permanent contributions of a living writer, especially one as creative and young as Rabe. He just turned 47 in March of 1987 and has much work ahead of him. But there is no disputing that his place in the American theatre is both high and unshakable. He has won almost every major honor given to our playwrights—a Tony, an Obie, a New York Drama Critics Circle Award, an American Academy of Arts and Letters Award, a Variety Poll Award, etc. And had one been given in 1972, no doubt Rabe would have received the Pulitzer, too. *Pavlo*, one of the most Brechtian American plays ever written, launched Rabe's career, revealing his extraordinary talent. In addition to earning him the Tony, *Sticks and Bones* brought the war and David Rabe squarely into the national consciousness in highly significant and timely ways. *Streamers* has rightly been called an American classic. And *Hurlyburly* made New York stage history, according to some of the most perceptive critics on the scene, again no mean accomplishment for Rabe. If Miller, Williams, and Albee form a first generation triumvirate in the American theatre, then Rabe securely stands with Mamet and Shepard as the triumvirate of the second generation of American playwrights since 1945.

Perhaps David Rabe will always be most famous for his so-called Vietnam trilogy—*Pavlo, Sticks*, and *Streamers* (I include this last play despite Rabe's avowed intention that *The Orphan* concluded the group). In his important study of American literature of the Vietnam War, Philip Beidler hailed Rabe as the most important playwright to deal with the war. Obviously, Rabe was not the first playwright to agonize over the war. But he was the first one to write so powerfully and so memorably about the ravages of the war on the battlefield and the home front. Rabe was largely responsible for bringing that confusing and confused war into the American theatres which had largely ignored it before him. His was a major dramatic— and sociological—achievement. His protagonists—Pavlo, David, Billy— were neither heroic nor popular but then neither was the war which their deaths protested. As long as America remembers the war and recalls the pangs of conscience that it inflicted, then plays like *Sticks and Bones* and *Streamers* will be studied and performed. *Sticks* earned the playwright one chapter at least in the history of broadcasting in America. The controversy surrounding Rabe's plays offers an ironically neat parallel to the controversy that gripped this country during the Vietnam War.

But it would be grossly misleading to label Rabe as a playwright of one cause or one war, to pigeonhole him as only "the Vietnam playwright." His work, especially in the last decade or so, has turned away from the war and explored another type of conflagration—the war at home. As I suggested earlier, Rabe's *Boom Boom Room*, screenplay *I'm Dancing as Fast as I Can*, and *Hurlyburly* form a second trilogy—perhaps some might want to replace the first or second title with Rabe's stunning *Goose and Tomtom* (the work most demanding comparison with David Mamet's plays). This second trilogy forms a major unit attacking the harrowing problems of drugs, betrayals, human bondage and victimization in urban America. If labels are still sought for Rabe, then these powerful dramas of a self-destructive America may earn him the title of "The Playwright of the New Lost Generation."

Unquestionably, along with Albee, Mamet, Shepard, and a group of other playwrights such as Beth Henley, Richard Foreman, and Lanford Wilson, Rabe is one of the most powerful voices in the American theatre. His reputation at home, as all would agree, is assured. His reputation abroad is growing and shows signs of becoming even greater, as his plays (such as *Streamers* and *Hurlyburly*) receive translations and performances. The foreign productions I cited are a sure sign of Rabe's growing international reputation.

In one interview Rabe told his listener that he had several boxes of unfinished plays and fiction at his home. Surely among these foul papers are several shining plays and at least that one novel he has promised the world for so many years. David Rabe is one of America's greatest living writers whose future is as bright as it is necessary to the American theatre.

NOTES

[1] I am indebted to Marsha Rabe, the playwright's sister, for much of my information about Rabe's early life. I also wish to thank Michael D. Gibson, the Archivist at Loras College, for his help.

[2] Barbara Hurrell, "American Self-Image in David Rabe's Vietnam Trilogy," *Journal of American Culture*, 4 (1981): 96.

[3] See Ira Simmons, "Oh, No . . . Another Success," *Courier Journal/Louisville Times*, July 10, 1976, "Scene": 21.

[4] For the stage history of Rabe's first play, see Tom Tully, "Loras Freshmen Stage Own Play," *The Lorian*, 34, no. 10 (Apr. 8, 1959): 10.

[5] Simmons, 21.

[6] Reprinted by permission of Loras College and David Rabe. All rights reserved.

[7] Ellen Kaye, "The Private War of David Rabe," *Philadelphia Inquirer Magazine,* Mar. 19, 1972: 20, does not mention a title.

[8] See Jonathan Takiff, "Phila. Co. Wins A Tip of the Hat," *Philadelphia Daily News*, Apr. 2, 1976: 30. See also Mary Martin Niepold, "Plays by Rabe, Lee Show Early Talent," *Philadelphia Inquirer*, Apr. 2, 1976, D: 7.

[9] I am indebted to Andrea A. Morgan, Coordinator of the Playwrights Program at the Rockefeller Foundation, for these details.

[10] See the *1970 Ayer Directory of Newspapers, Magazines, and Trade Publications*: 170.

[11] "The Basic Training of American Playwrights: Theatre and the Vietnam War," *Theatre*, 9 (Spring 1978): 30-37.

[12] "David Rabe's *The Orphan*: A Peripatetic Work in Progress," *Theatre Quarterly*, 7 (1977): 72-73.

[13] Samuel G. Freedman, "Rabe and the War at Home," *New York Times*, June 28, 1984, sec. C: 13.

[14] See the *1970 Ayer Directory of Newspapers, Magazines, and Trade Publications*, "Supplementary Information": 1653.

[15] Quoted in Marsha Cochran, "'I Didn't Think It Was Possible,'" *New Haven Register*, Apr. 30, 1972, "Arts and Leisure," 4: 1.

[16]I thank Nancy Johnson, the librarian at the American Academy and Institute of Arts and Letters, for sharing her file on David Rabe with me.

[17]For these and further details, see Frederick Smith, "Soviet Sticks and Stones for David Rabe," *New York Times,* Apr. 12, 1973: 56.

[18]Quoted in Mel Gussow, "2nd David Rabe to join *Pavlo Hummel* at Public Theatre," *New York Times*, Nov. 3, 1971: 43.

[19]Quoted in Charles McEwen, "David Rabe's *Orphan* Born Again," *Twin City Sentinel* [Winston-Salem, NC], Nov. 13, 1973: 11. I am indebted to McEwen for details about the North Carolina production.

[20]Quoted in Mike Jahn, "Ellen Greene Mixes Clubs and Theatre," *Jazz*, Feb. 10, 1975: 4.

[21]Quoted in Markland Taylor, "The Fates Seem to Dictate Rabe's Role as Playwright," *New Haven Register*, Feb. 7, 1976: 1.

[22]These comments come from the *Streamers* press leaflet distributed by Rank (#165); see also Clarke Taylor's "Playwright Rabe Cheered at Filmfest," *Los Angeles Times*, Oct. 12, 1983, VI: 2.

[23]Quoted in Phillip Bergson, "The Right Stuff," *What's On* [London], Mar. 22, 1984: 37.

[24]Quoted in Jay Newquist, "*Streamers* Author Ponders Play as Film," *New Haven Register*, Nov. 6, 1983, "Arts and Travel," D: 1.

[25]I am indebted to John Corry, "Rabe Disavows the *Goose* He Thought He Had Closed," *New York Times*, May 8, 1982: 17, for my information and quotations in this paragraph.

PRIMARY BIBLIOGRAPHY

PLAYS

1. *The Chameleon* (1959).

   Unpublished play written by Rabe when he was a freshman at Loras
   and performed on April 12, 1959 at Holy Trinity Auditorium,
   Dubuque

2. *Bonfire of Old Jackets* (1963).

3. *Bridges* (1963).

   Performed at workshop production at Villanova University

4. *Bones* (1969). Revised and written under title of *Sticks and Bones*
   (1972).

5. *Nor the Bones of Birds* (1970). Expanded and retitled *The Orphan.*

6. *The Basic Training of Pavlo Hummel. Scripts* [New York, NY], 1, no. 1
   (Nov. 1971): 56-92.

7. *The Basic Training of Pavlo Hummel.* New York: Samuel French, 1972.

8. *The Basic Training of Pavlo Hummel.* In *The Off-Off-Broadway Book.*
   Eds. Albert Poland and Bruce Mailman. Indianapolis: Bobbs-Merrill,
   1972. 461-94.

9. *The Basic Training of Pavlo Hummel.* Book Club Edition. New York:
   Viking, 1973. 6 leaves of plates.

10. *The Basic Training of Pavlo Hummel.* New York: Viking, 1973.

11. *The Basic Training of Pavlo Hummel.* In *The Basic Training of Pavlo Hummel and Sticks and Bones: Two Plays by David Rabe.* New York: Viking, 1973.

12. *The Basic Training of Pavlo Hummel.* In *The Basic Training of Pavlo Hummel and Sticks and Bones.* New York: Penguin Books, 1978.

13. *The Basic Training of Pavlo Hummel and Sticks and Bones.* Middlesex, England: Harmondsworth, 1978.

14. *The Basic Training of Pavlo Hummel.* In *The Obie Winners: The Best of Off-Broadway.* Ed. Ross Wetzsteon. New York: Doubleday, 1980. 261-369.

15. *The Basic Training of Pavlo Hummel.* In *Famous American Plays of the 1970s.* Introduction by Ted Hoffman. The Laurel Drama Series. New York: Dell, 1981. 29-116.

16. *The Basic Training of Pavlo Hummel.* In *The Longman Anthology of American Drama.* Ed. Lee A. Jacobus. New York: Longman, 1982. 618-52.

17. *Sticks and Bones.* New York: Samuel French, 1972.

18. *Sticks and Bones* (excerpt). In *The Best New Plays of 1971-1972.* Ed. Otis L. Guernsey, Jr. New York: Dodd, Mead & Company, 1972. 181-202.

19. *Sticks and Bones.* In *Plays for the Theatre: An Anthology of World Drama.* Eds. Oscar G. Brockett and Lenyth Brockett. 2nd ed. New York: Holt, Rinehart, 1974. 522-80.

20. *Sticks and Bones.* In *Best American Plays; Seventh Series, 1967-1973.* Eds. Clive Barnes and John Gassner. New York: Crown, 1975. 245-82.

21. *Sticks and Bones.* In *The Tony Winners.* Ed. Stanley Richards. New York: Dodd, Mead & Company, 1977. 737-834.

22. *Sticks and Bones: A Play in Two Acts.* New York: Samuel French, 1979.

23. *Burning* (1974).

  Workshop production of eight performances at the Public Theatre's Martinson Hall, 1974

24. *In the Boom Boom Room: A Drama in Three Acts.* New York: Samuel French, 1975.

25. *In the Boom Boom Room.* Book Club Edition. New York: Knopf, 1975. 4 pages of plates.

26. *In the Boom Boom Room.* New York: Knopf; distributed by Random House, 1975. 2 leaves of plates.

27. *In the Boom Boom Room* (excerpt). In *Contemporary Scenes for Student Actors.* Eds. Michael Schulman and Eva Meklu. New York: Penguin Books, 1980. 227-31.

28. *In the Boom Boom Room: A Play by David Rabe. Revised to the original two acts.* New York: Grove Press, 1986.

29. *The Orphan: A Play in Two Acts.* New York: Samuel French, 1975.

30. *The Crossing* (1963-1964).

  Unpublished one-act play performed by Philadelphia Company, April 1976; also done at Villanova around 1963

31. *Knives* (1967).

  A one-act play which contained seeds of other Rabe works, including *Streamers*

32. *The Guys* (1975).

  Earlier version of *Hurlyburly*

33. *Streamers.* Book Club Edition. Borzoi Book. New York: Knopf, 1975.

34. *Streamers.* New York: Knopf; distributed by Random House, 1975. 2 leaves of plates.

35. *Streamers*: *A Drama in Two Acts.* New York: Samuel French, 1977.

36. *Streamers.* New York: Knopf; distributed by Random House, 1977. 2 leaves of plates.

37. *Streamers* (excerpt). In *The Best Plays of 1975-1976.* Ed. Otis L. Guernsey, Jr. New York: Dodd, Mead & Company, 1976. 212-29.

38. *Streamers.* In *Plays for the Theatre: An Anthology of World Drama.* Eds. Oscar G. Brockett and Lenyth Brockett. 3rd ed. New York: Holt, 1979. 582-638.

39. *Streamers* (excerpt). In *Contemporary Scenes for Student Actors.* Eds. Michael Schulman and Eva Meklu. New York: Penguin Books, 1980. 362-66.

40. *Streamers.* In *Coming To Terms: American Plays & The Vietnam War.* Introduction by James Reston. New York: Theatre Communications Group, 1985. 1-66.

41. *Spin Off* (1983-1984).

    Earlier version of *Hurlyburly*

42. *Hurlyburly: A Play.* 1st Evergreen Edition. New York: Grove Press, 1985.

43. *Hurlyburly: A Play.* New York: Samuel French, 1985.

44. *Hurlyburly: A Play.* New York: Grove Press, 1985.

45. *Hurlyburly.* Book Club Edition. New York: Grove Press, 1985. 4 leaves of plates.

46. *Hurlyburly* (excerpt). In *The Best Plays of 1984-1985.* Ed. Otis L. Guernsey, Jr. New York: Dodd, Mead & Company, 1985. 96-123.

47. *Goose and Tomtom.* New York: Grove Press, 1987.

SCREENPLAYS

48. *Sticks and Bones* (1972).

    TV screenplay written by David Rabe, Joseph Papp, and Robert Downey, 1972

49. *First Blood* (1974-1975).

    Unpublished screenplay

50. *In the Boom Boom Room* (1975).

    Unpublished screenplay

51. *It Gave Everybody Something To Do* (1976).

    Unpublished screenplay

52. *The Prince of the City* (1978).

    Unpublished screenplay

53. *I'm Dancing as Fast as I Can* (1981).

    Unpublished screenplay

54. *Just Married* (1983).

    Unpublished screenplay

55. *Streamers* (1983).

    Unpublished screenplay

56. *Streamers*. Videorecording. Los Angeles: Media Home Entertainment, Inc., 1984.

    Videocassette release of the 1983 motion picture by Streamers International Distributors, Inc.

NOVELS

57. *Rumor* (1972).

    Unpublished novel; see Walter F. Naedele, #150.

58. *Recital of the Dog* (in progress 1986-87).

    See William Gale, #176; Michael Musto, #270.

SHORT STORIES

59. "'Walls of Blackness' by David Rabe Cops First Place." *The Crest* [student newspaper, Loras Academy], May, 24, 1956: 3, 4, 6.

    Prints Rabe's story

60. "When You're Eighteen." *The Spokesman* [literary magazine, Loras College] 57, no. 1 (1959): 44-46. Rpt. in *Today* [national Catholic magazine—Chicago], 15, no. 6 (Mar. 1960): 38-39.

61. "The Color of Bears." *The Spokesman*, 57, no. 2 (1959-60): 26-31.

62. "Nothing But the Sky." *The Spokesman*, 57, no. 3 (1960): 14-19.

63. "Beatnik." *The Spokesman*, 57, no. 4 (1960): 32-34.

64. "Jocko." *The Spokesman*, 57, no. 4 (1960): 45-53.

65. "Stomach." *The Spokesman*, 58, no. 1 (1960): 12-18.

66. "The Loudest Sound." *The Spokesman*, 58, no. 1 (1960): 54-60.

67. "Jack Be Nimble." *The Spokesman*, 58, no. 2 (1961): 18-23.

68. "The Last Moment." *The Spokesman*, 58, no. 2 (1961): 42-46.

69. "Napkins and a Coke Straw." *The Spokesman*, 59, no. 1 (1961): 8-13. Rpt. in *Today* [national Catholic magazine—Chicago], 17, no. 4 (Jan. 1962): 36-39.

70. "But the King Was Dead." *The Spokesman*, 59, no. 1 (1961): 53-57.

71. "After the Play Was Over." *The Spokesman*, 59, no. 2 (1962): 3-9.

72. "A Wash of Snow & Lye." *The Spokesman*, 59, no. 2 (1962): 80-85.

73. "Ben Schmidt's Old Shoes." *Mademoiselle*, Apr. 1974: 202-203.

POEMS

74. "Night." *The Crest* [student newspaper, Loras Academy], May 20, 1955: 2.

75. "Deathbed." *The Spokesman*, 57, no. 2 (1959-60): 33. Included in *Annual Anthology of College Poetry* (1960).

76. "I Loved Her." *The Spokesman*, 57, no. 3 (1960): 8.

77. "Boy, Seven." *The Spokesman*, 57, no. 3 (1960): 42.

78. "Adolescents." *The Spokesman*, 57, no. 4 (1960): 15.

79. "Knight Errant: 1960." *The Spokesman*, 58, no. 1 (1960): 46.

80. "Yes, I Remember." *The Spokesman*, 58, no. 1 (1960): 75.

81. "Boy/Man." *The Spokesman*, 59, no. 2 (1962): 28.

PREFACES AND AFTERWORDS

82. "Introduction." *The Basic Training of Pavlo Hummel and Sticks and Bones: Two Plays by David Rabe*. New York: Viking, 1973. ix-xxv.

83. "Author's Notes." *The Basic Training of Pavlo Hummel*. In *The Basic Training of Pavlo Hummel and Sticks and Bones: Two Plays by David Rabe*. New York: Viking, 1973. 103.

84. "Author's Notes." *Sticks and Bones*. In *The Basic Training of Pavlo Hummel and Sticks and Bones: Two Plays by David Rabe*. New York: Viking, 1973. 211-12.

85. "Afterword." *Hurlyburly*. New York: Grove Press, 1985. 161-71.

86. "Author's Note." *In the Boom Boom Room*. New York: Grove Press, 1986. 127-28.

NEWSPAPER ARTICLES

87. "The Cruelest Game." *Philadelphia Magazine* (Apr. 1969): 82-87, 142-43.

88. "A Wanderer Passes Through New Haven." *New Haven Register Sunday Pictorial* [Magazine], June 22, 1969: [8], 9, [10], 11.

89. "The Fine Art of Shaping Obstinate Clay." *New Haven Register Sunday Pictorial* [Magazine], July 13, 1969: 17-19.

90. "Weiss: Philosophy and The Fight." *New Haven Register Sunday Pictorial* [Magazine], Aug. 10, 1969: 6-7, 9.

91. "On Different Journeys." *New Haven Register Sunday Pictorial* [Magazine], Aug. 24, 1969: 8-9.

92. "Ahmed Sharif: Sour View of U.S. Criminology." *New Haven Register Sunday Pictorial* [Magazine], Sept. 7, 1969: 8-9, 11.

93. "Strenuous Test for Writers." *New Haven Register Sunday Pictorial* [Magazine], Oct. 5, 1969: 18-19, 21.

94. "Architects of Webs." *New Haven Register Sunday Pictorial* [Magazine], Oct. 12, 1969: 8, [9-13].

Rabe's introduction to photoessay by Gene Gorlick and John Degnall

95. "Merchants' Quest for Quality." *New Haven Register Sunday Pictorial* [Magazine], Oct. 19, 1969: 22-25, 27.

96. "Three Faces of Dissent and How They've Changed." *New Haven Register Sunday Pictorial* [Magazine], Dec. 14, 1969: Part I. "Multiple Viewpoints": 6, 7; Part II. "The Draft Information Center": 7-11; Part III. "Two Very Different Movies": 14-18.

97. "The Military Stance." *New Haven Register Sunday Pictorial* [Magazine], Dec. 14, 1969: 20-25.

98. "Conscientious Objector." *New Haven Register Sunday Pictorial* [Magazine], Dec. 14, 1969: 34-37.

99. "High Expansion Winter." *New Haven Register Sunday Pictorial* [Magazine], Jan. 25, 1970: 10, [11-14].

Unsigned article

100. "A Rainy Day in Hartford with Katherine Houghton." *New Haven Register,* Feb. 22, 1970, "Arts and Leisure," 4: 1, 4.

101. "A Life of Ordered Singularity." *New Haven Register Sunday Pictorial* [Magazine], Feb. 8, 1970: 15-17.

102. "Return to the Orient." *New Haven Register Sunday Pictorial* [Magazine], March 15, 1970: 20-21, [22], 23-25.

103. "Time Machine for Words." *New Haven Register Sunday Pictorial* [Magazine], Mar. 22, 1970: 6-7, 9.

104. "Artist Cimaglia's Obsession." *New Haven Register Sunday Pictorial* [Magazine], Apr. 26, 1970: 14-15, 17, [18], 19, 21-22, [23].

105. "The Great Inner (Space) Race." *New Haven Register Sunday Pictorial* [Magazine], June 7, 1970: [8], 9-11.

106. "Daytop's Dope Fiends." *New Haven Register Sunday Pictorial* [Magazine], June 14, 1970: 4-6, 8-9.

107. "'85 to 90 Per Cent, That's Total Cure, No Relapses.'" *New Haven Register Sunday Pictorial* [Magazine], June 14, 1970: 9-10.

108. "Indoctrination at Daytop." *New Haven Register Sunday Pictorial* [Magazine], June 21, 1970: [4], 5-9.

109. "Hostility Encounter." *New Haven Register Sunday Pictorial* [Magazine], June 21, 1970: 10-12, [13].

110. "Survivor of a Difficult Trip." *New Haven Register,* July 5, 1970, "Arts and Leisure," 4: 1, 7.

     Profile of John Clellon Holmes, a founder of the "Beat School of Poetry"

111. "New Theatre for the Adventurous." *New Haven Register,* July 12, 1970, "Arts and Leisure," 4: 1, 7.

112. "An Attorney's Look at Legal Bias." *New Haven Register Sunday Pictorial* [Magazine], Aug. 9, 1970: 4-7.

113. "A Strange and Wanton Game." *New Haven Register Sunday Pictorial* [Magazine], April 25, 1971: [8], 9-13.

114. "So We Got Papp in to See a Runthrough." *New York Times*, June 4, 1972, "Arts and Leisure," II: 1.

BOOK, PLAY, AND MOVIE REVIEWS

115. "The War. . . And What It Does To Men." *New Haven Register,* Oct. 20, 1968, "Arts and Leisure," 4: 4.

     Review of Martin Russ's *Happy Hunting Ground*

116. "A Gut Film. . . And Commercial." *New Haven Register*, May 11, 1969, "Arts and Leisure," 4: 3, 7.

Review of Martin Scorsese's film *Who's That Knocking at My Door*

117. "Bringing Joyce to the Stage." *New Haven Register*, June 15, 1969, "Arts and Leisure," 4: 1,4.

Review of University of Bridgeport's stage adaptation of James Joyce's *Finnegans Wake*

118. "*When the Water's Running*." *New Haven Register*, June 17, 1969: 31.

Review of Robert Anderson's play *You Know I Can't Hear You When the Water's Running* performed at Westport Summer Theatre

119. "The Unreachable." *New Haven Register*, July 27, 1969, "Arts and Leisure," 4: 4.

Review of Knut Hamsun's novel *Victoria*

120. "*South Pacific*." *New Haven Register*, Sept. 2, 1969, "Arts and Leisure," 4: 8.

Review of Westport Summer Theatre production

121. "Beyond the Power to Redeem." *New Haven Register*, Oct. 19, 1969, "Arts and Leisure," 4: 4.

Review of *Fat City* by Leonard Gardner

122. "A Long Wharf Premiere Is Impressive Off Broadway." *New Haven Register*, Nov. 9, 1969, "Arts and Leisure," 4: 3.

Review of American premiere of *A Whistle in the Dark*

123. "Search for an Eternal Name." *New Haven Register*, Dec. 28, 1969, "Arts and Leisure," 4: 1, 2.

Review of *Wanton Soup* performed at La Mama Theatre, New York

124. "Strindberg at Yale." *New Haven Register,* Jan. 15, 1970, "Arts and Leisure," 4: 18.

   Review of *Crimes and Crimes* performed by Yale Repertory

MISCELLANEOUS

125. Promo for "The Birdman of the Peabody" [forthcoming story in the *Pictorial*], *New Haven Register,* Aug. 1, 1969: 33.

   Unsigned

126. Promo for "Boys and Girls Together—Why?" [forthcoming story in the *Pictorial*], *New Haven Register,* Aug. 1, 1969: 33.

   Unsigned

127. "Each Night You Spit in My Face." *New York Times,* "Drama Mailbag," Mar. 18, 1973, 2: 3, 20.

   Addressed to Soviets who pirated *Sticks and Bones*

128. Blurb for Michael Herr's novel, *Dispatches.* New York: Knopf, 1977.

129. Letter of protest sent to Czechoslovakian leader Gustav Husak, Feb. 11, 1977.

   See Paul Hoffmann, "Czech Underground Literature Circulating Hand to Hand." *New York Times,* Feb. 15, 1977: 3

   Rabe is one of 54 signatories to protest arrests of dissidents

130. Lyrics to "Baby When I Find You." Lyrics to song included in *Sticks and Bones.* New York: Samuel French, 1979. 95.

TRANSLATIONS

131. *I Blinde* [*Sticks and Bones*]. Trans. Bjorn Endreson. Oslo, 1972.

132. *Bot es gitar* [*Sticks and Bones*]. Trans. Bakti Mihaly. 1974.

   Unpublished translation for Pesti Szinhazban, Budapest, Feb. 1974

133. *Knuppel und Knochen* [*Sticks and Bones*]. Trans. Joachim Brinkmann. Berlin: Felix Bernd Erben, 1975.

134. *O Uruwashi No Rakkasan Hiraiteo-Kure: Sutorimazu* [*Oh, Beautiful Parachute, Open: Streamers*]. Trans. Marie Kai. 1979.

   Translated for Seihai Theatre Company, Tokyo, May 31, 1979-June 8, 1979. (Copies available from Prof. Kai, 408 Demeure Tsudanuma, 3-16-30 Tsudanuma, Narashino-shi, Chiba Prefecture, Japan, 275)

135. *Soldat Hummel* [*Basic Training of Pavlo Hummel*]. Trans. Jan Maagaard. 1979.

   Translated for the Gladsaxe Teater production in 1979. (Copies available from Gladsaxe or Jan Maagard, H. C. Andersens Blvd. 7, 1553, Copenhagen)

136. *Bokire To Hone* [*Sticks and Bones*]. Trans. Marie Kai and K. Kurahashi. 1981.

   Translated for Mingei Company at Tokyo's Sabo Hall, Oct. 24 to Nov. 4, 1981

137. *Hurlyburly.* Trans. Bernd Samland. Berlin: S. Fischer Verlag, 1985.

138. *Hurlyburly.* Trans. Rossella Bernascone. In *Teatro Americano.* Genoa: Costa & Nolan, 1987.

139. *Chutes Libres* [*Streamers*]. Trans. Henri Behar, 1987.

For planned Paris production, Spring 1988. (Write to Henri Behar, 26 Gramercy Park West, Room 8A, New York, NY 10003)

INTERVIEWS

140. "Rabe Speaks." *The Villanovan*, 44, no. 16 (Feb. 5, 1969): 7, 11.

141. Gussow, Mel. "2nd David Rabe to Join *Pavlo Hummel* at Public Theatre." *New York Times*, Nov. 3, 1971: 43.

142. Fields, Sidney. "Viet Vet, Teacher, Author." *New York Daily News*, Nov. 15, 1971: 50.

143. "Rabe." *New Yorker*, Nov. 20, 1971: 48-49.

144. Berkvist, Robert. "If You Kill Somebody. . ." *New York Times*, Dec. 12, 1971, II: 3.

145. Michener, Charles. "The Experience Thing." *Newsweek*, Dec. 20, 1971: 58, 61. Rpt. in *The Loras Alumnus*, 22, no. 2 (Feb. 1972): 1.

146. Tallmer, Jerry. "The Basic Training of David Rabe." *New York Post,* "This Week in Entertainment," Mar. 11, 1972, 2: 15.

147. Glover, William. "David Rabe Was Ready." *New Haven Register*, Mar. 19, 1972: 8.

148. Kaye, Ellen. "The Private War of David Rabe." *Philadelphia Inquirer Magazine*, Mar. 19, 1972: 18-20, 26, 27, 31. Rpt. in *Villanova Alumnus*, 34, no. 6 (June 1972): 1, 11.

149. Glover, William. "Rabe One New Playwright Not to Be Found Napping." *New Orleans Times-Picayune*, Apr. 2, 1972, II: 13.

150. Naedele, Walter F. "The Basic Training of David Rabe, Soldier-Playwright." *Philadelphia Sunday Bulletin*, "Amusements and Travel," Apr. 2, 1972, 5: 1, 2, 3.

151. Cochran, Marsha. "'I Didn't Think It Was Possible.'" *New Haven Register,* "Arts and Leisure," Apr. 30, 1972, 4: 1, 5.

152. Brockway, Jody. "Defining the Event for Myself." *After Dark,* 5 (Aug. 1972): 56-57.

153. Wahls, Robert. "The Competitors." *New York Sunday News*, Apr. 1, 1973, II: 8.

154. Cultural-News Department. *"Boom Boom Room* and the Role of Women." *New York Times*, Nov. 24, 1973: 22.

    Interview with Rabe and actress Madeline Kahn

155. Kramer, Carol. "Plays by Rabe, Power by Papp." *Chicago Tribune,* Dec. 9, 1973, II: 12.

156. Adcock, Joe. "Rabe Cagey About the Intentions of *Orphan.*" *Philadelphia Evening Bulletin*, Mar. 5, 1974: 33.

157. Vogel, Caryn. "David Rabe: 'Playwriting taught by one's life.'" *Indiana Daily Student* [campus newspaper Indiana University], Nov. 14, 1975, II: 7.

158. Taylor, Markland. "The Fates Seem to Dictate Rabe's Role as Playwright." *New Haven Register*, Feb. 1, 1976, "Arts and Leisure," 4: 1, 4.

159. Berkvist, Robert. "How Nichols and Rabe Shaped *Streamers.*" *New York Times*, Apr. 25, 1976, II: 1, 12.

160. Gussow, Mel. "Rabe is Compelled 'To Keep Trying.'" *New York Times*, May 12, 1976: 34.

161. Kelly, Kevin. "*Streamers* Brings Rabe Confidence." *Boston Globe,* May 23, 1976, A: 8, 13.

162. Simmons, Ira. "Oh, No. . . Another Success." *The Courier Journal/Louisville Times*, "Scene," July 10, 1976: 7, 21.

163. Prochaska, Bob. "David Rabe: 'there's no audience that ever experiences anything I haven't experienced when I wrote it.'" *Dramatics*, 48 (May-June 1977): 18-20.

164. Weller, Sheila. "Jill Clayburgh Wants It All." *McCall's*, Mar. 1980: 27-28, 31, 32, 100.

165. "An Interview with David Rabe." In *Streamers* [Sept. 1983]: 20-23; "An Interview with Robert Altman": 12-15.

    Press leaflet prepared by Manson International in Hollywood and distributed by Rank Film Distributors in the U. K.

166. Taylor, Clarke. "Playwright Rabe Cheered at Filmfest." *Los Angeles Times*, Oct. 12, 1983, VI: 2.

167. Newquist, Jay. "*Streamers* Author Ponders Play as Film." *New Haven Register*, "Arts and Travel," Nov. 6, 1983, D: 1.

168. Bennetts, Leslie. "Interview with Rabe." *New York Times*, May 11, 1984, III: 2.

169. Christiansen, Richard. "Is Our Destiny Our Doom? Playwrights Give an Answer." *Chicago Tribune*, May 20, 1984, XIII: 16.

170. Dudar, Helen. ". . . And as Rabe Sees Hollywood." *New York Times*, June 17, 1984, 2: 1, 5.

171. Freedman, Samuel G. "Rabe and the War at Home." *New York Times*, June 28, 1984, C: 13. Rpt. *Biographical Service, New York Times*, 15 (June 28, 1984): 843-44.

172. [Freedman, Samuel G. and Michaela Williams.] "A Conversation Between Neil Simon and David Rabe: The Craft of the Playwright." *New York Times Magazine*, May 26, 1985: 37-38, 52, 56, 57, 60, 61, 62.

173. Freedman, Samuel G. and Michaela Williams. "Playwright's Craft: Views from Tony Nominees." *Columbus Dispatch* [Ohio], June 2, 1985, F: 1.

Condensed version of interview with Neil Simon and Rabe in #172
above

174. Kleiman, Dena. "A Revival That May Not Revive." *New York Times*,
Aug. 19, 1986, sec. 3: 13.

   Rabe discusses *Goose and Tomtom*

175. O'Brien, Jerry. "From a Conversation with Playwright David Rabe."
Trinity Repertory Company Playbill, Dec. 1986: 18-21, 23, 25.

   Interview took place on Oct. 31, 1986

176. Gale, William K. "This *Hurlyburly* is the Real One." *Providence
Sunday Journal,* Dec. 14, 1986, "Arts," I: 1, 4.

   This interview was occasioned by the production of Rabe's play by
   Trinity Rep in Providence

177. Savran, David. "An Interview with David Rabe." *In Their Own
Words: Contemporary American Playwrights.* New York: Theatre
Communications Group, 1987.

SECONDARY BIBLIOGRAPHY

RELEVANT BIBLIOGRAPHIES

178. Barnes, Clive. "Off-Broadway." *Theatre 4: The American Theatre 1970-1971.* New York: Scribner's, 1972. 36.

179. Bronner, Edwin. *The Encyclopedia of the American Theatre 1900-1975.* South Brunswick, NJ: A. S. Barnes, 1980. 59, 445, 572, 586.

180. Calloway, Catherine. "Vietnam War Literature and Film: A Bibliography of Secondary Sources." *Bulletin of Bibliography,* 43 (Sept. 1986): 149-158; Rabe is included only on page 150 under "Drama."

     Lists 22 items on drama about Vietnam War

181. Carpenter, Charles A. *Modern Drama Scholarship and Criticism 1966-1980: An International Bibliography.* Toronto: University of Toronto Press, 1986. 76.

     Includes 13 items on Rabe

182. Eckert, Edward and William J. Searle. "Creative Literature of the Vietnam War: A Selective Bibliography." *Choice* (Jan. 1987): 725-35; Rabe is included on page 729.

     Sticks, Pavlo Hummel, and *Streamers* are summarized under section on "Drama"

183. Eddleman, Floyd Eugene. *American Drama Criticism, Supplement II.* Hamden, CT: Shoe String, 1976. 133-34.

   Lists selected play reviews

184. _____. *American Drama Criticism: Interpretations 1890- 1977.* Hamden, CT: Shoe String, 1979. 311-13.

   Lists selected reviews of five Rabe plays—*Pavlo, Sticks, Streamers, Orphan,* and *Boom Boom Room*

185. Harris, Leonard. "Broadway." *Theatre 5: The American Theatre 1971-1972.* New York: Scribner's, 1973. 24

   Sticks and Bones

186. Hughes, Catharine, ed. *New York Theatre Annual 1976-1977.* Detroit: Gale, 1978. I: 53, 139.

   Pavlo Hummel, Streamers

187. _____. *New York Theatre Annual 1977-1978.* Detroit: Gale, 1979. II: 59.

   Pavlo Hummel

188. King, Kimball. *Ten Modern American Playwrights: An Annotated Bibliography.* New York: Garland, 1982. 186-96.

   Includes 18 items of Rabe criticism and 69 theatre reviews

189. Newman, John. *Vietnam War Literature: An Annotated Bibliography of Imaginative Works About Americans Fighting in Vietnam.* Metuchen, NJ: Scarecrow Press, 1981. 104-105.

   Summarizes plots of *Pavlo Hummel* and *Sticks*

190. Smith, Susan Harris. "Twentieth-Century Plays Using Classical Mythic Themes: A Checklist." *Modern Drama*, 29 (Mar. 1986): 127.

   Includes *The Orphan* under Orestes myth

191. *Theatre Profiles/1.* New York: Theatre Communications Group, 1973. Et passim.

192. *Theatre Profiles/3.* Ed. Marsue Cumming. New York: Theatre Communications Group, 1977. 2, 6, 24, 108, 120, 150, 196.

193. *Theatre Profiles/4.* Ed. David Skal. New York: Theatre Communications Group, 1981. 5, 41, 50, 57, 66, 129.

194. *Theatre Profiles/5.* Ed. Laura Ross. New York: Theatre Communications Group, 1982. 144.

195. *Theatre Profiles/6.* Ed. Laura Ross. New York: Theatre Communications Group, 1984. 149.

196. Willis, John, ed. *Theatre World: 1984-1985 Season.* Vol. 41. New York: Crown, 1986. 8, 61, 184.

197. _____. *Theatre World.* Vol. 40 (1983-84). 170.

198. _____. *Theatre World.* Vol. 38 (1981-82). 98, 186.

199. _____. *Theatre World.* Vol. 37 (1980-81). 210.

200. _____. *Theatre World.* Vol. 36 (1979-80). 90, 205, 216.

201. _____. *Theatre World.* Vol. 34 (1977-78). 173, 226.

202. _____. *Theatre World.* Vol. 33 (1976-77). 70, 154, 184, 200.

203. _____. *Theatre World.* Vol. 32 (1975-76). 78, 132, 212.

204. _____. *Theatre World.* Vol. 31 (1974-75). 129.

205. _____. *Theatre World.* Vol. 30 (1973-74). 121, 233.

206. _____. *Theatre World.* Vol. 29 (1972-73). 86, 145, 214, 230.

207. _____. *Theatre World.* Vol. 28 (1971-72). 36, 118.

BIOGRAPHY

208. Ames, Wilmer. "Restless Jill Clayburgh." *People*, Nov. 5, 1979: 68, 70-71.

209. "Another Hit behind Him, Rabe Turns to Film." *Dubuque Telegraph Herald*, Jan. 24, 1977: 7.

210. Announcement about Rabe as Lorasman. *Loras Alumni Newsletter*, Aug. 1971: 4.

211. "Art-Theatre—Across the Drama Desk." *New Haven Register*, May 26, 1972, sec D: 3.

    Rabe to win John Gassner Medallion for playwriting

212. "A Year Broadway is Busy Forgetting." *Philadelphia Inquirer*, June 22, 1985: 8.

213. Ball, A. L. "Clayburgh Off-Camera: Just Plain Jill . . . ?" *Redbook*, Apr. 1982: 76, 78.

214. "Band." *The Log 1957* [Yearbook of Loras Academy]: 117.

215. "Band." *The Log 1958* [Yearbook of Loras Academy]: 7.

    "David Rabe, Trumpet Player"

216. Barnes, Clive. Introduction and Biography. *Streamers*. In *Best American Plays; Eighth Series, 1974-1982*. Ed. Clive Barnes. New York: Crown Publishers, Inc., 1983. 403.

217. Biographical sketch. *1961 Purgold* [Loras College Yearbook]: 52.

218. Biographical sketch. *1962 Purgold* [Loras College Yearbook]: 59.

219. "Births: News of Record." *Dubuque Telegraph Herald*, Mar. 11, 1940: 2.

    Rabe's birth announcement

220. Bordman, Gerald. "David Rabe." *The Oxford Companion to American Theatre.* New York: Oxford, 1984. 564.

221. Bruckner, D. J. R. "Playwrights in Search of Dramatic Language." *San Francisco Chronicle*, July 28, 1985: 39.

222. Calta, Louis. "Critics Vote 2 Papp Shows Best of Year." *New York Times*, May 23, 1972, sec. L: 34.

223. "Clayburgh Has Miscarriage." *Milwaukee Journal*, Oct. 25, 1980, "People," sec. I: 2.

224. Cochran, Marsha R. "Playwright David Rabe, Director Barnet Kellman: *The Register* Brought Them Together." *New Haven Register*, Aug. 25, 1974, sec. D: 3, 9.

    Discusses Rabe's relationship with Kellman, director of the New American Theatre Ensemble and their friendship in working on *The Orphan*

225. Collins, William. "*Big River* Tops Tony Nominations." *Philadelphia Inquirer*, May 7, 1985, sec. E: 1.

226. "D. Rabe." *The Log 1955* [Yearbook of Loras Academy]: 46.

227. "David Rabe." *The Log 1956* [Yearbook of Loras Academy]: 45.

228. "David Rabe." *The Log 1957* [Yearbook of Loras Academy]: 74.

229. "David Rabe." *The Log 1958* [Yearbook of Loras Academy]: 30.

230. "David Rabe . . ." *The Lorian*, 39 no. 1 (Jan. 18, 1962): 3.

    Rabe's story "Napkins and a Coke Straw" published in *Today*

231. "David Rabe." *Current Biography*, 34 (July 1973): 29-32.

232. "David Rabe." *Encyclopedia of World Theater*. New York: Charles Scribner's & Sons, 1977. 223.

233. "David Rabe." *Who's Who in America*, 43 (1984-85). 2671.

234. "David Rabe Named Winner of Hull-Warriner Award." *New York Times*, Dec. 4, 1971: 23.

235. "David Rabe: All the War's a Stage." *Playboy*, Aug. 1972, "On the Scene": 168-69.

236. Ellis, Joshua. "Rabe Play to be Produced in New York." *The Villanovan*, 46, no. 30 (May 5, 1971): 9.

Basic Training of Pavlo Hummel

237. "English." *The Log 1957* [Yearbook of Loras Academy]: 40.

238. "Ex-*Register* Man's Play Wins Tony Nomination." *New Haven Register*, Apr. 4, 1972: 19.

239. "Ex-*Register* Writer Wins $3000 Prize for His Two Plays." *New Haven Register*, Dec. 5, 1971: 31A.

240. "Football: Loras-3—Lacrosse Logan-0; Loras-6 Dowling-7." *The Log* 1957 [Yearbook of Loras Academy]: 145, 146- 47.

    Rabe's performance on the football team

241. "Football: Loras-0—Alleman-19; Loras-0—East Waterloo-0; Loras-21—Logan-6; Loras-28—Campion-18." *The Log 1958* [Yearbook of Loras Academy]: 79.

    Rabe's performance on the football team

242. Gent, George. "Arts Award Goes to Absent Papp." *New York Times*, May 26, 1972: 20.

243. Gussow, Mel. "A Rich Crop of Writing Talent Brings New Life to the American Theater." *New York Times*, Aug. 21, 1977, sec II: 1.

244. _____. "Productive Papp Follows the Writers' Lead." *New York Times*, Mar. 4, 1974, sec. L+: 38.

245. "Hail the Chiefs . . ." *The Lorian*, 37, no. 13 (May 12, 1960): 1.

   Rabe is among new editors of Loras College's literary magazine, *Spokesman*

246. Harmetz, Aljean. "New York Police Graft Film Topic." *New York Times*, July 13, 1978, sec III: 22.

   Rabe to write screenplay for movie *Prince of the City*

247. Hart, James D. "David Rabe." *The Oxford Companion to American Literature*. 5th Edition. New York: Oxford University Press, 1983. 623.

248. Hartnoll, Phyllis. "David Rabe." *The Oxford Companion to the Theatre*. New York: Oxford University Press, 1983. 677.

249. Henry, William A., III. "Playwright Rabe in Profile." *Boston Globe*, Apr. 19, 1972: 28.

250. Herbert, Ian, ed. "David Rabe." *Who's Who in the Theatre*. Vol. 1. Detroit: Gale Research, 1981. 558.

251. Hirsch, Dale. "Rabe, Varsity Fullback, Takes Literary Awards." *The Crest* [Loras Academy student newspaper], Oct. 26, 1956: 4.

252. "Hollywood Newlyweds: Making Marriages Work." *US*, 3, no. 3 (May 29, 1979): 30, 31.

253. Hughes, Catharine. "Did Vietnam Spoil David Rabe?" *America*, 134 (May 15, 1976): 432.

254. "Jill's House." *Philadelphia Inquirer*, Aug. 9, 1978, sec. D: 11.

255. Johnson, Elaine. "Oscars Something Special for Dubuque Couple." *Dubuque Telegraph Herald*, Mar. 9, 1980: 1.

256. "Joseph Papp Gets Big Ideas. An Interview with Ross Wetzsteon." *American Theatre*, Sept. 1986: 11-17, 50.

257. Kaplan, Mike, ed. "David Rabe." *Variety International Show Business Reference*. New York: Garland, 1981. 225.

258. _____. "David Rabe." *Variety's Who's Who In Show Business*. New York: Garland, 1983. 224.

259. Kaye, Phyllis Johnson, ed. "David Rabe." *National Playwrights Directory*. Waterford, CT: Eugene O'Neill Theater Center, 1981. 330-31.

260. Kelly, Kevin. "*Streamers* Brings Rabe Confidence." *Boston Globe*, May 23, 1976, sec. A: 8, 13.

261. Kroll, Jack. "Clayburgh Touch." *Newsweek*, Oct. 8, 1979: 69-70.

262. Lawson, Carol. "Elizabeth Taylor to Make Theatrical Debut." *New York Times*, Oct. 15, 1980: 18.

263. Linfield, Susan. "Zen and the Art of Film Acting." *American Film*, July-Aug. 1986: 28-33.

     Interview with William Hurt who played Eddie in *Hurlyburly*

264. Little, Stuart W. *Enter Joseph Papp: In Search of a New American Theater*. New York: Coward, McCann & Geoghegan, 1974. 136-63, 194-99, 203-205, 240-46, et passim.

     Contains detailed study of Papp's problems with CBS over *Sticks and Bones*; numerous references to Rabe

265. _____. *Off-Broadway: The Prophetic Theater*. New York: Coward, McCann & Geoghegan, Inc., 1972. 261, 288.

266. "Loras in the News." *The Loras Alumnus*, 28, no. 1 (Aug. 1976): 5.

267. "Loras Student's Works Accepted for Anthology." *The Lorian*, 37, no. 6 (Jan. 13, 1960): 4.

Rabe's poem "Deathbed" to be included in *Annual Anthology of College Poetry*

268. Mann, Roderick. "Jill Clayburgh on Center Stage." *Los Angeles Times*, Mar. 27, 1979, sec. IV: 10.

269. Morite, Charles, ed. "David Rabe." *Current Biography Yearbook 1973*. New York: H. W. Wilson Co., 1973. 339-41.

270. Musto, Michael. "La Dolce." *Village Voice*, Apr. 7, 1987: 42.

Briefly mentions Rabe's novel in progress, *Recital of the Dog*; also refers to Rabe's dinner companions at Grove Press party

271. "News Notes." *The Loras Alumnus*, 34, no. 2 (Spring-Summer 1984): 30.

272. "News Notes." *The Loras Alumnus*, 36, no. 1 (Fall 1985): 31.

273. "Nichols, Streep Get Heartburn." *Miami Herald*, June 16, 1985, sec. K: 6.

Includes a quotation from Rabe

274. Niepold, Mary Martin. "Plays by Rabe, Lee Show Early Talent." *Philadelphia Inquirer*, Apr. 2, 1976, sec. D: 7.

Rabe's *The Crossing* to be staged by Philadelphia Company

275. "1961 *Spokesman* Editors Named." *The Lorian*, 38, no. 13 (May 19, 1961): 3.

Rabe selected as editor of Loras College literary magazine, *Spokesman*

276. Panella, Vince. "Rabe's Plays Done Off-Broadway and He's Right On!" *Dubuque Telegraph Herald*, Dec. 5, 1971: 41.

277. "Papp Slates Ex-*Register* Staffer's Play." *New Haven Register*, Apr. 25, 1971, sec. D: 3.

   Basic Training of Pavlo Hummel

278. "Poet John Logan Meets Students." *The Lorian*, 39, no. 3 (Nov. 2, 1961): 5

   Rabe interviews poet Logan who visits Loras

279. *Proceedings of the American Academy of Arts and Letters and The National Institute of Arts and Letters.* Second series, no. 25. New York, 1975. 16.

   "Presentation of Awards by Jacques Barzun, President of the Institute" contains the citation accompanying Rabe's award written by Kurt Vonnegut, a member of the committee that chose Rabe

280. Rabe poses for ad. *Esquire*, Aug. 1987: 99

   Rabe models cardigan, shirt, and diver's watch

281. "Rabe Rates Raves in New York." *The Villanovan*, 47, no. 11 (Nov. 17, 1971): 1.

282. "Rabe Returns with Flying Streamers." *Globe and Mail* [Toronto], May 14, 1976: 14.

283. "Rabe, Slaughter Win Honors." *The Lorian*, 37, no. 9 (Mar. 9, 1960): 8.

   Rabe's story "When You're Eighteen" will be published in *Today Magazine*

284. Rockefeller Foundation. *The President's Review and Annual Report 1981.* New York, 1981. 37.

   Rabe listed as one of eight authors to receive an award for playwriting

285. Santa, Jay. "More Good News for Rabe's Folks." *Dubuque Telegraph Herald*, May 26, 1977: 17.

286. Schier, Ernest. "David Rabe is Having a Good Month Despite CBS's Cancellation of His Play." *Philadelphia Evening Bulletin*, Mar. 8, 1973: 28.

287. _____. "David Rabe's Tony Award Well-Deserved." *Philadelphia Evening Bulletin*, Apr. 27, 1972: 26.

288. _____. "Villanova's David Rabe: Impressive." *Philadelphia Evening Bulletin*, Oct. 27, 1970: 21.

   Early assessment of Rabe's talents

289. Shepard, Richard F. "250 Playwrights Protest Equity's Rules on Fees." *New York Times*, May 8, 1980, sec. III: 19.

290. "Special Citation Voted by Critics to Rabe Play." *New York Times*, May 25, 1972, sec L+: 52.

291. "*Spokesman*." *1961 Purgold* [Loras College Yearbook]: 124-25.

   Comments on Rabe's work on Loras College literary magazine

292. "*Spokesman* Staff Members Named." *The Lorian*, 38, no. 3 (Oct. 20, 1960): 8.

293. Stitt, Milan. "Gratitude Must Be Paid." *Horizon*, Dec. 1984: 17.

294. Syse, Glenna. "A Rare Talk with Mike Nichols." *Chicago Sun-Times*, Apr. 24, 1984: 47.

   Nichols's relationship with Rabe is included

295. Takiff, Jonathan. "Phila. Co. Wins A Tip of the Hat." *Philadelphia Daily News*, Apr. 2, 1976: 30.

296. "Track." *The Log 1956* [Yearbook of Loras Academy]: 116.

297. Tully, Tom. "Loras Freshmen Stage Own Play." *The Lorian*, 34, no. 10 (Apr. 8, 1959): 10.

Staging Rabe's first play, *The Chameleon*

298. Vallely, J. "It's My Turn." *Rolling Stone*, Nov. 27, 1980: 54-57.

Review of film *It's My Turn* with profiles on stars Weill, Clayburgh, and Douglas

299. "Varsity Football." *The Log 1956* [Yearbook of Loras Academy]: 90, 94, 95.

300. "Varsity Track." *The Log 1957* [Yearbook of Loras Academy]: 166.

301. "Villanova Man Makes His Mark." *Philadelphia Inquirer*, Apr. 24, 1972: 8.

302. Wakeman, John, ed. "David Rabe." *World Authors: 1970- 1975*. New York: H. W. Wilson, 1980. 666-69.

303. "Why is This Man Laughing?" *Boston Globe*, May 14, 1978, sec. L: 4.

304. Wilson, Edwin and Alvin Goldfarb. *Living Theatre: An Introduction to Theatre History*. New York: McGraw Hill, 1983. 353.

305. "Winners in Annual Loras Literary Contest Announced." *The Crest* [Loras Academy student newspaper], May 20, 1955: 1.

Rabe wins first prize in poetry contest for "Night"

306. Woodside, Christine. "Busy Actress Says, 'I'm Just a Mom.'" *The Patent Trader* [Mt. Kisco, NY], Feb. 20, 1987, sec. A: 1, 7.

Story on Jill Clayburgh and her activities as wife and mother

307. Wright, David. "Rabe Teeters at Pinnacle of Drama Career." *Dubuque Telegraph Herald*, July 29, 1973: 44.

308. Zito, B. L. "Jill Clayburgh: Dancing as Fast as She Can." *American Premiere*, 3 (Apr. 1982): 12-15+.

CRITICAL STUDIES: AN ANNOTATED SURVEY

309. Adler, Thomas P. "Blind Leading the Blind: Rabe's *Sticks and Bones*
      and Shakespeare's *King Lear*." *Papers on Language and Literature*,
      15 (1979): 203-206.

      Rabe is indebted to *King Lear* "for certain symbols, character
      configurations, and thematic motifs." Chief among these are parallels
      between the blinded David and Gloucester as well as Cordelia (a
      "moral authority"); and Ozzie and Lear (both deny an honest child—in
      the inventory scene of Act II of *Sticks* and in the mock trial scene in
      Lear). The character of David, however, shows "one of Rabe's
      deficiencies, and perhaps finally his most serious"—David is "so
      arrogant in his moral superiority—something Cordelia never is—that
      the play is without any core of empathic identification."

310. American Assembly, Columbia University. *The Performing Arts and
      American Society*. Englewood Cliffs, NJ: Prentice-Hall, 1978. 107.

      Sticks came to Broadway from the New York Shakespeare Festival,
      "New York's own very distinctive resident theater."

311. Ariizuma, Norioki. "Vietnam War Plays." In *The Traditional and the
      Anti-Traditional Studies in Contemporary American Literature*. Ed.
      Kenzaburo Ohashi. Tokyo: The Tokyo Chapter of the American
      Literature Society of Japan, 1980. 191-200.

      Rabe is discussed within the literary tradition established by writers'
      responses to the war.

312. Asahina, Robert. "The Basic Training of American Playwrights:
      Theatre and the Vietnam War." *Theatre*, 9 (Spring 1978): 30-37; 35-

37 concentrate specifically on Rabe.

While journalists controlled the public perception of the war and
dramatists avoided it or turned their plays into polemics, Rabe was
"the only playwright really concerned with the art of the theater rather
than with the form or the content of the media." Although Rabe
escaped the "journalistic snares" of autobiography and "advocacy,"
his plays display serious flaws. *Pavlo Hummel* and *Sticks* lack
"authenticity," are stuffed with "overblown symbolism," contain
"mysterious" characters (Zung or Ardell who in sunglasses suggests
"shades of Tiresias?"), and rely on "preexisting" story lines.
Streamers, however, "exhibits real dramatic movement" and offers a
"perfect metaphor." Like "parachutists at the mercy of their packers,"
characters in *Streamers* are divided between those "who will float"
and those "who will plunge" to their destiny.

313. Atkinson, Brooks, and Al Hirschfeld. *The Lively Years 1920-1973: A
     Half Century of the Most Significant Plays on Broadway.* New York:
     Da Capo Press, 1985. 299-302.

     Sticks "simmers with hatred" as it presents the effects of war on a
     family of strangers obsessively fearful of miscegenation. The entire
     play "emerges as a kind of evil hallucination in which the characters
     can never escape the privacy of their own experience." Allowing the
     audience no quarter, Rabe's play "gives the theatre distinction as a
     public forum." For the Lafayette Street audiences the play was
     "overwhelming"; on Broadway *Sticks* was "merciless." It deserves
     the honor of being "the play that made the most devastating case
     against national policy."

314. Barranger, Milly S. *Theatre Past and Present: An Introduction.*
     Belmont, CA: Wadsworth, 1984. 427, 452, et passim.

     Rabe's achievements are mentioned as part of a general survey of
     contemporary American theatre.

315. Beidler, Philip D. *American Literature and the Experience of Vietnam.*
     Athens: University of Georgia Press, 1982. 26, 88, 112-19, 179-82.

     Rabe's plays are acknowledged as being "the most important
     contributions to the dramatic literature of Vietnam during the period

1970-75." Beidler believes that they depict a "collective tragedy" proving that the horror of the war "had been implicit in the American character from the outset." *Pavlo Hummel* is a "mad, inexhaustible pastiche" of America's involvement in the war. Accompanied by Ardell ("a slangy, irreverent GI Virgil"), Pavlo in death as in life "experiences nothing." The family in *Sticks* protects the "whole American mythology of a happy life" which Rabe parodies and which the blind son punctures. *Streamers* is "about the effects of a 'memory' of something called Vietnam upon a group of soldiers who have never been there" but who experience its brutality stateside. Beidler concludes that Carlyle "brings out the dark latencies" found in the other characters.

316. Berkowitz, Gerald M. *New Broadways: Theatre Across America 1950-1980*. Totowa, NJ: Rowman and Littlefield, 1982. 83, 126, 136-38, 157.

Although he "ranks below" Shepard and supposedly has only "one thing to say," Rabe "dramatized the damage done to the American spirit by the Vietnam war more eloquently, perhaps, than any writer in any genre." In *Pavlo Hummel* the title character "confuses" manhood with self-destructive army rituals. Sticks discloses the evil that assaults everything the wholesome family and the nation symbolize. *Streamers*, "the darkest of the three" plays, reveals the "inescapable doom" foretold in its metaphoric title.

317. Bernstein, Samuel J. *The Strands Entwined: A New Direction in American Drama*. Boston: Northeastern University Press, 1980. 17-34, 139-40, et passim.

Bernstein first reviews the major criticism of *Sticks*, focusing on Rabe's promise as a writer and the perceived flaws in his art. Turning to an analysis of *Sticks*, he then compares it with works by Sophocles, Ibsen (especially *Ghosts*—David is like Oswald Alving), Conrad (*Heart of Darkness*), Eliot, Ionesco, and Van Itallie. Although *Sticks* savagely attacks American venality and false values, it is not simply an anti-American play. It is like a traditional tragedy in structure (especially in Rabe's use of the screen in the prologue and epilogue), in the symbolic presence of sickness and blight (in David), and in the use of Hank Grenwaller as the "demi-god" and "god devil" who, as the representative of "the American ethos," casts his dangerous shadow over the family.

Rabe has intertwined absurdism and realism so well that we cannot separate them; the realism is a "facade, a cover" for the ugliness of American culture as well as a "clue to the dark, unfriendly void that lies beneath." Rabe's realism is frightening; it never "allows us to relax" with the family. Bernstein concludes: "Brilliantly, Rabe has fused episodic incident and linear plot, associative image and cause and effect developments, poetry and prose, monologue and dialogue, comic and tragic impulses, in order to reveal a panorama of truths about American culture and about life and death itself."

318. Bigsby, C. W. E. *A Critical Introduction To Twentieth-Century American Drama.* Vol. 3 *Beyond Broadway.* New York: Cambridge University Press, 1985. 324-31, 417.

Bigsby contends that Rabe is "not best seen simply as a Vietnam playwright," even though unlike many contemporary dramatists, "the war and its effects lay at the heart of most of his major works." Rabe uses the war metaphorically to expose America's "profound uncertainties," cruelties, racism, and a "desperately uncommunal world." In *Pavlo Hummel*, Rabe's "target is not merely the moral and literal anarchy of war but equally that of the culture which wages it." Pavlo is confused, betrayed; Ardell is best seen as a "kind of chorus, commenting on the action, but never intervening." Similarly, *Sticks* is "not so much concerned with Vietnam as with the desperate attempt of its characters to deal with radical disjunction in their lives." Its "soap opera family" rejects David, whose fate is identical to many returning veterans because he threatens the insane mythos of the family. In *Streamers*, Vietnam again becomes a "dramatic device" to orchestrate the social "tensions" that "erupt in violence." Its metaphoric title refers to the men "having lost whatever values, whatever structures, that support their lives."

319. Bode, Walter. "David Rabe." *Contemporary Authors.* Ed. James Vinson. 2nd ed. New York: St. Martin's Press, 1983. 660-62.

Rabe's plays "define the structures and strictures of American life." He has a powerful sense of the "spoken word" and a great "facility in scenic structures." In *Pavlo Hummel* the dire message is that "the physical body is all that exists." *Sticks* tears away at "America's comforting and fatuous self-image." And *Streamers* contains "realistic" insights about America. But *Boom Boom Room* lacks the "precision" of Rabe's Vietnam plays.

320. Bonin, Jane F. *Major Themes in Prize-Winning American Drama.* Metuchen, NJ: Scarecrow Press, Inc., 1975. 83, 85, 86.

Like other anti-war plays, *Sticks* is a "striking example of a violent play which protests violence." In attacking the insensitivity of folks back home, David is like Chris in Arthur Miller's *All My Sons.*

321. Brockett, Oscar G., and Robert R. Findlay. *Century of Innovation: A History of European and American Theatre and Drama Since 1970.* Englewood Cliffs, NJ: Prentice-Hall, 1973. 715.

Pavlo Hummel, "considered by many the best play yet written about the Vietnam War," is discussed as one of the offerings of Papp's "controversial" theatre.

322. Brockett, Oscar. *"Streamers." Historical Edition. The Theatre: An Introduction.* New York: Holt, Rinehart, 1979. 400-404.

Pavlo Hummel questions the belief that "soldiering is the ultimate test of manhood," and *Sticks* attacks the "tribalistic tendencies of the American family" toward xenophobia. In *Streamers* Rabe questions another American myth—"Army life's the essence of masculinity"— by dramatizing the threats of homosexuality and violence, both "organic to Rabe's purposes." In its "compact and entirely realistic" style, *Streamers* reveals that Roger, Billy, and Richie evade "self-knowledge"; that the sergeants, who "best represent the Army," are not "authentic heroes and real men" but "pathetic" pranksters; and that Carlyle, "the most crucial character," is unconcerned about the masculinity myth and like a captured animal is "alternately affable and enraged." The symbol in Rabe's title, applicable to not only "parachutists but all humanity," raises "questions about the nature of the canopy that suspends us and keeps us from crashing fatally." An open chute symbolizes love. The final scene, which "gives shape and meaning to the play," shows the waste that results from following the myth.

323. Brooks, Colette. "In Pursuit of the Self: Actor and Society." *Yale/ Theatre*, 8 (Spring 1977): 94-103; 101-103 focus on *Sticks and Bones*.

   Robert Patrick's *Kennedy's Children* and *Sticks* are "simplistic and decidedly sentimental [;] they engender and then exorcise the sense of guilt that currently afflicts the country . . . ." *Sticks* frees the audience from necessary and painful self-analyses since it would identify with David instead of the complacent family Rabe misguidedly attacks. In fact, *Sticks* leads "only to a deceptively cathartic moment of self-congratulation." Rabe's "most pressing interest" is to portray David as the misunderstood Romantic poet-artist who, in the context of the "political realities" surrounding the play, is judged "offensive."

324. Brooks, Tom. "Blah-blah-blah." *1986-87 Humanities Booklet #3*: 6-9. Prepared through Rhode Island Committee for the Humanities for Trinity Repertory Company.

   Hurlyburly is not about drugs; it is about the characters' struggle with and over language itself. Language fails on both the semantic level (in accurately representing reality) and on the phatic level (in connecting speakers socially). These two functions of language often mix, get confused, and lead to confrontation. Eddie, for example, expects a phatic response from the television; and Phil's suicide note emphasizes that "the semantic content of language may bear no necessary relationship" to events in the characters' lives.

325. Brown, Janet. *Feminist Drama: Definitions & Critical Analyses*. Metuchen, NJ: Scarecrow Press, Inc., 1979. 17, 37-55.

   The Boom Boom Room displays a "feminist rhetorical motive" in picturing Chrissy in her struggle to obtain "autonomy" in a "socio-sexual" and oppressively patriarchal "hierarchy." The world of the go-go bars mirrors society in general—bleak, oppressive, despairing (for women and men alike). Identifying associational clusters occurring on various levels of the play, Brown concludes that women are presented as food for men's consumption, outsiders excluded from various institutions (prisons, hospitals, churches), and objects to be violently exploited by men. Susan and Guy, Chrissy's friends, seemingly occupy an "unusual position" in the hierarchy but in fact are really part of it because of their oppressive acts or sexual rivalry

with Chrissy. In the symbolic action of the play, Chrissy's attempts
to establish her selfhood are futile; her anger is "diffuse" and
ineffective as "each character attempts to impose a limiting sexual
role" on her. In the end she is a sacrificial victim to materialism, "an
impersonal sexual commodity." Brown concludes that the "total
inflexibility and final triumph of the unjust hierarchy" turn *Boom
Boom Room* into "a deterministic dramatic statement."

326. Bruckner, D. J. R. "Strong Language." *San Jose Mercury News*,
"Arts and Books," July 14, 1985: 12.

Rabe, Shepard, and Mamet have infused a new dramatic language into
the American theatre. The intensity of *Pavlo Hummel* can be
attributed to Rabe's "language more than time or place dislocations."
In *Sticks* the power of language is "even greater," especially in
Ozzie's "mad eloquence." In *Hurlyburly*, the characters are stripped
down to nothingness by the language they use. "As they diminish,
their language builds up a vision of the repulsive world they live in,
work in and believe in even as they are destroyed by it."

327. Brustein, Robert. "Contemporary American Theatre: The Importance
of Freedom." *Theatre Quarterly*, 3 (Apr.-June 1973): 31-35; Rabe is
discussed on 34.

Along with Shepard, Ribman, Fornes, Terrence McNally, Owens,
Adrienne Kennedy, and others, Rabe is part of a "large number of
good young writers with serious ambitions"; they are searching for
"an authentic poetic vision" but still have not written a "major play."
Paradoxically, the American theatre is experiencing an "unprecedented
freedom," yet it has "lost its power to reach us." As an example,
Brustein points out that *Sticks* attacks the very "national character" of
the middle-class audience who supports the play. One cannot help
wondering, concludes Brustein, if the audience is really "alive."

328. _____. "The Crack in the Chimney: Reflections on Contemporary
American Playwriting." *Theatre*, 9 (Spring 1978): 21-29.

Rabe is judged to be the "most typical and the most highly esteemed
of the younger generation of playwrights." Like Arthur Miller, he
deals with guilt, the family, and the responsibility of "his middle-class
characters for the crimes of the nation at large." Brustein draws

comparisons in theme and technique between *All My Sons* and the "semisurrealist" *Sticks*, "a relatively straightforward family drama," and concludes that Rabe's indictment of his audience by dwelling on its guilt has been savagely undercut by Christopher Durang in his *Vietnamization of New Jersey.*

329. ____. *Making Scenes: A Personal History of the Turbulent Years at Yale 1966-1979.* New York: Limelight, 1984. 100, 154, 198, 239.

Scattered throughout Brustein's book are brief comments on Rabe as a reviewer (for the *Register*), Durang's parody of *Sticks and Bones* in his *Vietnamization of New Jersey*, and Rabe's reputation as a writer whose language accurately portrays and reflects military life.

330. Bryfonski, Dedria, and Phyllis Carmel Mendelson, eds. *Contemporary Literary Criticism, 8.* Detroit: Gale, 1978. 449-51.

In a section entitled "Sidelights," a pastiche of reviewers' comments on Rabe's plays reflects the variety of critical responses they have elicited. This overview concludes with the sentence: "If Kalem's assessment is right [*Time*, May 3, 1976], then the unopened parachute is an appropriate metaphor for the whole of Rabe's work."

331. Christiansen, Richard. "Gun-shy Rabe Makes Triumphant Return to New York Stage." *Houston Chronicle*, Aug. 8, 1976: 17.

The "large metaphor" for *Streamers* is the story of the Viet Cong caught in the bunker with an exploding grenade. At the beginning of the play, Rabe "figuratively tosses a grenade on stage" to the audience. Analyzing the characters, and finding that "they are all at war with themselves," Christiansen maintains that in some ways *Streamers* is a "sentimental work" in presenting "familiar characters."

332. Clifton, Merritt, Coordinating Editor. *Those Who Were There: Accounts of the War in Southeast Asia, 1956-1975 & Aftermath.* Paradise, CA: Dustbooks, 1984. 160-61.

Found here is a brief summary of *Pavlo Hummel* and *Sticks* that notes that David's "physical disability counts for almost nothing in comparison to what the parents regard as a moral failing."

333. Coale, Sam. "Phone Booths in the Shopping Mall in Your Head." *1986-87 Humanities Booklet #3*: 1-3. Prepared through Rhode Island Committee for the Humanities for Trinity Repertory Company.

In *Hurlyburly* "language can lie; it can distort and spiral inward." Victims of the Information Age, Rabe's characters speak of deals, dreams, and misdeals, all of which get lost in a "kind of incestuous labyrinth."

334. Cohn, Ruby. *New American Dramatists: 1960-1980*. New York: Grove Press, 1982. 31-36.

Rabe's plays have a "stylistic rather than thematic consistency." *Pavlo Hummel* and *Sticks* (which is "more sentimental and broadly satiric") have predominantly "straightforward plots." *The Orphan* offers "tedious confusion" as Rabe "reaches for myth" to create a "more positive hero." The "obverse" of Pavlo, Chrissy (*In the Boom Boom Room*) is more aware of being a victim. Everyone tries to "martyrize Chrissy; her very name is a Christian derivative." The mask in the last scene conceals her previously "gullible face." *Streamers* is Rabe's "least pretentious and most coherent play," an honest reflection of "the Army in the 1970s." Cohn concludes that it is only Rabe's "seriousness that might offend on Broadway."

335. Collins, William B. "Will Rabe's Plays Break Theater's Silence About Vietnam War?" *Philadelphia Inquirer*, Jan. 23, 1972, sec G: 1, 6.

Pavlo Hummel and *Sticks*, which show that the theatre is at last turning to the war, "are more considerable as art than as polemics" and reveal that Rabe is "writing not so much about Vietnam as from Vietnam." Pavlo's plight is presented in "highly theatrical terms." But *Sticks* is a "quieter, more coherent and deeper play" that is "about love as well as war."

336. _____. "Durang's Satiric *Vietnamization* Seems to Lack Direction." *Philadelphia Inquirer*, Apr. 6, 1982, sec C: 10.

Collins draws a number of comparisons between *Sticks and Bones* and *Vietnamization*, pointing to the ways in which Durang's plot and characters attack Rabe's.

337. Cooper, Pamela. "David Rabe's *Sticks and Bones*: The Adventures of
     Ozzie and Harriet." *Modern Drama*, 29 (Dec. 1986): 613-25.

     Agreeing with Robert Asahina (# 312), Cooper observes that Rabe's
     play "contains an ironic and satirical comment on the ability of jour-
     nalism to tell the truth." Although the absence of television coverage
     of the war in the 1980s "muffles the impact of the play for a contem-
     porary audience," Rabe's "controlled fury" throughout *Sticks* reveals
     a "profound mistrust of the media." Through the fictional Nelsons
     Rabe attacks a "consumer society" that has clearly "reduced family life
     to supply and demand." The family's clichéd thinking and language
     (filled with "euphemisms and advertising jargon") is ultimately
     responsible for the war and cannot explain or appreciate "profound
     human experience." Attacking television and "its products," Rabe
     stresses the ways Harriet's obsession with food exposes "the
     commercial mother's shallow expression of love." Father Donald
     glibly provides the family with "instant spiritual gratification." The
     sickly Hank Grenweller "signals the rottenness of a powerful,
     mythologized ideal of American manhood: athletic, healthy, and
     strong." Ozzie's "language of stereotyped machismo" reflects the
     American combative savagery of Vietnam. (Later, Ozzie "slips into
     David's lyrical style of speech.") The "ripest and fullest expression of
     violence" is embodied in Rick ("a virtual eating machine") who has
     "the lowest level of linguistic usage." Zung's presence in the Nelson
     house symbolizes the plague that the family itself spreads: she also
     symbolizes David's "projected desires and his failure of nerve."

     David's "phantasmagoric, poetic style" contrasts with the family's
     clichés as he searches for truth. The returning son is both an invader
     and a victim; he is, however, "too ambiguous to be either a hero or
     martyr." David discovers that the world is deterministic and sees
     "identity as nothingness, a hole." The title of Rabe's play questions
     the truth of the nursery rhyme ("sticks and stones may break my
     bones . . .") as it "affords a clue to the major stylistic strategy of the
     play itself"; the setting represents both realism (downstairs) and
     symbolism (the imaginary walls of David's bedroom upstairs).

338. Counts, Michael Lee. *The Twentieth-Century American Homecomer*.
     Diss., CUNY, 1983. Ann Arbor: UMI, 1984. 83-19755.

     In analyzing plays dramatizing a soldier returning home, Counts

identifies some major themes: adjustment to society; society's
reception of the homecomer; reception of the soldier by spouse,
fiancee, or other loved one; the homecomer as a ghost or spirit; and
homecomers from more than one war. These themes are traced in
Sticks and works by other playwrights.

339. "David Rabe." *Charivari* [Felix Bloch Publishers Bulletin], 123 (May
     1972): 1.

     Rabe's *Pavlo Hummel* touches the most sensitive nerves of America
     as it is engulfed in the unpredictable chaos of the Vietnam War. Pavlo
     suffers the fate of someone caught in the mechanistic world of war,
     and he is harshly ground down. In *Sticks* no one wants to or can
     understand the pained David.

340. Donohue, John W. "*Sticks and Bones* on TV." *America*, Sept. 1,
     1973: 120.

     Supplying background information on the airing of *Sticks* in August
     1973, Donohue finds that CBS's decision was wise, for the play is
     "usefully" abrasive. *Sticks* "suggests that the engine really powering
     the war was racism," and in its technique the play combines
     "allegorical substance and colloquial form." Rabe can clearly be seen
     as one of a new breed of Catholic-educated authors whose work is
     "gifted."

341. Freedman, Samuel G. "America Making About-Face on Vietnam."
     San Francisco Chronicle, "Datebook," Apr. 28, 1985: 17, 21.

     Beginning with a synopsis of the film *Uncommon Valor*, Freedman
     then reflects on how "the Vietnam War is affecting the popular culture
     and fine art of America today." Focusing on films, an exhibit of
     Vietnam art ("Vietnam: Reflexes and Reflections"), television, fiction,
     theatre, and poetry, Freedman sketches the changing views of
     Vietnam and the American soldier over the last three decades. Among
     these changes are that the American soldier who was the "war criminal
     of the 1960s" is "the hero of the 1980s," that Vietnam itself has
     moved from a "safe subject" to a "trendy one," that the "anti-war
     movement has come in for skepticism," and that Vietnam art (closely
     associated with World War I literature) is "more personal than

polemical." Regarding the possibility of "a period of healing" taking place, Rabe is quoted as saying: "The phase now . . . is to make up a tolerable explanation for Vietnam. Our appetite is for a substitute answer, not the real answer. We'll salve ourselves."

342. Frymer, Murry. "Fear and Change on Stage: 'When I was Growing Up, Gays in . . . Plays were Criminals.'" *San Jose Mercury News*, Jan. 10, 1986, sec D: 1.

David A. DeLong, the director for the City Lights production of *Streamers*, believes that a gay director "can provide a sensibility to *Streamers* that others might miss." While there is a gay theme in the play, *Streamers* is "more a story about fear—racial, homophobic, combat-related . . . ."

343. Gawlik, Jan Pawel. "Rzecz O Nieprzystosowaniu." ["A Case of Maladjustment."] Playbill for *Jak Brat Bratu*, Teatr Stary, Krakow, Mar. 6, 1973.

Rabe's play offers a dual genealogy and a dual meaning. On the surface it deals with the war and the price a man pays for it. This theme belongs to the good school of American drama that can be traced to Albee and Miller. But a second, deeper element concerns the moral aspect of the play. Rabe presents a conflict of conscience and milieu. David, a former murderer and rapist, now sees reality in its true form. His otherness (he is a stranger who poses a threat) conflicts with the middle-class ideals of consumption his family espouse. Thus the play deals with the drama of maladjustment. Rabe's hero belongs to an old archetype going back to Antigone who says no to mendacity, preferring death to compromise. We must feel solidarity with David.

344. Grabes, Herbert. "Das experimentelle Theater in Amerika seit den fruhen 60er Jahren." In *Das Amerikanische Drama*. Ed. Gerhard Hoffmann. Berne: Franke, 1984. 245-46, 51.

Rabe's plays (especially *Sticks* and *Streamers*) and dramatic technique are analyzed and Rabe is seen as a contributor to experimental theatre in America.

345. Guthmann, Edward. "*Rundown*/Forgotten Anxieties of Vietnam Revived." *San Francisco Chronicle*, "Datebook," June 23, 1985: 42-43.

As a part of this review of Robert Auletta's *Rundown* Rabe's works are briefly mentioned. According to Auletta, *Rundown* is "more impressionistic, less grounded in realism" than Rabe's trilogy. Moreover, he continued, "Rabe's plays are more about combat, about being a soldier." Auletta's play is more concerned with the "'post-traumatic stress' of the Vietnam veteran."

346. Hassan, Ihab. *Contemporary American Literature, 1945-1972*. New York: Frederick Ungar, 1973. 177.

Recognizing that "some of the best dramatists of the seventies are Black," Hassan also admits that "two new white playwrights deserve special notice"—David Rabe and Michael Weller.

347. Hertzbach, Janet S. "The Plays of David Rabe: A World of Streamers." *Essays on Contemporary American Drama*. Eds. Hedwig Bock and Albert Wertheim. Munich: Hueber, 1981. 173-86.

Hertzbach identifies key metaphors, themes, and topical issues in Rabe's plays. Violence, racism, the family, terror, and the lack of alternatives to destructive streamers become the "central metaphor" in his plays; the "controlling metaphor" in *Pavlo Hummel* is the army ritual. Pavlo, the "classic loser," searches in vain for heroism; the structure of the play represents his "self-centered confusion and failure to develop." In *Sticks*, "domestic violence is as terrible" as the battlefield variety, for the family becomes a "potential minefield." A major flaw in *Sticks* is David's arrogance; he learns only to hate, not to grow.

Exhibiting "intellectual gamesmanship," *The Orphan* also emphasizes that "the source of all corruption is the family," but the mythological connections Rabe insists upon are not entirely convincing. Chrissy (*In the Boom Boom Room*) inhabits an "urban jungle" where go-go cages represent "physical and mental imprisonment." Unlike Rabe's military protagonists, though, she lacks "vitality," and the play may reveal Rabe's inability to write about events and character "not directly associated with the war." Because it is "straightforward" and "structurally" more coherent, *Streamers* is a "more persuasive" play than the others. Like Pavlo and David, Carlyle is "the Rabean grenade" ready to explode. Aside from *Streamers*, Rabe's plays may be locked into the times they depict.

348. _____. "David Rabe." *Critical Survey of Drama: English Language Series*. Ed. Frank N. Magill. Englewood Cliffs, NJ: Salem Press, 1984. IV: 1545-54.

Reiterating the points made in her 1981 essay above, Hertzbach classifies Rabe's dramas as "war plays" reflecting the "turbulent era" of the 1960s and 1970s. Up to *Hurlyburly*, the confusion in the lives of Rabe's characters is "figured, institutionalized, and sometimes justified by ritualistic activities that are symbolic of their alienation and lack of choice rather than of the communal experience and support that ritual ordinarily celebrates." *Hurlyburly* shows "both a continuation and a break with" Rabe's previous works. Although set in the new jungle of Hollywood, *Hurlyburly* does not attempt the "sort of ironic ritual which pervades his earlier plays."

349. Hoffman, Ted. Introduction. *Famous American Plays of the 1970s*. New York: Dell, 1981. 20-21.

The metaphor in *Pavlo Hummel* applies to both war and domestic experiences. Although the play has a "traditional" plot suggesting "a fable, an epic tale," it is told as if the middle-class Pavlo has to relive his life again and again "until the details become illuminating." Rabe is neither a "'protest' playwright nor an affirmer. He is mordant and paradoxical . . . ."

350. Homan, Richard L. "American Playwrights in the 1970's: Rabe and Shepard." *Critical Quarterly*, 24 (Spring 1982): 73-82.

Rabe's style progresses from nonrepresentational staging characteristic of the 1960s to a new realism used "to challenge our everyday sense of reality." Language, which is inadequate to express our needs, becomes "a form of conflict." As a manifestation of that conflict, "the horror of violence can be juxtaposed with the assumptions of everday life." In *Pavlo Hummel* and *Sticks*, military and civilian worlds merge through the "contradictory sides" of Rabe's "unified" fictional creations.

351. Hughes, Catharine. *American Playwrights 1945-75*. Chapter 8: "David Rabe." New York: Pitman, 1976. 81-87, 103.

Although praising Rabe ("the most significant playwright to appear since Albee"), Hughes finds major weaknesses in his work. *Pavlo Hummel* has "so many layers that the focus is at times diffused." The "weakest element" in the play, however, is Ardell who is "never fully integrated or defined." Pavlo, though, is credible ("neither a bad guy nor a good guy"). David's bitterness in *Sticks* (an odd combination of "menace and melodrama") is not made sufficiently clear to the audience. *The Orphan* is "vastly more flawed" because of "murkiness and intellectual clutter." *In the Boom Boom Room* offers powerful writing coexisting with tedious action; Chrissy is too inarticulate to sustain an audience's interest. She is "yet another in a long line of Marilyn Monroe figures."

352. _____. *Plays, Politics, and Polemics*. New York: Drama Book Specialists / Publishers, 1973. 77-82.

Pavlo Hummel is not "polemical"; Rabe "avoids both easy sentimentality and facile point scoring." He does not take sides as far as the grotesqueries of war are concerned; for him "war is a tragicomic nightmare in which no one can really win." It is wrong, therefore, to see Pavlo as becoming dehumanized. In Rabe's more "complex" presentation, this "gung ho" and "mixed up . . . oddball" is used by the Army which "gives him the occasion to cultivate his basic capacity for the inhumane."

353. Hurrell, Barbara. "American Self-Image in David Rabe's Vietnam Trilogy." *Journal of American Culture*, 4 (1981): 95-107.

After briefly tracing the growing interest in Vietnam in American popular entertainment, Hurrell describes the Dubuque of his boyhood, the vision of America he was exposed to, and Rabe's views of writing about the war. Historically, America's wars were just and her veterans respected and honorable. Not so in Vietnam. "The extent to which individuals (and, by extension, whole countries) will go to preserve a self-image, no matter how distorted, is the constantly recurring motif" in Rabe's trilogy. The battle between "incompatible" images is existentially translated into a "struggle between 'self' and 'other.'" Rabe's protagonists (with whom Rabe has a number of significant traits in common) find the self threatened by hostile others—the war-sanctioning church and the racist family in *Sticks*, fellow soldiers in *Streamers*, or the Vietnamese themselves in *Pavlo Hummel*. The spiritual and psychological crisis these protagonists experience in attempting to "bolster flawed images" absurdly results in death.

354. Jackson, Graham. "The Theatre of Implication." *Canadian Theatre Review*, 12 (1976): 41.

In the Boom Boom Room is briefly discussed in light of its implications for gay theatre.

355. Jacobus, Lee A. "David Rabe's *The Basic Training of Pavlo Hummel* (1971)." *The Longman Anthology of American Drama*. Ed. Lee A. Jacobus. New York: Longman, 1982. 615-17.

Rabe's views about the war "have remained complex." Like many other American plays, *Pavlo Hummel* ("fascinating on many grounds") raises the question of innocence. Pavlo is "weird"; he is "not a figure who can be taken symbolically or allegorically and he is definitely not modeled after Rabe himself." A brief contrast of *Pavlo Hummel* with Bronson Howard's *Shenandoah* establishes great differences in world view and theme between these two American plays.

356. Kauffmann, Stanley. "Sunshine Boys." *New Republic*, May 26, 1973: 22.

Theatre critics (the "Sunshine Boys") are guilty of "overpraising" writers like Rabe (elevating a "small talent" into a large one) and then denigrating the dramatists' later work. Kauffmann claims, though, that Rabe's most recent play (*The Orphan*) "was merely infested with the disease that had been evident in the two earlier ones." It is a "ludicrous" work and the worst part of the play is the language. *Pavlo Hummel* is "one more good-hearted sentimental undergraduate play about the horrors of war . . . using stale expressionist fantasy and even staler rhetoric to prove its humanitarianism and high-mindedness." *Sticks* is a "mixed bag" written "in sharp pop-art style" but overflowing with "purple speeches."

357. _____. "*Sticks and Bones*," *New Republic*, Dec. 4, 1971: 22. Rpt. in *Persons of the Drama: Theater Criticism and Comment.* New York: Harper & Row, 1976. 224-26.

Rabe's earlier produced *Pavlo Hummel* was "another sincere anti-war play which proved that sincerity was not enough." The "mode" of *Sticks* is "pop art" and its dialogue "trivia swollen into threat." David's "river of rhetoric" is dyed a "college-dormitory purple" and Ozzie's "arias" are "faded Tennessee Williams." Rabe's "vision is insufficient" because his message is too obvious; Rabe "generally has more skill in the way that he says things than perception in what he has to say."

358. _____. "Molehills." *New Republic*, June 12, 1976: 20-21. Rpt. "*Streamers*" in *Theatre Criticisms.* New York: Performing Arts Journal Publications, 1983. 30-32.

Rabe is a "playwriting mole" whose "artistic gifts are insufficient to turn his commonplace precepts into strong dramatic emblems." The events in *Streamers* are not unique to the Vietnam era; they could have occurred earlier and in other places. Rabe uses "gimmicks" and inflated symbolism; his "dialogue is equally unsteady." Even Mike Nichols, who uses the stage "adroitly," becomes "less interesting, in his choices, in his shrinking compass."

359. Kellman, Barnet. "David Rabe's *The Orphan*: A Peripatetic Work in Progress." *Theatre Quarterly*, 7 (1977): 72-93.

Called an "unusual casebook study" in a headnote, this article chronicles the "genesis" of Rabe's *Orphan* by one of its directors. Kellman tells "the story of the writing of *The Orphan*, its development through no fewer than five productions, and [his] collaboration with the playwright during part of the process." In tracing the history of the play, Keller begins with *The Bones of Birds*, a one-act play performed at Villanova University. *The My Lai Book Report*, an unpublished "collage-like" document reflecting Rabe's attempt to review books on the subject, gave the playwright "the starting point for the second act of *The Orphan*." The New York Shakespeare Festival production was unpopular with critics and disappointing to both Jeff Bleckner, who directed it, and to Rabe himself. Enlisting

Rabe's help, Kellman revised the script and staged a new and "final"
Orphan at the North Carolina School of the Arts in 1975. Major
problems Kellman (and Rabe) confronted were the characterization
and motivation of Orestes, the dramatic necessity of two
Clytemnestras, the effect of Agamemnon (he is both "kingly" and
"fool"), the integration of the Family of Furies into the action, and the
staging of the play, including "the largest problem"—the altar.
Rewriting the play made it more moving and workable; in revising the
second act, for example, there was "fashioned a vessel to contain and
carry the play's thematic cargo to its destination." Kellman notes
"there is much to be said for seeing *The Orphan* as two plays—the
first act, Agamemnon's, the second act, Orestes', the play of the
father and the play of the son."

360. Kerr, Walter. "David Rabe's 'House' Is Not a Home." *New York
Times*, May 2, 1976, sec. 2: 5. Rpt. in *Journey to the Center of the
Theatre.* Chapter 1: "Dying Together." New York: Knopf, 1979.
134-37.

Starting with a review of a production of *Streamers* ("Rabe's most
successful play to date"), Kerr argues that the metaphoric use of
"house" is central to "Rabe's consistent view of his troubled
universe." In Rabe's dramas, houses have turned into "slaughter-
houses." Nor does this view have anything "to do really, with the
Vietnam War as such," which Rabe uses as "the most readily available
background." Rabe's message is that "We are all—black, white,
straight, queer, parents, children, friends, foes, stable, unstable—
living together in the same 'house.' And we cannot do it." We
"violate" each other with unrelenting despair. The asperity of Rabe's
message about our house has driven audiences out of the theatre or
left them sitting there "in numb horror."

361. Kiernan, Robert F. *American Writing Since 1945: A Critical Survey.*
New York: Frederick Ungar, 1983. 86, 88-89, 90.

Rabe, Mamet, and Shepard are "probably the most important
American dramatists of the 1970s." *Pavlo Hummel* and *Sticks* happily
avoid "antiwar rhetoric" and sentimentality, but the latter unfortunately
is "too much a product of the guilt complex" of the period and is thus
easily satirized by Christopher Durang's *Vietnamization of New
Jersey. Streamers*, which concerns the "exclusivity of groups,"

escapes Rabe's previous "capricious lyricism and straining symbolism" and shows that Rabe's "forte is realism."

362. Klein, Maury. "Misdeals." *1986-87 Humanities Booklet #3*: 3-6. Prepared through Rhode Island Committee for the Humanities for Trinity Repertory Company.

Rabe's characters are seen against the historical background of deal making essential to the market economy fueling the American Dream. Eschewing the "traditional values that hold society together," the Hurlyburlyites barter for better dreams and wait for "the next possibility, the Big Score." They are the "wave of the future" in the American market society.

363. Kohler, Klaus, "Das 'Underground Theatre.'" In *Studien zum amerikanischen Drama nach dem zweiten Weltkrieg*. Eds. Eberhard Bruning, Klaus Kohler, and Bernhard Scheller. Berlin: Ruthen and Loeing, 1977. 178-213; Rabe is discussed on 209-11.

Kohler provides a Marxist interpretation of *Sticks and Bones* focusing on the decadent American family which destroys the truth-searching son.

364. Kolin, Philip C. "David Rabe's *Streamers*." *The Explicator*, 45 (Fall 1986): 63-64.

Streamers explores an "archetypical theme—the rite of passage into manhood." Playing a crucial role in this rite are "the destructive father figures"—in both the army and civilian life. These men are guilty of "paternal crimes" (abandonment, violence, cruelty) against the young soldiers in the *Streamers* barracks. Other Rabe plays dramatize the father-son relationships, too.

365. _____. "Staging *Hurlyburly*: David Rabe's Parable for the 1980s." *The Theatre Annual*, 41 (1986): 63-78.

Hurlyburly is a bleak parable of the Hollywood cocaine culture "symbolizing contemporary American society caught up in the hurlyburly of dehumanization and despair." A study of Rabe's "provocative dramaturgy" focusing on the "acoustical, visual, and physical elements" in the play illustrates how these twin themes are raised and emphasized. Rabe's characters play games and "unintentionally confront destiny." They lead meaningless lives of "severed connections, aborted relationships." Perhaps more than any other American play, *Hurlyburly* reveals the variety and abundance of "pharmaceutical experiments" characters can indulge in. The setting of the Hollywood house, surrounded outside by encroaching vegetation and cluttered inside with Hollywood props, becomes "the new battleground of the 1980s (replacing the actual Vietnam of *Pavlo Hummel* or the Army barracks of *Streamers*)."

In *Hurlyburly* "language loses significance and sincerity" as characters shout at each other, exchange nonsense words in lieu of meaningful ones, and turn words into "combative weapons." The stage business involving telephone conversations also emphasizes the verbal hurlyburly. The way the characters dress—in tattered, patched clothing—or appear disheveled further suggests "their frazzled lives." In their movements and gestures, Rabe's Hollywoodites unleash their aggression; they pace in anxiety and anger or whirl in desperation. The collection of Hollywood props reflect the characters' despair and cluttered lives. Near the end of the play, "visual and verbal elements create a Rabean emblem of the comic horrors of Eddie's life." The dictionary ("the most important Hollywood prop") symbolizes many of "the negatives elevated to a position of importance in America today."

366. Lebdai, Benaouda. "The Representation of the Vietnam War in Western Theatre." *Proceedings of the International Conference in Comparative Drama.* Eds. David Konstan and Charlotte El-Shabrawy. Cairo: American University in Cairo Press, 1984. 150-64. Rabe is discussed on 161-63, 164.

At the end of a discussion of Vietnam literature Lebdai considers two plays which deal with "the presence of Vietnam in American society"—*Sticks* and Robert Patrick's *Kennedy's Children.* The theme of *Sticks* is "the reinsertion of the soldier into society," and in that "nightmare" world the family denies the identity of its own son who is never regarded as heroic. Rabe attacks "an army which considers every soldier a mere number." Throughout the play David "is the living memory of the war within his family."

367. Little, Stuart. "Joe Papp Seeks a Bigger Stage." *Saturday Review*, 55 (Feb. 26, 1972): 43-44.

Little briefly explains how Papp came to stage *Pavlo Hummel*, selected Jeff Bleckner to direct the play, and why he decided to move *Sticks* to Broadway. *Pavlo Hummel* has "rapid-fire dialogue" and "a magma of military slang." In a play "studded with such overt brutality there is perhaps no greater crime than the understated neglect by brother and mother," as Pavlo learns.

368. _____. *Off-Broadway: The Prophetic Theatre.* New York: Coward, McCann, 1972. 261, 288.

Rabe's work, especially *Sticks*, is briefly discussed in the chapter on "Popular Theater of Joseph Papp."

369. McDonald, David. "The Mystification of Vietnam: David Rabe's *Sticks and Bones*." *Cultural Critique*, 3 (Spring 1986): 211-34.

Sticks poignantly confronts the mystery that Vietnam introduced in the American consciousness—"in the sense of not knowing, of refusing to know or repressing and denying what is known; in the sense of never having been there or having been there and no longer being there; in the sense of lack or inability to produce an adequate image or representation of the meaning of Vietnam; and finally, in the sense of spectacle itself as the sustaining illusion of American ideology." This mystification is the controlling force behind "the significant absences in the play." Through parody Rabe reveals an absence of home and of family (they are "theatrical identities as copies of themselves"). David himself is "absent from home and Vietnam." Zung represents the Vietnam that Americans have tried to "displace." Hank Grenweller is the lost "ideal." And Father David, the exorcist who is a parody of a priest, knows nothing and is "replaced by nothingness."

Moreover, "we are displaced by the very signs that should give us identity"—photos, televisions, telephones, etc. The opening scene with the home movies—perhaps showing Ricky in the future as the father of two children watching the wounded Uncle David— reveals how "the future itself has the quality of something repeated." Like the unrepresented violence in Greek tragedy, David's blank movie of Vietnam emphasizes the family's refusal to see "David's consciousness" and the "inner vision" of the horror of war he offers. In both the "dionysiac orgies" and in the reversal of roles (David becoming the father, for example), we can see that "Oedipal conflict dominates the action, even as the conventional Oedipal drama is parodied." The "most sinister moment" in the play occurs when David attempts to rape Harriet. Ultimately, though, in parodying the family Rabe "limits the range of his criticism of the America that waged the Vietnam War." This parody unfortunately leads to an inadequate explanation and assessment of responsibility for the war.

370. McInerney, Peter. "Straight and Secret History in Vietnam War Literature." *Contemporary Literature*, 22 (Spring 1981): 187-204; see 190-91 for a discussion of Rabe.

Rabe's blurb for Michael Herr's novel *Dispatches* identifies for praise the blend of the poetic and the "bureaucratically camouflaged" language aptly characterizing "the American experience" in Vietnam.

371. Marranca, Bonnie. "David Rabe's Viet Nam Trilogy." *Canadian Theatre Review*, 14 (Spring 1977): 86-92.

Claiming that *Streamers, Pavlo Hummel*, and *Sticks* are "not anti-war plays," Marranca believes that Rabe is interested in the "*effect* of the Viet Nam experience on ordinary individuals." His plays "expose the turmoil of American life, and his characters represent attitudes toward heroism, maleness, alienation, violence, racism and interpersonal communication." *Streamers*, a "modern day well-made play," depicts "random violence" with "documentary realism." Marranca regards Richie as "the real villain," labels the sergeants "comic figures," and calls attention to Rabe's characteristic use of "poetic metaphor." *Pavlo Hummel* also erupts into violence but uses "semi-realistic" techniques. The loser Pavlo is a pawn of the system, and Ardell is his "inner voice." *Sticks* launches Rabe's "indictment of the American family" through the "gallery of grotesques" unable to communicate. Marranca finds that the "father-son conflict . . . dominates the play." Insisting that Rabe "never tries to make it easy for us," Marranca characterizes the trilogy as "the drama of moral rage" and hears in Rabe "the voice of the American consciousness."

372. Metcalf, William A. *A Search for the Causes of Violence in Selected Plays of David Rabe and Sam Shepard Compared to the Patterns of*

Violence Found in Rollo May's "Power and Innocence: A Search for the Sources of Violence." Diss., Univ. of Minnesota, 1982. Ann Arbor: UMI, 1986. PUV 83-01971.

Argues that "Rollo May's *Power and Innocence* . . . might prove useful to theatre artists attempting to produce plays of this period." Metcalf attempts "to present the life view developed by Rollo May and place it side by side with the views created by two playwrights of the period" in order "to determine if the playwrights and psychologists share common viewpoints about violence." A chapter each is devoted to the following plays by Rabe: *Pavlo Hummel, Sticks, In the Boom Boom Room, The Orphan*, and *Streamers*.

373. Mordden, Ethan. *American Theatre.* New York: Oxford University Press, 1981. 301, 318-19, 330.

Mordden succinctly reviews Rabe's fortunes in the theatre, his association with Joseph Papp, and the "neater justice" of Christopher Durang's *The Vietnamization of New Jersey*, a satiric parody of *Sticks*. A "hot playwright," Rabe's calling card may be that he is "the only prominent dramatist still writing in the social guilt complexes of the 1960s." Rabe is like "a lively Arthur Miller, especially in *Sticks and Bones*, a family play (Miller's choice of genre) . . . ."

374. Nyren, Dorothy, Maurice Kramer, and Elaine Fialka Kramer, eds. *Modern American Literature.* New York: Frederick Ungar, 1976. IV: 388-93.

This reference work reprints excerpts from reviews of Rabe's plays by the following critics: Harold Clurman, Jack Kroll, Henry Hewes, Gerald Weales, Gil Lazier, John Simon, Stanley Kauffmann, and Julius Novick.

375. Olszewski, Joseph Francis. "American Theater in the Sixties and Seventies: The Non-Broadway Stage and Its Playwrights." Diss. St. Louis Univ. *DAI,* 42 (Apr. 1982): 4500-A.

Analyzing plays by Rabe, Shepard, Mamet, Albee, and Lanford Wilson as cultural documents, Olszewski finds them valuable documents for students of American studies.

376. Patterson, James A. "David Rabe." In *Dictionary of Literary Biography.* VII, Part 2. *Twentieth-Century American Dramatists.* Ed. John MacNicholas. Detroit: Gale Press, 1982. 172-78.

As he summarizes the plots of five Rabe plays, Patterson identifies the strengths and weaknesses of each. Overall, Rabe is a "playwright of exceptional quality and promise"; his themes are "compellingly topical" and his language is "mordantly humorous and strangely lyrical." *Pavlo Hummel* shows a "surreal carnival of death" in which Pavlo is an "anti-hero," Ardell his "alter ego," and Tower an "archetypical figure." A major "shortcoming" of the play is "a confusion of styles." Similarly, *Sticks* is a "black comedy" but its style is a "major defect." Rabe's satire is double-edged, directed against the typical American family and those who endorse that "self image." While *The Orphan* contains some fine writing, the play "does not have the narrative energy to overcome the speciousness of its central idea." *In the Boom Boom Room* is "static" because Chrissy has little insight into herself or her "self worth." Appearing in a mask at the end of the play, she "is stripped of all vestiges of identity." Rabe's "most powerful" play is *Streamers*, which has the "promise of becoming a new American classic." Like *Pavlo Hummel*, *Sticks*, and *In the Boom Boom Room*, *Streamers* is "unschematic, violent, and often strangely lyrical" but unlike them it "is wholly realistic."

377. Phillips, Jerrold A. "Descent into the Abyss: The Plays of David Rabe." *West Virginia University Philological Papers*, 25 (Feb. 1979): 108-17.

For Rabe "existential nothingness" is "the core of all existence." The confused Pavlo unsuccessfully tries to discover identity and meaning in the army, yet "soldiering, the idea of mission, the revenge of slain buddies, all become senseless, devoid of any significance." He learns his lesson only by confronting, and being the victim of, his own mortality. In *Sticks*, David's "blindness is symbolic"; after his Vietnam experiences he can "no longer find any meaning in middle-class suburban existence." Conversely, David's family is blind to the horrors of Vietnam that he brings home with him. But while Harriet and Rick remain unchanged, Ozzie is transformed into a "nihilist" whose values are shattered. *In the Boom Boom Room* dramatizes Chrissy's "mental disintegration"; she is "surrounded by people who offer her definitions of existence that reinforce her own incapacity to

discover meaning." These individuals find "ways of adjusting to their
emptiness" by using others (especially Chrissy) sexually. In the last
scene, Chrissy's mask represents "her acceptance of nothingness." In
Streamers it is Cokes who makes "the descent into nothingness."
Two major images—blood and streamers (or signs of "impending
death")—underscore the "meaninglessness of all life."

378. Reston, James, Jr. "Introduction." *Coming to Terms: American Plays
& The Vietnam War*. New York: Theatre Communications Group,
1985. x.

Discusses *Streamers* in context of the war and in relationship to other
Vietnam War plays.

379. Riley, Carolyn, ed. *Contemporary Literary Criticism* 4. Detroit: Gale,
1975. 425-28.

Offers brief selections from the following critics: Henry Hewes,
Stanley Kauffmann, Julius Novick, Harold Clurman, Marilyn Stasio,
Gerald Weales, and Catharine Hughes.

380. Rosen, Carol Cynthia. "The Theater of Institutions: The
Reconstruction of the Total Institution on the Modern Stage." Diss.,
Columbia University, 1975. *DA*, 36(1975): 2813A.

381. _____. *Plays of Impasse: Contemporary Drama Set in Confining
Institutions*. Princeton: Princeton University Press, 1983. 236-50
(*Pavlo Hummel*); 250-59 (*Streamers*).

The "entropic" *Pavlo Hummel* and *Streamers* are plays of impasse in
presenting a "claustrophobic, no-exit situation" within a "setting
engulfing the individual." In comparing Rabe's plays with Arnold
Wesker's, Rosen studies Pavlo's character (he is "a misplaced
Everyman" whose "predecessors are vaudeville types"), the
"dreamlike" structure of the play, and also its "kaleidoscopic stage
design." The symbolic action is used to "heighten the effect of
regimentation, fragmentation, and loss," found in the act of basic
training itself. Pavlo's first act transformation exists on four levels—
the "naturalistic, sociodramatic, ritualistic, and symbolic." Pavlo is
lost in the illogical dream world of war demythified by Rabe. Even

"more profoundly," *Streamers* portrays "experience as a no-exit conceit." It has a "doubleness, its representational presentation and its sudden lurch beyond logic." The "loss of logic," the "organization of the audience response" to violence, and the impossibility of human contact characterize *Streamers* as a play of impasse. Rabe's cruel jokes uncover a "system which promises nothing."

382. Sanders, Joseph Elwood. "Modern American War Plays." Diss., UCLA, 1975. *DA*, 36(1975): 07A.

Pavlo Hummel* and *Sticks* are among some 20 plays extensively studied against the historical changes in the presentation of war and warfare in American drama.

383. Schafer, Jurgen. *Geschichte des amerikanischen Dramas im 20. Jahrhundert*. Stuttgart: Kohlhammer, 1982. 168-69.

Rabe is seen as an innovator in the American theatre.

384. Schier, Ernest. "Rabe Learns How to Write for Stage and Survive." *Philadelphia Evening Bulletin*, Apr. 6, 1976: 37.

Schier confirms "what is already known in local circles, that Rabe at 31 is a dramatist of considerable force and vision with a major career ahead of him." Not an ordinary anti-war play, *Pavlo Hummel* is a masterly "psychological" study of how men seek their own death. The play "questions not only war and military machines but all systems invented by men that are destructive of life." Schier admits that Pavlo is "not somebody it is easy to care about."

385. _____. "Villanova's David Rabe: Impressive." *Philadelphia Evening Bulletin*, Oct. 27, 1970: 21.

Assessing Rabe's early career, Schier praises *The Orphan* and *Bones*. Both plays reveal Rabe's "grasp of stagecraft that enabled him to skillfully handle dramatic situations . . . with multiple characters . . . carrying out action on several psychological levels at once." According to Schier, "there may be no other playwright in America writing against violence with as much passion and sense of commitment as David W. Rabe."

386. Schulz, Franz. "Amerikakritik in Edward Albee's *The American Dream*." In *Amerikanisierung des Dramas und Dramatisierung Amerikas*. Eds. Manfied Siebold and Horst Jimmel. Frankfort, 1985. 174.

   Briefly mentions *Sticks* and *Pavlo Hummel* as satires.

387. Simard, Rodney. *Postmodern Drama: Contemporary Playwrights in America and Britain*. Lanham, MD: University Press of America, 1984. 117-30.

   While exploring various influences on Rabe (absurdism, existentialism, epic theatre), Simard compares and contrasts Rabe's themes and techniques with those found in Albee, Beckett, Pinter, Shaffer, and Shepard. Characteristic of postmodern theatre, Rabe's plays "are structured in multiple layers of reality, dramatizing the conflict of subjective perceptions." Labeling the plays "contemporary moralities," Simard agrees with Jerrold Phillips (#377) that Rabe's "doomed protagonists" are swallowed by existential nothingness. In *Pavlo Hummel*, the war is "tangential"; Rabe is interested in "a realistic absurdity presented impressionistically." Ardell thus becomes "a projection of Pavlo's mind," and "the circularity of plot" is a sign of Pavlo's fate. The Albee-like family in *Sticks* is threatened by David's interior truth as the play moves "from absurdism to the level of existential reality." *Boom Boom Room*, which is "the touchstone of Rabe's canon to date," takes place in Chrissy's mind offering another instance of the character's descent into the abyss. The misleading realism of *Streamers* conceals the false sense of order in the external world of the army. Identifying Cokes as "the central character," Simard claims that "each character makes the mistake of looking at others and seeing himself." The streamers of the title "represent the failed realities of each character as he faces destruction from independent and personal causes." Believing that Rabe's "thematic range is the most limited and his experimentation the most narrow" of the major postmodern playwrights, Simard concludes that the playwright cannot be securely or comfortably placed in any one camp.

388. Stuart, Jan. "Reminders of A War." *American Theatre*, 1 (Mar. 1985): 23.

Noting the abundance of current plays about Vietnam, Stuart observes that Rabe's work—especially in the early 1970s—disproved the claim that "Americans don't like to be reminded of Vietnam."

389. Vorlicky, Robert Harvey. "America's Power Plays: The Traditional Hero in Male Cast Drama." Diss., University of Wisconsin-Madison, 1981. *DA*, 42(1981): 4451A.

Streamers is one of the 13 plays Vorlicky analyzes for patterns of heterosexual communication on stage. Like Mamet's *American Buffalo*, *Streamers* dramatizes the characters' inability to establish meaningful personal relationships and interactions.

390. Weales, Gerald. "Rampant Rabe." *Commonweal*, Mar. 10, 1972: 14-15.

Rabe is "the most successful serious playwright to turn up in the American theater in recent years." His Pavlo is a "mixture of two pacifist stereotypes"—the "clown, the foul-up, the yardbird, the victim-hero and also the sacrificial innocent of the sentimental anti-war play." However, Pavlo is too "dumb" to exist "outside" comedy. *Sticks*, a better, more dramatically emotional play, is "about the peculiarly American habit of refusing to see, to hear, to admit the ugly and the painful." Weales explores the differences (in characterization, plot, and technique) between Miller's *All My Sons* and *Sticks*. He finds that *Sticks* admirably attacks "the obvious fakery of television to question the reality of middle-class America."

391. _____. "Drama." In *Harvard Guide to Contemporary American Writing*. Ed. Daniel Hoffman. Cambridge: Harvard University Press, 1979. 427.

Rabe is briefly mentioned as one of the new American playwrights to whom attention is being given.

392. Werner, Craig. "Primal Screams and Nonsense Rhymes: David Rabe's Revolt." *Educational Theatre Journal*, 30 (Dec. 1978): 517-29.

Viewing Rabe's works within the larger tradition of American "disunities," Werner finds that "the problem of language lies at the center" of Rabe's Vietnam plays. *Pavlo Hummel*, "a classic work of the American imagination," employs the "Language of Brutality" to expose Pavlo to contradictions (life-in-death, black/white, humanity and brutality) that he cannot resolve and which reduce him to excrement. *Sticks* employs the "Language of Evasion" which results in "almost total isolation for every family member." The fact that Zung is an illusion poignantly demonstrates that "David's insights rest on a lie." The "Collapse of Metaphor" in *Streamers* leads to a "concrete reality" in which characters cannot protect themselves through abstractions (or fictions) and from which they cannot escape death. Rabe's vision of the world is "basically pessimistic."

393. Wilson, Edwin. *The Theater Experience.* 3rd ed. New York: McGraw-Hill, 1985. 325.

Pavlo Hummel "personifies a number of troubled young people who grew up in the difficult period of the 1960s and early 1970s."

394. Winner, Carole Ann. "A Study of American Dramatic Productions Dealing with the War in Vietnam." Diss., University of Denver, 1975. *DA*, 36 (1975): 5645A.

Classifying their plays about the war into various categories based upon production and themes, Winner believes that only the work of Daniel Barrigan, Terrence McNally, and David Rabe investigate the true reasons behind the war. *Pavlo Hummel* presents a picture of an unheroic soldier while *Sticks* attacks America's foolish endorsement of the war. Rabe's plays contain universal themes.

395. Zeigler, Joseph Wesley. *Regional Theatre: The Revolutionary Stage.* Minneapolis: Univ. of Minnesota Press, 1973. 229.

In surveying Papp's fortunes at the New York Shakespeare Festival and on Broadway, Zeigler mentions *Sticks* and Papp's dispute with and his eventual break with CBS.

STICKS & BONES, INCLUDING *BONES*

396. "A Dazzling New Play. Go At Once!" *New York Times*, Mar. 12, 1972, sec. 2: 3.

    Ad containing excerpts from 14 New York reviews

397. "A Dismal Performance by Critics." *Philadelphia Inquirer*, May 29, 1972: 10.

    Discusses the mistake in tallying Drama Critics Award votes

398. Adcock, Joe. "*Sticks and Bones* is an Experience." *Philadelphia Evening Bulletin*, June 28, 1974, sec. A: 19.

    Ibsen-Shaw Festival, Randor High School

399. Africano, Lillian. "*Sticks and Bones*." *The Villager* [Greenwich Village], Nov. 25, 1971: 9.

    Anspacher Theatre

400. Albrecht, Ernest. "*Sticks and Bones*: Message Haunts." *The Home News* [New Brunswick, NJ], Nov. 8, 1971: 25.

    Anspacher Theatre

401. "Amerika no Gendaibyo Egaku; Mingei ga *Bokire to Hone*" [Mingei Presents *Sticks and Bones*; American "Modern Illness" Depicted]. *Mainichi Shinbun* [Tokyo], Evening Ed., Oct. 26, 1981: 9.

402. Andras, Barta. "*Bot es gitar*: David Rabe szinmuve a Pesti Szinhazban." *Magyar Nemzet*, Mar. 2, 1974: 4.

403. Andras, Rajk. "*Bot es gitar*. Amerikai szimu a Pesti Szinhazban." *Nepszava*, Feb. 8, 1974: 4.

404. Anna, Foldes. "Tudositasok A Valosagrol." *Nok Lapfa*, 9 (1974): 10-11.

    Pesti Szinhazban, Budapest

405. Armstrong, Douglas. "Is New Play Offensive?" *Milwaukee Journal*, Apr. 16, 1973, sec. II: 1.

    Milwaukee Repertory Theater

406. "Award-Winning Play at Experimental Theatre." *Daily Herald-Telephone* [Bloomington, IN], Nov. 9, 1973: 3.

    Indiana University production directed by Andrew Apter

407. Baker, Russell. "U.S.-Approved Happiness." *New York Times*, Mar. 11, 1973, sec. IV: 15.

408. Barnes, Clive. "Order of Merit." *London Times*, Apr. 29, 1972: 13.

409. _____. "Stage: A Most Gifted Playwright at the Anspacher." *New York Times*, Nov. 9, 1971: 60.

410. _____. "Theater: A Most Gifted Playwright." *New York Times*, Nov. 8, 1971: 53.

411. _____. "Theater: *Sticks and Bones* at Golden." *New York Times*, Mar. 2, 1972: 33.

412. Beaufort, John. "Controversial Drama Will Air Tomorrow after Being Vetoed." *Christian Science Monitor*, Aug. 16, 1973: 16.

413. _____. "Can Stage Buck Success?" *Christian Science Monitor*, Mar. 3, 1973: 123, 125.

414. _____. "Television Pressures from 50's to 70's." *Christian Science Monitor*, Mar. 8, 1973: 10.

415. Botto, Louis. "*Sticks and Bones*." NBC TV. Nov. 6, 1971.

416. Bourne, Michael. "Ozzie, Harriet, David and Pain in T300 Drama *Sticks & Bones*." *Daily Herald-Telephone* [Bloomington, IN], Nov. 12, 1973: 15.

    Indiana University production in the T300 Theatre

417. Brown, Les. "CBS Flunks the Papp Test." *Variety*, Mar. 14, 1973, "Radio-Television": 39, 51.

418. _____. "Wood, CBS-TV Head, Defends 'Mature' Shows." *New York Times*, Oct. 16, 1973: 87.

419. Brukenfeld, Dick. "The Nuclear Family of Ozzie & Harriet." *Village Voice*, Nov. 11, 1971: 57.

420. Buscher, Henry P., Jr. and John Ralph. Letters on C.B.S. Cancellation. *New Orleans Times-Picayune*, Mar. 15, 1973, sec. I: 10.

421. Calta, Louis. "Broadway to Get *Sticks and Bones*." *New York Times*, Jan. 28, 1972: 22.

422. _____. "Fund Buying $50,000 in Tickets." *New York Times*, Feb. 15, 1972: 26.

423. "CBS Cancels *Sticks and Bones*." *New Haven Register/Journal-Courier*, Mar. 7, 1973: 2.

424. "CBS Cancels Viet Nam Play." *Chicago Tribune*, Mar. 7, 1973, sec 3: 17.

425. "CBS Drops Viet Drama." *Christian Science Monitor*, Mar. 8, 1973: 10.

426. "CBS Puts Off Papp's *Sticks and Bones*." *New York Times*, Mar. 7, 1973, sec. L: 87.

427. "CBS Reschedules *Sticks and Bones*." *Philadelphia Inquirer*, July 14, 1973, sec B: 9.

428. Childs, James. "Coming to Grips with Mom's Apple Pie." *New Haven Register/Journal-Courier*, Nov. 14, 1971, sec. D: 1,7.

429. _____. "Dramatist Rabe Husbands His Words." *New Haven Register/Journal-Courier*, Oct. 31, 1971, sec. D: 1, 7.

430. Clarke, Constance. "*Sticks and Bones*." *Applause*, Dec. 1, 1971: 24.

     Anspacher Theatre

431. Clurman, Harold. "Theatre." *Nation*, Nov. 22, 1971: 539-40.

432. Collins, William B. "Will Rabe's Play Break Theater's Silence About Vietnam War?" *Philadelphia Inquirer*, Jan. 23, 1972, sec. C: 1,6.

433. _____. "Why Were Pulitzer Drama Jurors Silent?" *Philadelphia Inquirer*, May 4, 1972: 13.

434. Craig, Randall. "Plays in Performance—Experimental." *Drama: QTR* (Spring 1978): 70.

     Theatre at New End

435. "Critics Circle Picks *Sticks* Best Drama." *Los Angeles Times*, May 24, 1972, sec. IV: 15.

436. Curley, Arthur. *Library Journal*, 98 (Feb. 1, 1973): 432.

     Book review

437. Cyclops. "At Last, Here Comes *Sticks and Bones* (Maybe)." *New York Times*, Aug. 12, 1973, sec. II: 17.

     Cartoon included

438. "Der Regiseur fur Rabes *Willkommen*." *Neue Zurcher Zeitung*, May 10, 1973: 41.

Schauspielhaus, Zurich

439. "Die Familie oder die unschuldigen Morder." *Die Tat* [Zurich], May 14, 1973: 5.

Schauspielhaus, Zurich

440. Doan, R. K. "Many CBS Affiliates Reacting Negatively to *Sticks and Bones*." *TV Guide*, Aug. 4, 1973: A-1.

441. _____. "CBS Decides to Air *Sticks and Bones* Five Months After Originally Scheduled Date." *TV Guide*, July 28, 1973: A-1.

442. _____. "CBS's *Sticks and Bones* and *Maude* Abortion Episode Blacked Out by Many Local Stations." *TV Guide*, Sept. 1, 1973: A-1.

443. Doup, Carol. "Bury *Bones* and Give Us All a Rest." *Indiana Daily Student* [campus newspaper Indiana University], Oct. 11, 1973: 7.

Indiana University production

444. Drake, Sylvie. "*Sticks and Bones* by South Coast Rep." *Los Angeles Times*, Jan. 24, 1974, sec. IV: 10.

445. "Drama Critics' Recount Deposes 'Winning' Play." *New York Times*, May 24, 1972: 52.

446. "Drama Critics to Give Rabe Special Citation." *New Haven Register/ Journal-Courier*, May 26, 1972: 58.

447. Dubrow, Rick. "Drama About Blind Viet Vet is On Again." *Philadelphia Inquirer*, July 18, 1972: 6D.

448. Dunn, Clara. "*Sticks and Bones*." *The North Side News* [Atlanta], Mar. 23, 1976: 5.

Academy Theatre

449. Ellis, Joshua. *"Sticks and Stones." The Villanovan* [campus newspaper Villanova University], 44, no. 17 (Feb. 12, 1969): 7, 8.

Original Villanova production of *Bones*

450. "Engeki Jihyo." *Higeki Kigeki* [Tokyo monthly review], Jan. 1981: 90-92.

Discussions by Nobuo Miqashita and Ryoko Okazaki

451. Ervin, Szombathelyi. *"Bot es gitar.* Bemutato a Pesti Szinhazban." *Magyar Hirlap*, Feb. 7, 1974: 6.

452. Fox, Terry Curtis. "I'll Take Ozzie." *Village Voice*, July 4, 1977: 86.

GAP Theatre

453. Frankel, Haskel. "New York Stage: Ozzie, Harriet—And Vietnam?" *The National Observer*, Nov. 20, 1971: 25.

Anspacher Theatre

454. Gabor, Mihalyi. "A rettenet hazhoz jon. David Rabe: *Bot es gitar* a Pesti Szinhazban." *Szinhaz*, 7, no. 5 (May 1974): 13-15.

455. Gagnard, Frank. *"Sticks and Bones." New Orleans Times-Picayune,* July 7, 1972, sec. II: 6.

456. Gaver, Jack. "Reviewer Says TV Undercuts *Sticks and Bones." New Haven Register*, Aug. 17, 1973: 5.

457. Gent, George. "C.B.S. Reschedules *Sticks and Bones." New York Times*, July 14, 1973: 55.

458. _____. "Johnson of F.C.C. Hits Nixon Policy." *New York Times*, Mar. 10, 1973: 62.

459. _____. "Rabe Protests Soviet *Sticks & Bones." Philadelphia Evening Bulletin*, Mar. 15, 1973: 19.

460. _____. "*Sticks and Bones* Pirated in Soviet Protested by Rabe." *New York Times*, Mar. 13, 1973: 31.

461. Gill, Brendan. "Real Play, False Play, No Play." *New Yorker*, Mar. 11, 1972: 82.

462. Glover, William. "Critics Err in Tally; *Season* Wins Award." *New Haven Register*, May 25, 1972: 3.

463. _____. "*Follies* Tops Tony Entries." *Los Angeles Times*, Apr. 5, 1972, sec IV: 17.

464. _____. "Rabe Is Hailed Again; This Time On Broadway." *New Haven Register/Journal-Courier*, Mar. 2, 1972: 14.

465. _____. "Rabe's Second Play Draws Critics' Praise." *New Haven Register/Journal-Courier*, Nov. 8, 1971: 4.

466. _____. "Viet War Vet Becomes Top Playwright." *Miami Herald*, Mar. 4, 1972, sec. B: 12.

467. Gottfried, Martin. "*Sticks & Bones*. . . a Striking and Original Play." *Women's Wear Daily*, Nov. 8, 1971: 14. Rpt. in *NYTCR, 1971*: 164.

     Anspacher Theatre

468. Gottlieb, Richard. "Bone-Weary." *Distant Drummer* [Philadelphia], 24 (Feb. 20-Mar. 5, 1969): 5.

     Original Villanova production of *Bones*

469. Gray, Fanum. "*Sticks & Bones* Outstanding Production." *Atlanta Constitution*, Mar. 17, 1976, sec. B: 4.

     Academy Theatre

470. Green, Harris. "Newcomers and Oldtimers." *The New Leader,* Dec. 13, 1971: 30.

     Anspacher Theatre

471. Griffin, William. "*Sticks and Bones*." *Sign* [Passionist Fathers, Union City, NJ], 52 (Nov. 1972): 34.

472. "Grim TV Play about War Veteran Postponed in US." *London Times*, Mar. 8, 1973: 5.

473. Gyorgy, Karpati. "David Rabe." *Lobogo*, Feb. 20, 1974: 4.

    Pesti Szinhazban, Budapest

474. "Half of CBS-TV Stations Won't Show Antiwar Drama." *New Haven Register/ Journal-Courier*, Aug. 16, 1973, sec. D: 1+.

475. Harris, Harry. "Savage *Sticks and Bones* Arrives at Last." *Philadelphia Inquirer*, Aug. 17, 1973: 5C.

476. _____. "Tony-Winning Play Postponed by CBS." *Philadelphia Inquirer*, Mar. 8, 1973: 2D.

477. Harris, Leonard. "*Sticks & Bones*." WCBS TV. Nov. 10, 1971. Rpt. in *NYTCR, 1971*: 166.

478. _____. "*Sticks & Bones*." WCBS TV. Mar. 1, 1972. Rpt. in *NYTCR, 1972*: 365.

479. Hart, Susan. "Award Winner Plays at Academy Until April 10." *The DeKalb New/Era* [GA], Apr. 8, 1976: 9.

480. Hewes, Henry. "Only Winter is White." *Saturday Review*, Nov. 27, 1971: 70-71.

481. Hickey, N. "Joseph Papp Signs with ABC to Do at Least Two ABC Theatre Productions (TV Teletype New York)." *TV Guide*, Nov. 17, 1973: 2.

482. Hughes, Catharine. "An American Nightmare." *America*, 126 (Mar. 18, 1972): 294-95.

483. _____. "*Sticks and Bones*." *Progressive* [Madison, WI], 36, no. 3 (Mar. 1972): 44.

484. Hutton, Geoffrey. "Moral of this Play is Stark and Clear." *The Age* [Melbourne, Australia], Sept. 27, 1972, "Arts": 2.

Melbourne Theatre Company, Russell Street

485. Istvan, Karcsai Kulcsar. "*Bot es gitar.*" *Tukor*, Feb. 19, 1974: 12.

Pesti Szinhazban, Budapest

486. Julia, Szekrenyesy. "Minden Oke!" *Elet es Irodalom,* 10 (1974): 12.

Pesti Szinhazban, Budapest

487. W.K. "Wojskowe dramaty Davida Rabe'a." *Dialog* (Warsaw), no. 9 (1976): 166-67.

488. Kalem, T. E. "Air-Conditioned Hell." *Time*, Nov. 22, 1971: 93. Rpt. in *NYTCR, 1971*: 164-65.

489. Kauffmann, Stanley. "*Sticks and Bones.*" *New Republic*, Dec. 4, 1971: 22, 36.

Anspacher Theatre

490. Kay, Doug. "*Sticks and Bones.*" WRFG, **fm** 89.3. Atlanta, Mar. 29, 1976.

Academy Theatre

491. Kerr, Walter. "David Has Never Been Alive." *New York Times*, Mar. 12, 1972, sec. II: 3.

492. _____. "Unmistakably a Writer—Why, Then, Does His Play Stand Still?" *New York Times*, Nov. 14, 1971, sec. II: 1, 3.

493. Koehler, Robert. "*Sticks and Bones*: Back Home and On the Front." *Los Angeles Times,* Feb. 6, 1985, sec. VI: 7.

494. Krebs, Albin. "A.C.L.U. Decries C.B.S. Over Play." *New York Times*, Mar. 9, 1973: 75.

495. _____. "C.B.S. Chief Defends Decision to Postpone *Sticks and Bones*." *New York Times*, May 24, 1973: 91.

496. _____. "C.B.S. Stations Balk on *Sticks and Bones*." *New York Times*, Aug. 17, 1973: 63.

497. _____. "5 Diverse Groups Urge Action to Counter Censorship of TV." *New York Times*, Aug. 30, 1973: 67.

498. _____. "Paley, C.B.S. Chairman, Personally Vetoed Showing of *Sticks and Bones*." *New York Times*, Mar. 20, 1973: 78.

499. Kriegsman, Alan M. "The *Sticks* Fracas: Weakened Spine, but No Fractures." *Washington Post*, Aug. 26, 1973, sec. G: 3.

500. Kroll, Jack. "*Sticks & Bones*." *Newsweek*, Nov. 29, 1971: 109-10. Rpt. in *NYTCR, 1971*: 162.

501. Kuhn, Christopher. "Dieser Vietnam—Heimkehrer schockte niemanden." *Tages-Anzeiger* [Zurich], "Kultur," May 12, 1973: 21.

     Schauspielhaus, Zurich

502. Lazier, Gil. *Educational Theatre Journal*, 24 (May 1972): 197.

     Anspacher Theatre

503. Lewis, Emory. "Antiwar Drama, *Sticks and Bones*, Opens on Broadway." *The Record* [Bergen Co., NJ], Mar. 2, 1972, sec. B: 8.

504. _____. "*Sticks and Bones*: A Blunt Look at War." *The Record* [Bergen Co., NJ], Nov. 8, 1971, sec. A: 23.

     Anspacher Theatre

505. Lichenstein, Grace. "C.B.S. Head to Speak Out on T.V.'s Rights." *New York Times*, Sept. 26, 1973: 82.

506. Lifton, Robert Jay. "Heroes and Victims." *New York Times*, Mar. 28, 1973, sec. L+: 47.

507. Little, Stuart W. "Joe Papp Seeks a Bigger Stage." *Saturday Review*, Feb. 26, 1972: 40-44.

508. LoSecco, John. "*Sticks and Bones*." *The Cooper Pioneer* [New York], 51, no. 4 (Nov. 21, 1971): 7.

    Anspacher Theatre

509. Mausson, Danny. "*Sticks and Bones*." WRNG Radio. Atlanta, Mar. 14, 1976.

    Academy Theatre

510. Mayhead, Gerald. "A Lost Play About a Lost War." *The Herald* [Melbourne, Australia], Sept. 27, 1972, "The Arts": 19.

    Melbourne Theatre Company, Russell Street

511. "MFA Series to Continue with *Sticks and Bones*." *Daily Texan*, Dec. 2, 1975: 13.

    University of Texas at Austin

512. Miklos, Apati. "Pesti Szinhaz. *Bot es gitar*." *Film Szinhaz Muzsika*, Feb. 9, 1974: 7-8.

513. Mishkin, Leo. "*Sticks and Bones* on B'way." *The Morning Telegraph* [New York], Mar. 3, 1972: 3.

514. Mitgang, Herbert. "Creativity and the Public." *New York Times*, Apr. 9, 1973: 37.

515. Miyaskita, S. N. and R. Okazaki. "Engeki Jihyo." *Higeki Kigeki*, Jan. 1981: 90-92.

    Mingei Company

516. Neuhaus, Hellmut "*Sticks and Bones*." *Zeitschrift fur Anglistik und Amerikanistik*, 24 (1976): 243.

517. "Nichols, Blydan, Linda Hopkins Win Tony Awards." *Philadelphia Inquirer*, Apr. 24, 1972: 8.

518. Novick, Julius. "The Basic Training of Ozzie & Harriet." *Village Voice*, Mar. 9, 1972: 58, 62.

519. O'Brien, Jim. "CBS Play Anti-Climactic." *Philadelphia Daily News*, July 18, 1973: 29.

520. O'Connor, John J. "How About Some Backbone?" *New York Times*, Mar. 18, 1973, sec. II: 19.

521. ____. "These Little Pressure Groups Went to Market—With a Club." *New York Times*, Sept. 2, 1973, sec. II: 11.

522. ____. "T.V.: *Sticks and Bones*." *New York Times*, Mar. 9, 1973: 74.

523. Oliver, Edith. "Off Broadway: Twice Hail." *New Yorker*, Nov. 20, 1971: 114, 119.

524. Oppenheimer, George. "Blind among the Blind." *Newsday*, Nov. 8, 1971, sec. A: 7.

525. Osztovic, Levente. "Some Leftovers and a Remarkable New Play." *New Hungarian Quarterly*, 61 (Spring 1976): 217.

526. Palmer, Howard. "Vietnam Play is a Song of Words." *Sun News Pictorial* [Melbourne, Australia], Sept. 27, 1972: 33.

Melbourne Theatre Company, Russell Street

527. Panella, Vincent. "David Rabe is Broadway's Best." *Dubuque Telegraph Herald*, Apr. 24, 1972: 1.

528. "Papp and CBS End Contract to Produce Dramatic Specials." *New York Times*, June 27, 1973: 111.

529. "Papp Axed by CBS, But *Sticks* Still Up in Air." *Variety*, June 27, 1973: 1, 70.

530. Phillips, McCandish. "*Sticks and Bones, Verona* Win Tonys; Gorman, Sada Thompson Cited for Acting." *New York Times*, Apr. 24, 1972: 40.

531. Polier, Rex. "CBS Postpones *Sticks and Bones* After Affiliates Balk." *Philadelphia Evening Bulletin*, Mar. 7, 1973, "Around the Dials": 10.

532. ____. "Questions on *Sticks and Bones*." *Philadelphia Evening Bulletin*, July 17, 1973, sec. B: 21.

533. ____. "*Sticks & Bones* Finally Gets Aired." *Philadelphia Evening Bulletin*, Aug. 17, 1973, "Around the Dials": 50.

534. Popkin, Henry. "How Did *Sticks and Bones* Fare in Moscow?" *Christian Science Monitor*, May 26, 1973: 14.

535. "Program Pressure." *New York Times*, Aug. 24, 1973, Editorial: 32.

536. "Rabe's Drama Named Best Play." *Philadelphia Inquirer*, May 21, 1972: 5.

537. Ramsdell, Sheldon. "Surrender to the Bully-Boys." *New York Post*, Mar. 10, 1973: 28.

538. Reif, Rita. "Fortunately, It's a House that Needs Some Work." *New York Times*, Apr. 17, 1972: 28.

539. Reiss, Curt. "Trinken, Essen, Halsdurchshneiden." *Die Welt*, "Culture," May 16, 1973: 16, 30.

     Schauspielhaus, Zurich

540. Reyher, Loren. "Scathing *Sticks* Ugly, Devastating." *Wichita Beacon*, Mar. 1, 1974, sec. A: 8.

     Wichita State University

541. "Right of CBS to Cancel Show." *New Orleans Times- Picayune*, Mar. 10, 1973, sec. I: 10.

542. Rollin, Betty. "*Sticks & Bones*." NBC TV. Mar. 1, 1972. Rpt. in *NYTCR, 1972*: 365.

543. Rost, Gertrude Sanders. "Suppressed Reminder." *New York Times*, Mar. 20, 1973: 38.

    Letter about cancellation of special

544. "Russian Literati View Downbeat on David Rabe's Critical Attitude." *Variety*, Mar. 23, 1973: 71, 75.

545. Sahl, Hans. "Ein Weisser Rabe." *Die Welt* [Berlin], Apr. 6, 1973: 23.

    Schauspielhaus, Zurich

546. Saito, Tomoko. "Homu Dorama no Dento" [Tradition of Home Drama]. *Teatro* [Tokyo], Jan. 1981: 34.

547. Sanders, Kevin. "*Sticks & Bones*." WABC TV. Nov. 7, 1971. Rpt. in *NYTCR, 1971*: 165.

548. Schier, Ernest. "Villanova Has Fine Play, Playwright." *Philadelphia Evening Bulletin*, Feb. 11, 1969: 33.

549. Schnabel, Dieter. "Ein mattes *Willkommen* fur ein Stuck Boulevard—Realismus." *Nachtausgabe* [Frankfurt], May 17, 1973: 6.

    Schauspielhaus, Zurich

550. Seelmann-Eggebert. "Heimkehr aus Vietnam." *Darmstadter Echo*, June 28, 1973: 80.

    Schauspielhaus, Zurich

551. Shabad, Theodore. "*Sticks and Bones* Wins Favor in Soviet." *New York Times*, Mar. 12, 1973: 36.

552. "Show Business." *Milwaukee Journal*, Mar. 14, 1973, II: 14.

553. Simon, John. "Domestic Infernos." *New York*, 4 (Nov. 22, 1971): 76.

554. _____. "Theatre Chronicle." *The Hudson Review*, 25 (Spring 1972): 89-90.

Anspacher Theatre

555. Singer, Samuel. "Play Focuses Anger on War, Racial Snubs." *Philadelphia Inquirer*, Feb. 7, 1969: 24.

Original Villanova production of *Bones*.

556. Smith, Frederick. "Soviet Sticks and Stones for David Rabe." *New York Times*, Apr. 12, 1973: 56.

557. Smith, Helen. "Academy Will Produce Rabe's *Sticks and Bones*." *Atlanta Constitution*, Mar. 6, 1976, sec. T: 8.

Academy Theatre

558. "Special Citation Voted by Critics to Rabe Play." *New York Times*, May 25, 1972: 52.

559. Stark, John. "*Sticks and Bones* is Just Too Much." *San Francisco Examiner-Chronicle*, June 10, 1975: 27.

560. Stevenson, Isabelle, ed. *The Tony Award*. New York: Arno Press, 1975. 117.

561. ["*Sticks*"]. *Frainich Shinbun* [Tokyo]. Oct. 26, 1981.

Mingei production

562. "*Sticks and Bones*." *New York Times*, Nov. 12, 1971: 52.

Half page ad with excerpts from the critics

563. "*Sticks and Bones*." *New York Times*, Feb. 6, 1972, sec. 2: 3.

Half page ad for the play

564. "*Sticks and Bones*." *New York Times*, Aug. 17, 1973, Editorial: 30.

565. *Sticks and Bones*. *Playbill*, 9, no. 2 (Feb. 1972).

John Golden Theatre

566. "*Sticks and Bones* Air Date Seen as Victory for Wood." *Variety*, July 18, 1973: 25.

567. "*Sticks and Bones* Opens Thursday on IU Campus." *Bloomington-Bedford Sunday Herald-Times*, Nov. 4, 1973: 48.

Experimental Theatre of Indiana University

568. "*Sticks and Bones* Stirs Little Local Comment." *Philadelphia Evening Bulletin*, Aug. 18, 1973, sec. B: 4.

569. "*Sticks and Bones* to Open at Academy Fri." *Atlanta Daily World*, Mar. 11, 1976: 6.

Academy Theatre

570. "*Sticks and Bones* Wins Tony Award for Rabe." *New Haven Register/Journal-Courier*, Apr. 24, 1972: 6.

571. "*Sticks* Nixed By 38 CBS-TV Affils; Many Delaying It." *Variety*, July 25, 1973: 21.

572. Stothard, Peter. "*Sticks and Bones/Streamers*." *Plays and Players*, 25 (Apr. 1978): 24-25.

Theatre at New End

573. Strayton, Richard. "Trips to the Dark Side of the American Dream." *Los Angeles Herald Examiner,* Feb. 12, 1985, sec. C: 5.

Theatre 40, Los Angeles, directed by Flora Plumb

574. Sullivan, Dan. "Critic Takes a Skeptical Look at the Tony Awards." *Los Angeles Times*, May 7, 1972: 26.

575. "Support for Public T.V. Grows as More Viewers Pledge Aid." *New York Times*, Feb. 21, 1973: 87.

576. Taikeff, Stanley, Harry Katz, and Paul Treat II. *New York Times*, Sept. 2, 1973, "Letters to the Editor," sec. II: 10.

577. Takada, Jo. "Jugatsu no Shingeki" [Stages in October]. *Mainichi Shinbun* [Tokyo], Evening Ed., Nov. 4, 1981: 7.

578. Tallmer, Jerry. "Casualty: America." *New York Post*, Mar. 2, 1972: 23. Rpt. in *NYTCR, 1972*: 364-65.

579. Tamas, Barabas. *"Bot es gitar.* Bemutato a Pesti Szinhazban." *Esti Hirlap*, Feb. 5, 1974: 2.

580. Tamas, Koltai. "Szinhazi Estek: *Bot es gitar.* Bemutaro a Pesti Szinhazban." *Nepszabadsag*, Feb. 12, 1974: 7.

581. Terry, Thomas. "Heimkehr ins Klischee." *Der Tagesspiegel* [Berlin], May 26, 1973: 4.

     Schauspielhaus, Zurich

582. "The Show that Won't Go On." *New York Post*, Mar. 7, 1973: 42.

583. Thomas, Barbara. "Family Folds Under Weight of War in *Bones.*" *Atlanta Constitution*, Mar. 17, 1976, sec. D: 4.

     Academy Theatre

584. Tighe, Mike. "CBS Puts Off 'Untimely' Rabe Play." Dubuque *Telegraph Herald*, Mar. 7, 1973: 1.

585. _____. "CBS Right for the Wrong Reason on *Sticks*?" Dubuque *Telegraph Herald*, Mar. 11, 1973: 48.

586. "Tony Awards Go to *Follies, Gentlemen.*" *Los Angeles Times*, Apr. 24, 1972, sec I: 5.

587. "TV Probe Sought." *New Haven Register/Journal-Courier*, Aug. 17, 1973: 2.

588. Wardle, Irving. "*Sticks and Bones*: New End." *London Times*, Feb. 1, 1978: 9.

Theatre at New End

589. Warren, Steve. "*Sticks and Bones*." *Creative Loafing* [Atlanta], Apr. 10, 1976: 10.

Academy Theatre

590. _____. "*Sticks and Bones* and *Night Club*." WGKA Radio. Atlanta, Mar. 18, 1976.

Academy Theatre

591. Watkins, Richard A. "Making No Bones About *Sticks and Bones*." *New York Times*, Apr. 1, 1973, "TV Mailbag," sec. II: 19.

Letter in favor of not airing play

592. Watt, Douglas. "*Sticks and Bones*." *New York Daily News*, Mar. 2, 1972: 85. Rpt. in *NYTCR, 1972*: 364.

593. _____. "*Sticks & Bones* Brings the Vietnam War Home." *New York Daily News*, Nov. 8, 1971: 64. Rpt. in *NYTCR, 1971*: 163.

594. Watts, Richard. "Soldier's Homecoming." *New York Post*, Nov. 8, 1971: 48. Rpt. in *NYTCR, 1971*: 165.

595. Weiner, Bernard. "Top Production of Family Satire." *San Francisco Chronicle*, June 10, 1975: 40.

596. White, Jean M. "91 Stations Won't Show Controversial War Drama." *Miami Herald*, Aug. 16, 1973, sec. E: 9.

597. Whittaker, Herbert. "*Sticks and Bones*: the Words Really Hurt." *Globe and Mail* [Toronto], Nov. 17, 1973: 32.

Marc Diamond's Hart House

598. Wilk, Gerald H. "Amerikanischer Hinkemann: *Sticks and Bones* beeindruckt New York." *Der Tagesspiegel* [Berlin], Dec 7, 1971: 4.

599. Williams, Bob. "On the Air." *New York Post*, Mar. 9, 1973: 77.

600. "*Willkommen*." *Neue Zurcher Zeitung*, May 12, 1973: 17.

    Schauspielhaus, Zurich

601. Wilson, Richard. "CBS's TV Reject." *New Orleans Times-Picayune*, Mar. 10, 1973, sec. I: 10.

602. Woodruff, Elizabeth. "*Sticks and Bones*." Mutual Broadcasting Network. Mar. 2, 1972.

603. Young, B. A. "*Sticks and Bones*." *Financial Times* [London], Feb. 1, 1978: 13.

    Theatre at New End

604. Zimmermann, Leda. "*Sticks and Bones*: Dry, Brittle . . . Deadly Drama." *Amherst Student* [campus newspaper], Mar. 13, 1978: 9.

BRAT BRATU

(Pirated Russian version of *Sticks and Bones* performed at the
Sovremennik Theatre in Moscow in November 1972.)

605. Anastasyev, A. "Sud'ba Teatra i Oprometchivost Kritiki." *Teatr*, 9
       (1976): 93-101.

606. Chernenko, S. "Eto Udivitel'niye Aktyory. . ." *Sovetskiy Ekran*, 1
       (1973): 16-17.

607. Komissarzhevsky, Viktor. "Etot Zhestokiy, Zheztokiy Mir" [Cruel,
       Cruel World]. *Pravda*, Jan. 6, 1973: 3+.

608. Nedelya. "Put' k Spektaklyu." *Izvestiya* (supplement), #48 (1972):
       10.

609. Silyunas, B. "Teni v Meshchanskom Rayu." *Komsomolskaya
       Pravda*, Jan. 18, 1973: 3.

THE BASIC TRAINING OF PAVLO HUMMEL

610. Agidius, Henrik. "Tipasnings-vanskeligheder." *Herlev Bladet*, Mar. 28, 1979, sec. 2: 23.

Gladsaxe Teater, Copenhagen

611. Anja. "*Soldat Hummel* pukler for at blive en helt." *Politiken* [Copenhagen], Mar. 9, 1979, sec. 3: 2.

Gladsaxe Teater, Copenhagen

612. "Antihelt i Gladsaxe." *Berlingske Tidende,* Mar. 14, 1979, sec II: 18.

Gladsaxe Teater, Copenhagen

613. P. J. B. "Soldater-Kammerater 1 Gladsaxe." *Ekstra Bladet* [Copenhagen], Mar. 16, 1979: 12.

Gladsaxe Teater, Copenhagen

614. Barnes, Clive. "A New Pavlo Hummel." *New York Times*, Dec. 7, 1971: 55.

615. _____. "New York Notebook: A Trifle Quiet Around the Edges." *London Times*, Dec. 18, 1971: 9.

616. _____. "Stage: Rabe's *Basic Training of Pavlo Hummel.*" *New York Times*, Apr. 25, 1977: 38. Rpt. in *NYTCR, 1977*: 254-55.

617. _____. "Theater: *Training of Pavlo Hummel.*" *New York Times*, May 21, 1971: 25.

618. *The Basic Training of Pavlo Hummel. Playbill*, Apr. 1977.

619. *"The Basic Training of Pavlo Hummel." New York Times*, May 16, 1971, sec. 2: 25.

620. Beaufort, John. *"The Basic Training of Pavlo Hummel." Christian Science Monitor*, May 5, 1977: 23. Rpt. in *NYTCR, 1977*: 256.

621. _____. "Stage: Matthew with Music, Pinter Reprise, Antiwar Tract." *Christian Science Monitor*, May 24, 1971: 4.

622. Beecroft, Jennifer. *"Basic Training* in the Drama Department." *California Aggie* [campus newspaper, University of California—Davis], Jan. 25, 1985: 6.

623. Bonosky, Phillip. "Basic Training for a Patriotic Corpse." *Daily World*, June 4, 1971: 8.

624. Brukenfeld, Dick. "And He Won't Come Back When It's Over, Over There." *Village Voice*, May 27, 1971: 65, 87.

625. Carr, Jay. *"Pavlo's* Better Than Ever." *Detroit News*, May 15, 1977, sec. J: 50.

    Greektown Attic Theatre

626. Childs, James. "A Soldier's Basic Training for Death." *New Haven Register*, May 30, 1971, "Arts and Leisure," sec. D: 3.

627. "Christoffer Brosom unheldig helt." *Bagsvaerd Folkebald-Soborg-Folkebald*, Mar. 14, 1979: 27.

    Gladsaxe Teater, Copenhagen

628. Clurman, Harold. "Theatre." *Nation*, 212 (June 7, 1971): 733.

629. _____. "Theatre." *Nation*, 224 (May 14, 1977): 602-603.

630. Collins, William B. *"Pavlo Hummel* Brings Vietnam War to Phila. Stage." *Philadelphia Inquirer*, Apr. 6, 1972: 17.

631. "Critics Applaud Play by Former *Register* Writer." *New Haven Register*, May 22, 1971: 15.

632. Curley, Arthur. *Library Journal,* 98 (Feb. 1, 1973): 432.

     Book review

633. Drake, Sylvie. "*Pavlo* Comes to the West Coast." *Los Angeles Times*, Feb. 11, 1973: 45.

634. Ekeroth-Petersen, Tom. "Den hablose helt og nar." *Villabyerne*, Mar. 21, 1979: 15

     Gladsaxe Teater, Copenhagen

635. Everfelt, Flemming. "En march pa stedet." *Frederiksborg Amts Avis*, Mar. 16, 1979: 9.

     Gladsaxe Teater, Copenhagen

636. "Explodes with Dynamite." *New York Times*, June 27, 1971, sec. D: 6.

     Ad for *Pavlo* with excerpts from critics

637. Falk, J. "Krig og ufred i Gladsaxe." *Politiken*, Mar. 14, 1979, sec. 2: 8.

638. Frankel, Haskel. "At the Theatre: Mr. Rabe's GI is No Everyman." *The National Observe*r, May 24, 1971: 17.

639. M. G. "Christopher Bro Kaemper for sit teater som en antihelt." *Journalistforbundets* [Ravnsborggade], Mar. 13, 1979: 15.

     Gladsaxe Teater, Copenhagen

640. Gereben, James. "UH Play Gives Newsreel, Not Drama, of War." *Honolulu Star Bulletin*, Dec. 8, 1972, sec. D: 11.

     University of Hawaii—Manoa

641. Gill, Brendan. "The Theatre: In Praise of Song." *New Yorker*, May 2, 1977: 91.

642. Glover, William. "Al Pacino as Pavlo Hummel." *Los Angeles Times*, May 10, 1977, sec. IV: 8.

643. Gottfried, Martin. "*The Basic Training of Pavlo Hummel* . . . an Extraordinary Play." *Women's Wear Daily*, May 21, 1971: 33. Rpt. in *NYTCR, 1971*: 259.

644. _____. "Powerful *Training* of Al Pacino." *New York Post*, Apr. 25, 1977: 22. Rpt. in *NYTCR, 1977*: 255.

645. _____. Review of *Pavlo Hummel* at the Public Theater. WINS—New York. May 21, 1971.

    Available from TV-Time Recordings, Inc. (1937 Barnes Ave., Bronx, NY 10462)

646. Grimme. "Kun civilister er laverest ende end rekrutter." *Aktuelt* [Copenhagen], Mar. 16 1979.

    Gladsaxe Teater, Copenhagen

647. Gussow, Mel. "The Basic Training of Al Pacino." *New York Times*, June 5, 1977, sec. VI: 21.

648. Hansen, Tove. "Den fodte taber." *Kristeligt Dagblad* [Copenhagen], Mar. 20, 1979: 6.

    Gladsaxe Teater, Copenhagen

649. Heldman, Irma Pascal. "Papp's Social Dramas Aren't Pap." *The Wall Street Journal,* Nov. 30, 1971: 200. Rpt. in *NYTCR, 1971*: 163.

650. Herbach, Mitchell D. ". . .*Pavlo Hummel*: A Powerful Anti-War Play." *Arts & Sciences*, Dec. 16, 1971: 5,14.

651. Hewes, Henry. "Taps for Lenny Bruce." *Saturday Review*, July 10, 1971: 36.

652. Huddy, John. "Pacino, *Pavlo Hummel* in a Wasted Exercise." *Miami Herald*, May 4, 1977, sec. B: 8.

653. Hughes, Catharine. "An American Nightmare." *America*, 126 (Mar. 18, 1972): 295-96.

654. Hurst, John V. "*Hummel*: A Search for Sense and Self." *Sacramento Bee*, Jan. 19, 1985, sec. A: 16.

      University of California—Davis

655. Hurwitt, R. "*Pavlo*." *Berkeley Barb* [Berkeley, CA], 28, no. 15 (Apr. 26, 1979): 10.

656. Hvidt, Erik. "Lille mand, hvad nu?" *Weekend-Avisen* [Copenhagen], Mar. 23, 1979: 20.

      Gladsaxe Teater, Copenhagen

657. Johansen, Birthe. "Fra de amerikanske overskudslagre." *Holbaek Amts Venstreblad*, Mar. 27, 1979: 15.

      Gladsaxe Teater, Copenhagen

658. _____. "Fri os fra de gronne baretter." *Roskilde Tidende* [Roskilde], Mar. 21, 1979.

      Gladsaxe Teater, Copenhagen

659. Judson, Horace. "Rags of Honor." *Time*, Apr. 24, 1972: 66.

660. "K." "Rat for usodet." *Gladsaxe Bladet*, Mar. 21, 1979: 17.

      Gladsaxe Teater, Copenhagen

661. Kalem, T. E. "Exit a Simple Soul." *Time*, May 9, 1977: 50. Rpt. in *NYTCR, 1977*: 257.

662. Kelly, Kevin. "*The Basic Training of Pavlo Hummel*." *Boston Globe*, May 15, 1977, sec. L: 9.

663. Kerr, Walter. "He Wonders Who He Is—So Do We." *New York Times*, May 30, 1971, sec. II: 3.

664. _____. "Watching a Star Wrestle a Zero." *New York Times*, May 8, 1977, sec. I: 1.

665. Kissel, Howard. *"The Basic Training of Pavlo Hummel." Women's Wear Daily*, Apr. 25, 1977: 16. Rpt. in *NYTCR, 1977*: 256.

666. Klein, Alvin. Review of *Pavlo Hummel* at the Public Theater. WNET—New York. May 21, 1971.

    Available from TV-Time Recordings, Inc. (1937 Barnes Ave., Bronx, NY 10462).

667. Kragh-Jacobsen, Svend. "I skyggen af Vietnam." *Berlingske Tidende* [Copenhagen], Mar. 16, 1979, sec. II: 5.

    Gladsaxe Teater, Copenhagen

668. Kroll, Jack. "Pavlo Pacino." *Newsweek*, May 9, 1977: 50. Rpt. in *NYTCR, 1977*: 256.

669. _____. "This is the Army." *Newsweek*, June 14, 1971: 70. Rpt. in *NYTCR, 1971*: 260.

670. Kunkel, Jonathan. *"The Basic Training of Pavlo Hummel." The Pitt News* [campus newspaper University of Pittsburgh], Jan. 27, 1984: 14.

    Famous Rider/We're Entertainment

671. Lahr, John. "On-Stage." *Village Voice*, May 27, 1971: 57.

672. Mishkin, Leo. "Pavlo Hummel's Basic Training: War." *The Morning Telegraph* [New York], May 22, 1971: 3.

673. Mork, Ebbe. "Rosinen i Kanonfoden." *Politiken* [Copenhagen], Mar. 17, 1979, sec. 2: 8.

    Gladsaxe Teater, Copenhagen

674. Moser, Charlotte. "Equinox Casting Perfect in Rabe's 1st Viet play." *Houston Chronicle,* Nov. 11, 1977, "Amusements," sec. 4: 7.

675. Norris, Keith A. "Rabe from N.Y. to Philly." *The Villanovan,* 47, no. 24 (Apr. 12, 1972): 13.

New Locust Theatre

676. Oliver, Edith. "The Theatre: Off Broadway." *New Yorker,* May 29, 1971: 55.

677. Oppenheimer, George. "Stage: Salute to Pavlo." *Newsday,* May 21, 1971, sec. A: 1, 9.

678. Pacheco, Patrick. "Theater: On Broadway and Off." *After Dark,* June 1977: 24-25, 80.

679. Pilecki, Michelle. "Play Stirs Discomforting Memories." *Market Square* [Pittsburgh], Jan. 11, 1984: 12.

Famous Rider/We're Entertainment

680. Probst, Leonard. *"The Basic Training of Pavlo Hummel."* NBC TV. Apr. 25, 1977. Rpt. in *NYTCR, 1977:* 257.

681. _____. *"The Basic Training of Pavlo Hummel."* NBC TV. May 20, 1971. Rpt. in *NYTCR, 1971:* 260.

682. Pryor, Karen. "No Villains, No Heroes; *Hummel* Just Is." *Honolulu Advertiser,* Dec. 9, 1972, sec. C: 6.

University of Hawaii—Manoa

683. Raidy, William A. *"Pavlo Hummel* Exciting." *The Jersey Journal,* May 21, 1971: 26.

684. Rasch, Jane. "Et abent sar." *Land og Folk* [Copenhagen], Mar. 23, 1979: 10.

Gladsaxe Teater, Copenhagen

685. Rawson, Chris. "Sprawling *Pavlo Hummel* Gets Surprisingly Solid Production." *Pittsburgh Post-Gazette*, Jan. 9, 1984: 17.

Famous Rider/We're Entertainment

686. Ricco, Anthony Rice. "Compulsive Manhood." *The Sentinel* [San Francisco], 6, no. 8 (Apr. 20, 1979): 12.

Eureka Theatre Company

687. Rich, Alan. "Thank Heaven for Little Girls." *New York*, 10 (May 9, 1977): 63.

688. Schier, Ernest. "Misfit Becomes the Perfect Soldier." *Philadelphia Evening Bulletin*, Apr. 6, 1972, sec B: 15.

689. _____. "*Pavlo* Goes to New York." *Philadelphia Evening Bulletin*, Jan. 7, 1971: 36.

690. _____. "The Proving of Mr. Rabe." *Philadelphia Evening Bulletin*, May 21, 1971, sec. B: 37.

691. Schjeldahl, Peter. "Pursuing a Bogus 'Manhood.'" *New York Times*, July 11, 1971, sec. II: 1.

692. Schubeck, John. "*The Basic Training of Pavlo Hummel*." WABC TV. May 20, 1971. Rpt. in *NYTCR, 1971*: 260.

693. Silver, Lee. "*Pavlo Hummel* Opens at the Public/Newman." *New York Daily News*, May 21, 1971: 64. Rpt. in *NYTCR, 1971*: 258-59.

694. Smith, Susan H. "Fast-paced Opening for *Pavlo Hummel*." *Pittsburgh Press*, Jan. 7, 1984: 36.

Famous Rider/We're Entertainment

695. "*Soldat Hummel* pa Gladsaxe Teater." *Helsingor Dagblad*, Mar. 28, 1979: 14.

696. Sorensen, Viggo. "Den alt for gode soldat pa Gladsaxe Teater." *Jyllands-Posten* (*Morgenavisen*) [Viby, Denmark], Mar. 16, 1979,

sec. I: 14.

Gladsaxe Teater, Copenhagen

697. Sullivan, Dan. "The Evolution of a Fightin' Machine." *Los Angeles Times*, Feb. 20, 1973, sec. IV: 1.

698. Szekend, Marilyn. "Pavlo: One Man Against the Rest." *The Purdue Exponent*, Nov. 13, 1972: 3.

    Purdue University

699. Takiff, Jonathan. "Vet's *Pavlo* Looks at Army Brutality." *Philadelphia Daily News*, Apr. 6, 1972: 24.

700. Tauke, M. S. "Portrayal of *Pavlo* Effective." *Journal and Courier* [Lafayette, IN], Nov. 14, 1972, sec. B: 4.

    Purdue University

701. Tofte, Hans J. "Nar Krigsgalskaben besaetter antihelten." *Naestved Tidende* [Naestved], Mar. 15, 1979: 5.

    Gladsaxe Teater, Copenhagen

702. "Uheldig soldat." *Fyens Stiftstidende*, Mar. 10, 1979, sec. 2: 5.

    Gladsaxe Teater, Copenhagen

703. Uricchio, Marylynn. "Young Actors Get Grueling Lesson in Army Life for *Basic Training*." *Pittsburgh Post-Gazette*, Dec. 31, 1983: 17, 20.

    Famous Rider/We're Entertainment

704. Wallach, Allan. "Stage: Recasting a Success." *Newsday*, Dec. 28, 1971, sec. A: 7, 9.

705. Watt, Douglas. "Pacino Plays Dogface Pavlo in Revival." *New York Daily News*, Apr. 25, 1977: 25. Rpt. in *NYTCR, 1977*: 254.

706. Watts, Richard. "An Innocent in Vietnam." *New York Post*, May 21, 1971: 31. Rpt. in *NYTCR, 1971*: 258.

707. Weidman, Lisa. "*Pavlo Hummel* Another Hit for UCD." *Daily Democrat* [Woodland, CA], Jan. 19, 1985: 5.

    University of California—Davis

708. Wetzsteon, Ross. "Theatre: Onepenny Opera." *Village Voice*, May 16, 1971: 79.

709. _____. "*The Basic Training of Pavlo Hummel*." Introduction. *The Obie Winners: The Best of Off-Broadway*. Garden City, NY: Doubleday, 1980. 263-64.

710. Wilson, Edwin. "Name Performers Returning to Theatre." *The Wall Street Journal*, May 9, 1977: 22. Rpt. in *NYTCR, 1977*: 257.

711. Woock, Clare. "Theatre: Rabe's War." *Drummer/Daily Planet* [New York], June 24, 1971: 14.

THE ORPHAN

712. Africano, Lillian. "Rabe's *The Orphan*." *Villager* [New York, NY], Apr. 26, 1973: 7.

713. Albrecht, Ernest. *"The Orphan*—Last, Least of Rabe's Trilogy." *The Home News* [New Brunswick, NJ], Apr. 20, 1973: 17.

714. Announcement that *Orphan* will open Villanova Season. *Philadelphia Evening Bulletin*, Oct. 15, 1970: 24.

715. "Arts School Gets Grant." *Winston-Salem Journal* [NC], Jan. 4, 1975: 4.

     Appointment of Barnet Kellman to direct *The Orphan*

716. Bachrach, Judy. "Something is Myth-ing from this Play." *Philadelphia Inquirer*, Apr. 22, 1973, "The Arts," sec. G: 8.

717. Barnes, Clive. "Stage: Rabe's *The Orphan* Arrives." *New York Times*, Apr. 19, 1973, L+: 51.

718. Beaufort, John. "David Rabe's Play *Orphan* Hopscotches the Ages." *Christian Science Monitor*, Apr. 20, 1973: 14.

719. Bermel, Albert. "From Greece to America." *The New Leader*, June 11, 1973: 24-25.

720. Carragher, Bernard. "Rabe, Bleckner Aim to Keep Theater Vital." *New Haven Register/Journal-Courier*, Apr. 22, 1973, sec. 4: 1, 5.

721. Childs, James. "Rabe Drama Profound." *New Haven Register*, Apr. 29, 1973, "Arts and Leisure," sec. D: 3.

722. _____. "Today's Reality Turned in on Mythology." *New Haven Register*, Oct. 25, 1970, "Arts and Leisure," sec. D: 1, 7.

723. Collins, William B. "Manning's *Orphan* Makes a Statement but is a Failure." *Philadelphia Inquirer*, Mar. 18, 1974, sec. B: 4.

724. Ellis, Joshua. "Villanova Theatre Co. Opens Tonight with *The Orphan*, An Original Play by David Rabe." *The Villanovan*, 46, no. 6 (Oct. 14, 1970): 8.

725. _____. "David Rabe's *Orphan*: An Experiment in Form." *The Villanovan*, 46, no. 7 (Oct. 21, 1970): 8.

    Original Villanova production

726. Glover, William. "*Orphan* Attracts While it Annoys." *Los Angeles Times*, Apr. 21, 1973, sec. II: 9.

727. _____. "Rabe Misses Epic Drama but Effort Not Timid." *New Haven Register*, Apr. 19, 1973: 38.

728. Gottfried, Martin. "Rabe's *The Orphan*—You Can't Win 'em All." *Women's Wear Daily*, Apr. 19, 1973: 12. Rpt. in *NYTCR, 1973*: 252.

729. Hughes, Catharine. "The Greeks Revisited." *America*, May 12, 1973: 444-45.

730. Kalem, T. E. "The Vortex of Evil." *Time*, Apr. 30, 1973: 90. Rpt. in *NYTCR, 1973*: 251.

731. Kerr, Walter. "David Rabe Still Has Work to Do." *New York Times*, Apr. 29, 1973, sec. II: 1, 3.

732. Kroll, Jack. "Greek Salad." *Newsweek*, Apr. 30, 1973: 87. Rpt. in *NYTCR, 1973*: 251-52.

733. Lifson, David S. "Spotlight on Theatre." *The East Side Herald* [New York], May 18, 1973: 12.

734. McEwen, Charles. "David Rabe's *Orphan* Born Again." *Twin City Sentinel* [Winston-Salem, NC], Nov. 13, 1973: 11.

    North Carolina School of the Arts

735. *New York Shakespeare Festival Public Theatre Program Notes.* Apr. 18, 1973.

736. Nourse, Joan T. "*Orphan* Relates to Post-Vietnam World." *The Catholic Transcript*, May 4, 1973: 10.

737. _____. "Greek Myths with Modern Meanings." *The Catholic News*, May 3, 1973: 5.

738. Novick, Julius. "Manque Business." *Village Voice*, Apr. 26, 1973: 69.

739. Oliver, Edith. "The Theatre: Off Broadway." *New Yorker*, Apr. 28, 1973: 105.

740. "*The Orphan.*" *Variety*, May 9, 1973: 252.

741. Probst, Leonard. "*The Orphan.*" NBC TV. Apr. 18, 1973. Rpt. in *NYTCR, 1973*: 253.

742. Schier, Ernest. "A Lively Production of *Orphan.*" *Philadelphia Evening Bulletin*, Mar. 15, 1974: 49.

743. Simon, John. "Stinkweed Among the Asphodel." *New York*, Apr. 30, 1973: 98.

744. Takiff, Jonathan. "Papp to Work with Manning Street." *Philadelphia Daily News*, Feb. 6, 1974: 22.

745. Tomeo, Mark. "Rabe's *Orphan*—Breeding Violence, Passion." *The Villanovan,* 49, no. 20 (Mar. 20, 1974): 12.

    Manning Street Actors Theater

746. Wallach, Allan. "*Orphan* is Overburdened." *Citizen-Register* [Ossining, NY], Apr. 19, 1973: 35.

747. Watt, Douglas. "Rabe *Orphan* Ambitious Failure." *New York Daily News*, Apr. 19, 1973: 104. Rpt. in *NYTCR, 1973*: 250.

748. Watts, Richard. "The Ordeal of Orestes." *New York Post*, Apr. 19, 1973: 47. Rpt. in *NYTCR, 1973*: 250-51.

749. _____. "Notes on the Passing Season." *New York Post*, Apr. 28, 1973: 18.

750. Weil, Henry. "Theatre U.S.A." *Show Magazine*, Nov. 1973: 66.

IN THE BOOM BOOM ROOM,
INCLUDING *BOOM BOOM ROOM*

751. Albrecht, Ernest. "*Boom Boom Room:* We, Too, May Be Trapped in Go-Go Cage of Life." *Home News* [New Brunswick, NJ], Nov. 9, 1973: 36.

752. _____. "Go-Go Dancer's Other Dimensions Ugly." *Home News* [New Brunswick, NJ], Dec. 5, 1974: 34.

753. Antoine, Rick and Caryn Vogel. "*Boom Boom Room*: Topless Go-Go Girl Dances Her Way to Oblivion." *Indiana Daily Student* [campus newspaper Indiana University], Nov. 14, 1975, sec. 2: 7.

    Indiana University

754. Apter, Andrew. "*Boom Room* Numbing, Ugly But Well Done." *Daily Herald-Telephone* [Bloomington, IN], Nov. 15, 1975: 13.

    Indiana University

755. Barnes, Clive. "*The Boom Boom Room.* Anspacher, New York." *London Times,* Dec. 28, 1974: 7.

756. _____. "Stage: New Papp Home." *New York Times*, Nov. 9, 1973, sec. L: 31.

757. _____. "Theater: Rabe Revised." *New York Times*, Dec. 5, 1974: 55.

758. Besaw, Susan. "*Boom Boom Room.*" *Eagle* [Albany, NY], Aug. 1, 1974.

Williamstown Theatre Festival

759. Bonesteel, Michael. "Raw Rabe Lives at Live." *Evanston Review* [IL], Dec. 6, 1984, sec. D: 4.

Live Theatre, Evanston, IL

760. *Boom Boom Room. Playbill.* New York Shakespeare Festival, Lincoln Center, Vivian Beaumont Theatre, Vol. 10, Nov. 1973.

761. "*Boom Boom Room.*" *Booklist,* 72 (Nov. 1, 1975): 340.

Book review

762. "*Boom Boom Room.*" *New York Times,* Nov. 18, 1973, sec. 2: 3.

763. Bosworth, Patricia. "Joseph Papp at the Zenith-Was it Boom or Bust?" *New York Times,* Nov. 25, 1973, sec. II: 1.

764. Bowman, Piere. "At UH Theatre *Boom Boom Room*: a Dismal Failure." *Honolulu Star Bulletin,* Dec. 9, 1978, sec. A6: 1.

University of Hawaii—Manoa

765. Brockway, Jody, Phil Frankfield, and Josephine F. Florio. "*Boom* Hit Her Hard." *New York Times,* Dec. 9, 1973, "Drama Mailbag," sec. II: 9.

766. Buck, Richard M. *Library Journal,* 100 (Sept. 1, 1975): 1567.

Book review

767. Cann, Rebecca. "Burton to Host Bunnies and Yuppies." *Excalibur* [York University, Ontario, Canada], Mar. 20, 1986: 14.

Production at Burton Auditorium directed by Steven Gregg

768. Carlson, Don. W. "*Boom Boom Room*: Mostly Rat-A-Tat-Tat." *Kalamazoo Gazette,* Apr. 8, 1977, sec. A: 18.

769. Carr, Jay. "*Boom Boom Room*—Penetrating Despite Its Sprawl." *Detroit News*, Oct. 16, 1978, sec. B: 3.

Greektown Attic Theatre

770. *Choice,* 12 (Nov. 1975): 1171.

Book review

771. Christiansen, Richard. "Energy of Cast and Script Help Light a Fire in *Boom*." *Chicago Tribune*, Dec. 5, 1984: 4.

Live Theatre, Evanston, IL

772. Christon, Lawrence. "A Rabe Play 'That's Gonna Hit People.'" *Los Angeles Times*, July 3, 1977, "California": 51.

Group Repertory Theater

773. Clurman, Harold. "Theatre." *Nation*, 217 (Nov. 26, 1973): 572-73.

774. _____. "Theatre." *Nation*, 217 (Dec. 3, 1973): 603-604.

775. _____. "Theatre." *Nation*, 219 (Dec. 28, 1974): 701.

776. Collins, William B. "*Boom Boom Room*: Suffers from an Air of Insecurity." *Philadelphia Inquirer*, Nov. 9, 1973, sec. B: 4.

777. Craig, Randall. "Plays in Performance. Experimental [Square One]." *Drama*: *QTR*, 124 (Spring 1977): 61.

778. Drake, Sylvie. "*Boom Boom*: A Survival Story." *Los Angeles Times*, July 15, 1977, sec. IV: 1.

Group Repertory Theater

779. _____. "Jill Clayburgh in *Boom Boom*." *Los Angeles Times*, Apr. 19, 1979, sec. IV: 1.

Long Beach Theatre Festival production directed by Peter Flood

780. Engstrom, John. "Two Rabe Plays in Boston Premieres." *Boston Globe*, Mar. 31, 1983: 64.

Alley Theater, Cambridge, does *In the Boom Boom Room* and *Streamers*

781. Ensslin, Chip. "*In the Boom Boom Room*: A Modern American Tragedy." *Daily Tar Heel* [campus newspaper Univ. of North Carolina], Feb. 13, 1978: 4.

Carolina Union production directed by John Morrow

782. Feingold, Michael. "Rabe: Almost Poetry." *Village Voice*, Dec. 16, 1974: 101-102.

783. Gaver, Jack. "A Search for Identity in *Boom Boom*." *Los Angeles Times*, Nov. 16, 1973, sec. IV: 25.

784. Gill, Brendan. "Another Philadelphia Story." *New Yorker*, Nov. 19, 1973: 84.

Public Theatre

785. _____. "Off Broadway: The Second Time Around." *New Yorker*, Dec. 9, 1974: 69.

Lincoln Center

786. Glover, William. "*Boom Boom Room* is a Bomb." *Burlington County Times* [Willingboro, NJ], Nov. 10, 1973: 5.

787. _____. "Rabe's *Boom Boom Room*: Once Again A Bomb-Bomb." *New Haven Register*, Dec. 5, 1974: 40.

788. Goldman, Henry. "Student Play Offends Some Blacks." *Philadelphia Inquirer*, Dec. 18, 1983, sec. B: 7.

West Chester University, PA

789. Gottfried, Martin. "*Boom Boom Room*." *Women's Wear Daily*, Nov. 12, 1973: 30. Rpt. in *NYTCR, 1973*: 197.

790. _____. *"Boom Boom Room*: Revived." *New York Post*, Dec. 4, 1974: 74.

791. Greer, Edward G. "Features Broadway—On and Off." *Drama: QTR*, 112 (Spring 1974): 58.

    Lincoln Center

792. Griffin, William. *"The Boom Boom Room."* *Sign* [Passionist Fathers, Union City, NJ], 53 (Feb. 1974): 20.

793. Grubb, Kevin. *"In the Boom Boom Room."* *Dance Magazine*, 60 (Feb. 1986): 79.

    South Street Theatre

794. Hansen, Marrianne. *"Boom Boom Room* Features Solid Acting." *Daily Tar Heel* [campus newspaper Univ. of North Carolina], Feb. 12, 1978: 3.

    Carolina Union production directed by John Morrow

795. Harris, Leonard. *"Boom Boom Room."* WCBS TV. Nov. 8, 1973. Rpt. in *NYTCR, 1973*: 199.

796. Henshaw, Chris. *"In the Boom-Boom Room."* *Fun City* [Bloomington, IN], Nov. 14, 1975: 13-14.

    Indiana University

797. Hobe. "Battling Papp Berates Barnes; Bars Raidy From *Boom* Preview." *Variety*, Nov. 14, 1973: 63.

798. Holder, Geoffrey. *"Boom Boom Room."* NBC TV. Nov. 8, 1973. Rpt. in *NYTCR, 1973*: 200.

799. Horton, Charles. *"Boom Boom* Characters Aren't the Waltons." *Chapel Hill Newspaper*, Feb. 16, 1978: 9.

    Carolina Union production directed by John Morrow

800. Hughes, Catharine. "The Perils of Being Papp." *America*, 129 (Dec. 22, 1973): 485.

801. Jahn, Mike. "Ellen Greene Mixes Clubs and Theatre." *Jazz*, Feb. 10, 1975: 4.

    Anspacher Theatre

802. Johnson, Tracie. "Cast Excels in Rabe's Play." *Indiana Daily Student* [campus newspaper Indiana University], Nov. 17, 1975: 6.

    Indiana University production with Debbie Dorris as Chrissy

803. Joyce, Herman Alex. "In the *Boom Boom Room*." *Michael's Thing* [New York, NY], Dec. 1974.

804. Kalem, T. E. "Shallow Soul in Depth." *Time*, Nov. 19, 1973: 96-97. Rpt. in *NYTCR, 1973*: 198.

805. Karey, Gerald. "*Boom Boom Room* Misses Boat." *Asbury Park Press* [NJ], Nov. 10, 1973: 7.

806. Kauffmann, Stanley. "*Boom Boom Room*." *New Republic*, Dec. 1, 1973: 22, 33.

807. Kelly, Martin P. "Poor Play Outmatches the Acting." *Times-Union* [Albany, NY], Aug. 5, 1974: 14.

    Williamstown Theatre Festival

808. Kerr, Walter. "We Leave the Girl as We Found Her." *New York Times*, Nov. 18, 1973, sec. 2: 3.

809. Kisonak, Rick. "*Boom Boom* Flays Scenes." *Primo Times*, Nov. 17, 1975: 8.

    Indiana University production

810. Kriegsman, Alan M. "*Boom Boom Room*: The Latest Bombshell from Joe Papp." *Washington Post*, Dec. 2, 1973, sec. K: 1, 3.

811. Kroll, Jack. "Go-Go Gone." *Newsweek*, Dec. 16, 1974: 105.

812. ____. "Go-go in Hell." *Newsweek*, Nov. 19, 1973: 96. Rpt. in *NYTCR, 1973*: 199.

813. Lewis, Allan. "Theater at Lincoln Center: *Boom Boom Room* Opens Series." *New Haven Register/Journal-Courier*, Nov. 18, 1973, "Arts and Leisure," sec. D: 3, 5.

814. Lovell, Glenn. "Rabe's *The Boom Boom Room* Wildly Uneven and, Well, Boring." *San Jose Mercury*, July 2, 1977, sec. C: 4.

Quantum Leap production at Venetian Bakery Theater

815. Mitgang, Herbert. "Stage: Revised Version of *Boom Boom Room*." *New York Times*, Dec. 22, 1985, sec. 1: 59.

Orange Theater Company production at South Street Theater

816. Moes, Steve. "Rabe's 4th Play Draws Rave Reviews." *Dubuque Telegraph Herald*, Dec. 2, 1973: 43.

817. Morley-Priestman, Anne. "Square One *In the Boom Boom Room*." *The Stage and Television Today* [England], Dec. 16, 1976: 29.

818. Mueller, Roxanne T. "*Boom Boom Room* Slow but Has Splendid Moments." *Daily Iowan* [campus paper University of Iowa], Apr. 16, 1982: 7.

University of Iowa production directed by James Milton

819. Myers, Larry. "*In the Boom Boom Room*." *Stages*, Jan. 1986: 10.

Orange Theater Company production at South Street Theater

820. Nelsen, Don. "They Both Had Their Dreams." *New York Daily News*, Jan. 7, 1986: 35.

Orange Theater Company production at South Street Theater

821. Novick, Julius. "Papp Goes Boom at Beaumont." *Village Voice,* Nov. 15, 1973: 74.

822. Ogden, Jean. "On Stage." WBRW Radio. Somerville, NJ. Dec. 4, 1974.

823. Pombeiro, Beth Gillin. "*The Boom Boom Room* is Philadelphia-Inspired." *Philadelphia Inquirer,* Nov. 4, 1973, sec. I: 1, 8.

824. Popkin, Henry. "*Boom Boom* Comes Back No Better." *New Rochelle Reporter Dispatch,* Dec. 9, 1974, sec. B: 9.

825. Prout, Teresa. "*Boom Boom*; A Punishing, But Well-Done Production." *Durham Morning Herald* [NC], Feb. 19, 1978, sec. C: 24.

     Carolina Union production directed by John Morrow

826. Raidy, William A. "*Boom Boom* Bold, Beautiful." *The Star-Ledger,* Nov. 10, 1973: 12.

827. _____. "Cast Fails to Keep Step with Strong *Boom Boom*." *The Star-Ledger,* Dec. 5, 1974: 72.

828. _____. "Less Bang in *Boom Boom Room*." *Long Island Daily Press,* Dec. 5, 1974: 20.

829. _____. "A Room for the Doomed." *Long Island Daily Press,* Nov. 9, 1973: 18.

830. Rozmiarek, Joseph T. "The *Boom Boom* is a Bust." *Honolulu Advertiser,* Dec. 11, 1978, sec. B: 1.

     University of Hawaii—Manoa

831. Russell, Candice. "A Troubling Drama Worth Seeing." *Miami Herald,* July 22, 1978, sec. B: 5.

832. Sahl, Hans. "Sex und Sarkasmus mit Pop-Musik." *Die Welt* [West Berlin], Dec. 22, 1973: 15.

833. Sanders, Kevin. *"Boom Boom Room."* WABC TV. Nov. 8, 1973. Rpt. in *NYTCR, 1973*: 200.

834. Sauvage, Leo. "Un echec de Joseph Papp." *Le Figaro*, Jan. 3, 1974: 17.

     Lincoln Center

835. Schier, Ernest. *"Boom Boom Room* is Rabe's Finest." *Philadelphia Evening Bulletin*, Nov. 9, 1973, sec. B: 19.

836. "Second Company to Offer *Boom Boom Room." Transcript* [North Adams, MA], July 25, 1974: 20.

     Williamstown Theatre Festival

837. Simon, John. "Bad and Good Evenings." *New York*, 6 (Nov. 26, 1973): 92.

838. _____. "Theatre Chronicle." *Hudson Review*, 27 (Spring 1974): 85-86.

839. Starr, William W. "A Stark, Compelling Drama." *The State* [Columbia, SC], Dec. 10, 1980, sec. B: 12.

     University of South Carolina production

840. Stasio, Marilyn. *"Boom Boom Room." Cue Magazine* [New York], Nov. 19, 1973, "Theatre": 7.

841. Stein, Ellen. "A Depressing *Boom Boom Room." San Francisco Chronicle*, July 3, 1980, sec. C: 7.

842. Van Aken, K. R. "Oh the Vulgarity, Sordidness and Obscenity of It." *The Pitt News* [campus newspaper University of Pittsburgh], 80, no. 56 (Feb. 7, 1986): 12.

     Studio Theater

843. Wallach, Allan. "A Second Try by Papp." *Newsday*, Dec. 5, 1974, sec. I: 47.

844. Watt, Douglas. "Rabe's *Boom Boom Room* Bows." *New York Daily News*, Nov. 9, 1973: 82. Rpt. in *NYTCR, 1973*: 196.

845. Watts, Richard. "Career of a Nightclub Dancer." *New York Post*, Nov. 9, 1973: 62. Rpt. in *NYTCR, 1973*: 196.

846. Weales, Gerald. "The Stage: Boom Boom Pop." *Commonweal*, 99 (Dec. 14, 1973): 294-95.

847. _____. "Theatre Watch." *Georgia Review*, 40 (1986): 529-30.

Orange Theater Company production at South Street Theater

848. Weiler, A. H. "News of the Screen." *New York Times*, Dec. 9, 1973: 78.

849. Wilk, Gerhard. "Go-Go-Girl und die Urmutter: Neue Stucke auf New Yorker Buhnen." *Der Tagesspiegel* [West Berlin], Dec. 15, 1973: 4.

850. Williams, Gary Jay. "Dr. Chekov and Mr. Papp." *National Review,* Jan. 18, 1974: 90-91.

851. Wilson, Edwin. "Sad Saga of a Go-Go Dancer." *The Wall Street Journal*, Nov. 14, 1973: 26. Rpt. in *NYTCR, 1973*: 198.

852. Winer, Linda. "Flailing Away in the *Boom Boom Room*." *Chicago Tribune*, Jan. 16, 1976, sec. III: 7.

853. Young, B. A. "*In the Boom Boom Room*." *Financial Times* [London], Dec. 2, 1976: 3.

Square One Theatre

STREAMERS

854. Aaron, Jules. *Educational Theatre Journal*, 30 (May 1978): 271-73.

Westwood Playhouse, Los Angeles

855. "ACT Presents *The* [sic]*Streamers*." *The Medium* [Seattle], Aug. 3, 1977: 4.

A Contemporary Theatre

856. Armstrong, James. "Stunning *Streamers*." *After Dark* (July 1978): 25.

Cannery Theatre production directed by Milton Katselas

857. Ashley, Dottie. "USC Theatre's *Streamers* Provokes Thought, Comment." *Columbia Record* [SC], Feb. 21, 1979, sec. C: 2.

University of South Carolina

858. Aso, T. "Amerika no Ryoshin ni Mesu" [A Scalpel into the American Conscience]. *Teatro* [Tokyo monthly magazine], Aug. 1979: 42-43.

Seihai Theatre

859. Barber, John. "Vietnam Play Given with Courage." *Daily Telegraph* [London], Feb. 24, 1978: 13.

Round House Playhouse, Liverpool

860. Barnes, Clive. "The Stage: *Streamers*; Rabe Brings Vietnam Trilogy to a Close." *New York Times*, Apr. 22, 1976: 38. Rpt. in *NYTCR, 1976*: 264.

861. _____. "Theater: David Rabe's *Streamers* in New Haven." *New York Times*, Feb. 8, 1976, sec. L+: 45.

     Long Wharf Theatre

862. _____. "Theatre for a Holiday Mood." *New York Times*, May 28, 1976: C4.

863. Beaufort, John. "*Streamers*." *Christian Science Monitor*, Apr. 26, 1976: 27. Rpt. in *NYTCR, 1976*: 266.

864. Becker, Karen. "Vietnam: IU Play Examines War." *Daily Herald-Telephone* [Bloomington, IN], Oct. 6, 1978: 28.

     Indiana University production directed by Robert Verini

865. "Beihei no Fuan to Kyofu, Gekidan Seihai ga Jyoen" [Theatre Company Seihai Presents Fear and Scare of American Soldiers]. *Yomiruri Shinbun*, Evening Edition, May 23, 1979: 7.

866. Bennett, Alice Boatwright. "*Streamers* in N.H. 'Excellent, Intense.'" *New England Entertainment Digest*, Jan. 16, 1980: 10.

     Theatre by the Sea

867. "Betonamu o Toinaosu" [Re-examination of the Meaning of Viet Nam]. *Mainichi Shinbun*, Evening Edition, May 28, 1979: 7.

868. Boak, Ed. "A Cry Against the Misuse of Men." *Seattle Sun*, Aug. 10, 1977: 10.

     A Contemporary Theatre

869. Bone. "New Show in Stock. *Streamers*." *Variety*, Feb. 18, 1976: 121.

870. Brennan, Brian. *"Streamers."* *Calgary Herald*, Mar. 25, 1978, sec. A: 3.

Theatre Calgary production at the QR Centre

871. Bretz, Lynn. "Potent War Play to Open." *Lawrence Journal-World*, Sept. 30, 1979, sec. B: 9.

University of Kansas production directed by James Graves

872. Brown, Joe. "Stark, Savage *Streamers*." *Washington Post*, Aug. 2, 1985, sec. WE: 11.

Steppenwolf production at the Kennedy Center

873. Buck, Richard M. *Library Journal*, 102 (Apr. 15, 1977): 944.

Book review

874. Burke, Lorrie. *"Streamers* Depicts Realities of War." *The Daily Beacon* [campus newspaper University of Tennessee], Nov. 4, 1982: 4.

University Company's production directed by Thomas Cook

875. Calta, Louis. "Evans, Miss Snyder Win Derwent Awards." *New York Times*, May 28, 1976, sec. III: 23.

876. Campbell, R. M. *"Streamers."* *Northwest Arts: Fortnightly Journal of News and Opinion* [Seattle], 3, no. 14 (Aug. 12, 1977): 4, 8.

A Contemporary Theatre

877. Carr, Jay. "Something's Missing on American Stage: A Tragic Ingredient." *Detroit News*, Nov. 13, 1977, sec. E: 1, 4.

Greektown Attic Theatre

878. _____. *"Streamers* Flares with Agony of War." *Detroit News*, Nov. 7, 1977, sec. B: 7.

Greektown Attic Theatre

879. Cassidy, Claudia. "*Streamers*." WFMT Radio. Chicago, Apr. 3, 1977.

Goodman Theatre

880. "A Catalogue of Violent Plays." *Southern Theatre*, 28 (Spring 1987): 30.

Includes *Streamers* in a group of plays "with at least some aspects of violence woven into the story line"

881. Cedrone, Lou. "*Streamers* Message Unclear; *Caesar* Had Best Beware." *Baltimore Evening Sun*, Jan. 18, 1977, sec. B: 4.

Arena Stage

882. Chagy, John. "War—No Longer Heroic." *Buckhead Atlanta*, Mar. 8, 1979: 10.

Academy Theatre

883. Chase, Chris. "The Audience Can Almost Hear Him Ticking." *New York Times*, June 13, 1976, sec. 2: 5.

Interview with Dorian Harewood who played Carlyle

884. Chesley, R. "*Streamers*." *Gay Community News* [Boston, MA], 4, no. 23 (Dec. 4, 1976): 11.

Long Wharf Theatre

885. *Choice*, 14 (Oct. 1977): 1054.

Book review

886. Christiansen, Richard. "11th Street Does a Banner Job with *Streamers*." *Chicago Tribune*, Jan. 12, 1983, sec. IV: 6.

Studio Theatre production at Columbia College

887. _____. "Steppenwolf's Kinney Back Directing—with Big Success and a Few Doubts." *Chicago Tribune*, Jan. 23, 1983, sec. 6: 16-17.

888. _____. "Steppenwolf's *Streamers* Lights up Kennedy Center." *Chicago Tribune*, Aug. 1, 1985, sec. 5: 7.

889. _____. "*Streamers*: A Drama of Life and Death." *Chicago Daily News*, Apr. 1, 1977: 32.

Goodman Theatre

890. Clark, Buddy. Review of *Streamers*. WWWL Radio 94 **fm**. Miami, Mar. 27, 1978.

Players State Theater

891. Clay, Carolyn. "Beautiful *Streamers*." *Boston Phoenix*, Jan. 22, 1980, sec. 3: 1, 5.

Theatre by the Sea

892. Clouston, Erlend. "Lesson in Futility." *Liverpool Echo*, Feb. 2, 1978: 2.

893. Clurman, Harold. "Theatre." *Nation*, 222 (May 8, 1976): 574.

894. Coe, Richard L. "Explosive *Streamers*." *Washington Post*, Jan. 13, 1977, sec. C: 1.

895. Cohn, Fritzi. "Theatre by the Sea—*Streamers*." "Newscenter," WCSH TV. Portland, ME, Jan. 15, 1980.

896. Cole, Gloria. "*Streamers*: A Brutal, Powerful New Rabe Play." *Fairpress* [Norwalk, CT], Feb. 11, 1976: 55.

Long Wharf Theatre

897. Collins, William. "*Streamers* is a War Within." *Philadelphia Inquirer*, Feb. 10, 1976: 4B.

Long Wharf Theatre

898. Cowan, Janet. Review of *Streamers*. WIOD Radio. Miami, Mar. 27, 1978.

Lively Arts

899. Cushman, Robert. "The Whirlpool's Edge." *The Observer* [England], Feb. 26, 1978: 37.

Round House Playhouse, Liverpool

900. Craig, Randall. "Plays in Performance—Experimental." *Drama: QTR* 125 (Spring 1978): 69, 71.

Round House Playhouse, Liverpool

901. "Critics Select *Travesties* as Best Play of 1975-76." *New York Times*, May 12, 1976: 34.

902. Daly, Margaret. "Stunning Play Tastefully Treated." *Toronto Star*, July 7, 1977, sec. F: 1.

Theatre Plus production at St. Lawrence Centre

903. Day, Richard. "Craftsmanly New Play Treats Pre-Battlefield Violence." *Post* [Bridgeport, CT], Feb. 12, 1976: 27.

Long Wharf Theatre

904. De Frie, Marion. "*Streamers* Explores Violence with Limited Vision." *Philadelphia Gay News*, Mar. 6, 1976, sec. B: 12.

905. De Mott, Benjamin. "Prize Play." *Atlantic Monthly*, Dec. 1976: 108-109.

906. Dodds, Richard. "Look Back in Sadness." *New Orleans Times-Picayune*, May 18, 1978, sec. V: 11.

907. Doughty, Jane. "GI Blues: Did Anything Really Happen?" *Herald* [Everett, WA], Aug. 12, 1977, "Today's Living/People," sec. B: 5.

A Contemporary Theatre

908. Drake, Sylvie. "*Streamers* Garners Six Critics' Awards." *Los Angeles Times*, Mar. 21, 1978, sec. IV: 1.

909. Erdelyn, Joseph. "*Streamers* in Toronto: Disturbing Look at Harsh Fishbowl Existence." *Ottawa Citizen*, July 8, 1977: 36.

Theatre Plus production at St. Lawrence Centre

910. Faires, Robert. "*Streamers*: The Cost of War." *The Austin Chronicle* [Texas], 4, no. 22 (June 28, 1985): 31.

Capitol City Playhouse

911. Fleckenstein, Joan S. *Educational Theatre Journal*, 28 (Oct. 1976): 408-409.

Long Wharf Theatre

912. Frymer, Murry. "City Lights Scores with Powerful Drama—Sensitive *Streamers* Flies High." *San Jose Mercury News*, Jan. 13, 1986, sec. B: 11.

913. Fryten, David. "David Rabe's Fifth Play a Hit." *Dubuque Telegraph Herald*, Feb. 20, 1976: 7.

914. Gottfried, Martin. "Rabe's *Streamers*—Theater at Its Peak." *New York Post*, Apr. 22, 1976: 21. Rpt. in *NYTCR, 1976*: 265.

915. _____. "Streaming Through Life." *New York Post*, Feb. 9, 1976: 15.

Long Wharf Theatre

916. Grant, Zalin. "Vietnam as Fable." *New Republic*, 178 (Mar. 25, 1978): 24.

Book review

917. Gussow, Mel. "Stage: *Streamers* Revived at AMDA Stage One." *New York Times*, Sept. 20, 1979, sec. III: 16.

918. Haller, Scott. "Powerful *Streamers* Brings Vietnam back Home." *Yale Daily News*, Feb. 15, 1976: 5.

919. Hanson, Alice M. "Everyone Has a Bottom." *Chicago Tribune*, Apr. 26, 1977, sec. III: 2.

920. Hasegawa, Ryusei. "Torikumi wa Shinken daga Iwakan, Beijin no Knado, Jinshu Koete Tsutawaruka?" [Earnest Stage, But a Little Strangeness Beyond Our Understanding; Is It Possible to Revive the Deep Emotion Felt by the U.S. Audience on the Japanese Stage. Beyond Racial Gap?] *Tokyo Shinbun*, Evening Edition, June 5, 1979: 5.

921. Hawthorn, Maggie. "ACT's *Streamers* is Strong, Fine Theatre." *Seattle Post-Intelligencer*, Aug. 6, 1977: 5.

     A Contemporary Theatre

922. Hewes, Henry. "*Streamers* Author Opens Up." *Los Angeles Times*, "California," Dec. 11, 1977: 87.

923. _____. "To 'Disneyland' and Back." *Saturday Review*, Apr. 17, 1976: 48-49.

924. Hirsch, Sam. "*Streamers* Violent, Shocking in Nature." *Goldcoast Scene* [Miami], Mar. 31-Apr. 6, 1978: 8.

     Players State Theater

925. Hoffecker, Felicity. "LWT Premiere is Moving, Beautiful." *Stamford Weekly Mall and Shopper* [CT], Feb. 12, 1976: 24.

926. Holman, Rhonda. "*Streamers* Depicts Jarring Reality of Fears, Sadness in Vietnam War." *University Daily Kansan* [campus newspaper University of Kansas], Oct. 3, 1979: 6.

     University of Kansas production directed by James Graves

927. Holmes, Ann. "UH's *Streamers* Excellent Contemporary Theater." *Houston Chronicle*, "Amusements," Nov. 1, 1977, sec. 1: 11.

University of Houston production directed by Sidney Berger at the Attic Theater

928. Hughes, Catharine. "Did Vietnam Spoil David Rabe?" *America*, May 15, 1976: 432.

929. Igarashi, Y. and A. Fujita. "Engeki Jihyo" *Higeki Kigeki* [Tokyo monthly review], Sept. 1979: 116-17.

930. Issacs, Robert. "LWT's *Streamers* Kathartic." *Stratford News* [CT], Feb. 15, 1976.

    Long Wharf Theatre

931. Jacway, Taffy. "*Streamers* is Dynamic." *Globe-News* [Auburn, WA], Aug. 12, 1977: 12.

    A Contemporary Theatre

932. Jenkins, Tom. "Theatre by the Sea Scores with *Streamers*." *The Atlantic News*, Jan. 15, 1980: 7.

933. Johnson, Bryan. "*Streamers* a Winner with U.S. Imports." *Globe and Mail* [Toronto], July 7, 1977: 13.

    Theatre Plus

934. Johnson, Florence. "*Streamers*—A Sorry Affair." *New Haven Register/Journal-Courier*, Feb. 9, 1976: 2.

    Long Wharf Theatre

935. Johnson, Malcolm. "Rabe's *Streamers* at LWT." *Courant* [Hartford, CT], Feb. 15, 1976, sec. F: 12.

    Long Wharf Theatre

936. Johnson, Wayne. "*Streamers* is Tough, Grim Show." *Seattle Times*, Aug. 5, 1977, "Tempo": 1.

    A Contemporary Theatre

937. Jones, Everett. "Arena Stage Play is Taut Drama." *Journal Messenger* [Washington, DC], Jan. 14, 1977, sec. A: 7.

938. Jones, John Bush. "Self-Psychotherapy Burdens Play." *Kansas City Times*, Oct. 4, 1979, sec. E: 7.

     University of Kansas production directed by James Graves

939. Kai, Marie. "The Silken Knives that Rip through the Deep Blue Sky ...." Performance pamphlet for Seihai Theatre Company. May 31-June 8, 1979.

940. Kalem, T. E. "War Without End." *Time*, May 3, 1976: 75. Rpt. in *NYTCR, 1976*: 267.

941. Keating, Douglas J. "The Last in a Vietnam Trilogy, a Powerful Play." *Philadelphia Inquirer*, Oct. 8, 1979, sec. B: 4.

     University of Pennsylvania production at Harold Prince Theatre

942. Kehoe, Emanuel. "War Games." *Sunday Press* [Dublin], Oct. 8, 1978: 23.

     Eblana Theatre

943. Kelly, George. *"Streamers." Concord Monitor* [NH], Jan. 10, 1980: 25.

     Theatre by the Sea

944. Kelly, Kevin. "In New Hampshire, a Soul-Searing Play." *Boston Globe*, Jan. 14, 1980, sec. L: 10.

     Theatre by the Sea

945. _____. *"Streamers." Boston Globe*, Dec. 10, 1976, sec. L: 11.

     Long Wharf Theatre

946. Kerr, Walter. "Stage View: When Does Gore Get Gratuitous?" *New York Times*, Feb. 22, 1976, sec. 2: 1, 7.

947. Kincade, Phil. "The Chilling Violence in *Streamers* is Close to Reality." *Foster's Daily Democrat* [Dover, NH], Jan. 10, 1980: 23.

    Theatre by the Sea

948. Klein, Alvin. "*Streamers*." WNYC TV. Apr. 22, 1976.

949. Klein, Stewart. "*Streamers*." WNEW TV. Apr. 22, 1976.

950. Kloten, Edgar. "*Streamers* Flutters Down the Drain." *West Hartford News*, Feb. 12, 1976, sec. B: 3.

    Long Wharf Theatre

951. Kmetzo, Tom. "*Streamers* Scores Long Wharf Hit." *Republican* [Waterbury, CT], Feb. 8, 1976: 16.

952. Kriegsman, Alan M. "On Stage: The Plays Are the Thing." *Washington Post*, Jan. 23, 1977, sec. E: 14.

    Arena Stage

953. Kroll, Jack. "Three Cuts to the Quick." *Newsweek*, Feb. 23, 1976: 89, 91. Rpt. in *NYTCR, 1976*: 267.

    Long Wharf Theatre

954. Kurokawa, K. "Amerika fo Maki." (Chapter on the U.S. Theatre., no. 2 from a series titled "News from Abroad.") *Higeki Kigeki* [Tokyo monthly magazine], Nov. 1977: 66.

955. Lardner, James. "*Streamers*." *Washington Post*, Sept. 21, 1979, sec. C: 16.

956. Leeney, Robert J. "At Long Wharf: Emotion—and Blood." *New Haven Register/Journal-Courier*, Feb. 8, 1976, sec. A: 31.

957. Lindstrom, Pia. "*Streamers*." NBC TV, April 23, 1976.

958. "Liverpool: *Streamers*." *Stage*, Mar. 2, 1978: 15.

Round House Playhouse

959. Lochte, Dick. "Marx Bros. Does More Than Beat the Dead to Death." *Los Angeles*, 23 (Feb. 1978): 208.

Westwood Playhouse

960. Lynwander, Linda. "Writer Disagrees with Reviewer On *Streamers*." *Times* [Trumbull, CT], "Letter to Editor," Feb. 12, 1976: 5.

961. McCarthy, Bob. "Stage: *Streamers*." *B.A.R.* [San Francisco], June 8, 1978, II: 25.

Cannery Theatre production directed by Milton Katselas

962. Morin, Nanette. "*Streamers*." *The Current* [Newburyport, MA], Jan. 23-Feb. 5, 1980.

Theatre by the Sea

963. Mullins, Dennis. "*Streamers*: Shockingly Successful." *Wisconsin State Journal* [Madison], Mar. 5, 1981, sec. 2: 7.

University of Wisconsin Experimental Theatre

964. Munk, Erika. "*Streamers* is Rabe's Naif Play." *Village Voice*, May 3, 1976: 118.

965. Nelson, Liza. "A Steamy Flop at the Academy Theatre." *Atlanta Gazette*, Mar. 11, 1979: 13.

966. "New Rabe Drama to Open at LWT." *New Haven Register/Journal-Courier*, Dec. 7, 1975, "Arts and Leisure," sec. 4: 3.

Long Wharf Theatre

967. Novick, Julius. "*Streamers* is Rabe's Best Play." *Village Voice*, May 3, 1976: 118.

968. Nowlan, David. "*Streamers* at the Eblana." *The Irish Times* [Dublin], Oct. 3, 1978, "Arts and Studies": 8.

969. O'Dowd, Brian. "*Streamers*: On the Way to 'Nam." *Valley Scene* [Los Angeles], Dec. 29, 1977: 3

    Westwood Playhouse

970. Oliver, Edith. "Off Broadway: Trilogy's End." *New Yorker*, May 3, 1976: 76-77.

971. Payne, Deborah C. "*Streamers*." *Studies in American Drama, 1945-Present*, 1 (1986): 107-109.

    Steppenwolf production at Kennedy Center

972. Peter, John. "Trapped in the Twilight." *London Sunday Times*, Mar. 5, 1978: 38.

973. Peterson, Margaret. "*Streamers* Requires a Strong Stomach." *Gazette* [Montreal], Oct. 17, 1981: 55.

    McGill Players

974. Pevear, Elizabeth. "*Streamers* is Strong Medicine." *The Transcript*, Jan. 15, 1980, sec. 1: 2.

    Theatre by the Sea

975. Phinney, Kevin. "War's Emotions Fill Stage in *Streamers*." *Austin American-Statesman* [TX], July 6, 1985, sec. B: 12.

    Capitol City Playhouse

976. Pluff, James L. "Rabe's 'Bloodbath.'" *New Haven Register/Journal-Courier*, Feb. 12, 1976, Letter to the Editor: 22.

    Long Wharf Theatre

977. Porter, McKenzie. "Actors Struggle with 'Best Play's' Mediocrity." *Toronto Sun*, July 8, 1977, "Entertainment": 35.

978. Pound, Kate. "*Streamers* is Strong Vietnam War Drama." *University Daily Kansan*, Oct. 2, 1979: 10.

University of Kansas production directed by James Graves

979. Pronechen, Joseph. "A Very Brutal Play." *Times* [Trumbull, CT], Feb. 5, 1976: 6.

Long Wharf Theatre

980. "Rabe Returns with Flying *Streamers*." *Globe and Mail* [Toronto], May 14, 1976, "Entertainment": 14.

981. Raposa, David. "*Streamers* Pulls no Punches." *Free Press* [Boston], Jan. 15, 1980: 5.

Theatre by the Sea

982. Reed, Rex. "*Streamers* Shatters Broadway's Doldrums." *New York Daily News*, Apr. 23, 1976: 70.

983. Rhem, James. "Rabe's *Streamers* Worth Standing For." *The Capitol Times* [Madison, WI], Mar. 5, 1981, sec. PM: 16.

University of Wisconsin Experimental Theatre

984. Rich, Alan. "Hank Cinq and Hank Sunk." *New York*, 9 (May 10, 1976): 78.

Mitzi Newhouse Theatre

985. Richards, David. "Myths of Men and Manhood." *Washington Star*, Jan. 13, 1977, sec. D: 3.

Arena Stage

986. Richardson, Jack. "The Surprise of *Streamers*." *Commentary*, 62 (July 1976): 61-63.

987. Riley, Joe. "Lawton Snuffs out Candle of Provincialism." *Liverpool Daily Post*, "Review," Feb. 2, 1978: 3.

Round House Playhouse, Liverpool

988. Risser, James. "People Faint at Rabe's *Streamers*." *Des Moines Register*, Feb. 19, 1977, sec. A: 1, 4.

989. Rosenfeld, Megan. "Slam-Bang *Streamers*." *Washington Post*, Aug. 1, 1985, sec. B: 10.

Steppenwolf production at Kennedy Center

990. Roush, Matt. "Vietnam War Play to Portray 'Eternal Human Pageant.'" *Indiana Daily Student* [campus newspaper Indiana University], "Entertainment/Arts," Oct. 6, 1978: 15.

Indiana University production directed by Robert Verini

991. _____. "*Streamers* is a Journey from Locker Room Humor to Sorrow." *Indiana Daily Student* [campus newspaper Indiana University], Oct. 9, 1978: 15.

Indiana University production directed by Robert Verini

992. Rousuck, J. Wynn. "Violence Neutralizes Impact of *Streamers*." *Baltimore Sun*, July 31, 1985, sec D: 1.

Steppenwolf production at Kennedy Center

993. Rush, William H., Jr. "Unholy Mess." *New Haven Register*, Letter to the Editor, Feb. 22, 1976, sec. B: 1.

994. Rushe, Desmond. "Ugly Face of Army Brutalisation." *Irish Independent* [Dublin], Oct. 3, 1978: 7.

Eblana Theatre

995. Russell, Candice. "*Streamers*: Drama of War." *Miami Herald*, Mar. 19, 1978, sec. L: 1,5.

996. Salij, Marta. "*Streamers*: A Difficult Excellence." *The Drummer* [Knoxville, TN weekly entertainment paper], 2, no. 8 (Nov. 4-10, 1982): 1.

University of Tennessee University Company production directed by Thomas Cook

997. Sanville, Jim. "*Streamers* Excellent Show." *Press Herald* [Portland, ME], Jan. 9, 1980, sec. E: 2.

Theatre by the Sea

998. Sarmento, William. "*Streamers* America's Best Play in Years." *The Sun* [Lowell, MA], June 3, 1976: 41.

Mitzi Newhouse Theatre

999. Schier, Ernest. "David Rabe's Newest Play is Lean, Eloquent, Moral." *Philadelphia Evening Bulletin*, Feb. 10, 1976, sec. A: 40.

Long Wharf Theatre

1000. ____. "*Streamers* Needs More Confidence." *Philadelphia Evening Bulletin*, Oct. 4, 1979, sec. BK: 39.

University of Pennsylvania production at Harold Prince Theater

1001. "Seiha ga Bungakuza no Fujiwara Shinpei Enshutsu de Otoko-dake no Betonamu Geki!" [Seihai Presents Vietnam Play, with All Male Cast, Directed By Shinpei Fujiwara of Bungakuza Company]. *Shukan Myojo*, May 22, 1979: 50.

1002. Sharp, Christopher. "*Streamers*." *Women's Wear Daily*, Apr. 22, 1976: 36. Rpt. in *NYTCR, 1976*: 266.

1003. Sherbert, Linda. "*Streamers*." *Atlanta Constitution*, Mar. 21, 1986, sec. P: 2.

Gallery Theater

1004. Sheridan, Michael. "Drama of Blood and Honesty." *The Irish Press* [Dublin], Oct. 3, 1978: 4.

Eblana Theatre

1005. Simon, John. "Playwright's Progress." *The New Leader*, June 21, 1976: 21-22.

1006. Smith, Gus. "The Americans." *Sunday Independent* [Dublin], Oct. 8, 1978: 2.

Eblana Theatre

1007. Smith, Helen C. "Rabe's *Streamers*, New Peck Play Key Academy Season." *Atlanta Constitution*, June 19, 1978, sec. E: 3.

Academy Theatre

1008. _____. "*Streamers* Great If You Can Stand the Shock." *Atlanta Constitution*, Feb. 23, 1979, sec. B: 1, 11.

Academy Theatre

1009. Smith, Mark. "*Streamers* Offends, Captivates in Westwood." *Daily Forty-Niner* [Los Angeles], Jan. 24, 1978: 4.

Westwood Playhouse

1010. Stanton, Tom. "*Streamers* Offers Great Performances." *Kalamazoo Gazette*, Apr. 28, 1979, sec. A: 7.

Carver Center Arena Theater

1011. Stern, Alan. "Hunger Artists Make *Streamers* Explode." *Denver Post*, July 6, 1985, sec. C: 2.

Hunger Artists Metro Theatre

1012. Stone, Pam. "Academy Presents Atlanta Premiere of *Streamers*." *Entertainment* [Atlanta], Mar. 1979, sec. B: 1, 2.

1013. Stoneman, Donnell. "*Streamers* Grapples with Wasteful Violence." *Advocate* [San Mateo, CA], 96 (Aug. 11, 1976): 44.

Mitzi Newhouse Theatre

1014. Stothard, Peter. "*Sticks and Bones/Streamers*." *Plays and Players*, 25 (Apr. 1978): 24-25.

Liverpool Playhouse

1015. *Streamers. Playbill.* Apr. 1976. New York Shakespeare Festival, Lincoln Center, Mitzi E. Newhouse Theatre.

1016. *Streamers. Playbill.* Oct. 1976. New York Shakespeare Festival, Lincoln Center, Mitzi E. Newhouse Theatre.

1017. "*Streamers.*" *The Austin Chronicle* [TX] 4, no. 24 (July 26, 1985): 32.

Capitol City Playhouse

1018. "*Streamers.*" *Sender Freies Berlin* [Radio West Berlin]. Aug. 29, 1976.

Play is not about gays but about pressures on the young; Rabe bitterly accuses military establishment of brutality

1019. "*Streamers.*" *New York Times*, Apr. 30, 1976, sec. C: 3.

Full-page ad with excerpts from major New York critics

1020. "*Streamers*: A Wartime Drama." *St. Louis Globe Democrat*, Feb. 23, 1979, sec. B: 1.

1021. "*Streamers* Bloodshed is Only Shocking." *Recorder* [Clinton, CT], Feb. 26, 1976, "The Second Section": 11.

Long Wharf Theatre

1022. *"Streamers." Booklist*, 73 (May 1, 1977): 1316.

Book review

1023. *"Streamers." Kirkus Review*, 45 (Apr. 1, 1977): 413.

Book review

1024. Sullivan, Dan. "Death at Flarepoint in Rabe's *Streamers." Los Angeles Times*, Jan. 8, 1978, "California": 44.

1025. _____. "Richard Thomas in *Streamers." Los Angeles Times*, Dec. 16, 1977, "View," sec. IV: 1, 20.

1026. Syse, Glenna. "*Streamers* Inspires Rage and Boredom." *Chicago Sun-Times*, Apr. 1, 1977: 65.

Goodman Theatre

1027. Tate, Paul. "Theatre: David Rabe's *Streamers." New Haven Advocate*, Feb. 18, 1976: 10.

Long Wharf Theatre

1028. Taylor, Markland. "*Streamers*: A Theatrical Explosion." *New Haven Register,* Feb. 15, 1976, sec. D: 1, 2.

Long Wharf Theatre

1029. True, Linda. "*Streamers* at Theatre by the Sea." *Seacoast Scene* [Portsmouth, NH], Jan. 16, 1980: 14.

1030. von Maurer, Bill. "*Streamers*, a Shattering, Disturbing Drama." *Miami News*, Mar. 27, 1978, sec. D: 3.

Players State Theater

1031. Wahls, Robert. "Onstream With Rabe." *New York Daily News*, Apr. 25, 1976, "Leisure": 4.

1032. Wallace, Robert. "*Streamers*." *Body Politic: Gay Liberation Journal* [Toronto], 36 (Sept. 1977): 18.

Theatre Plus

1033. Wallach, Allan. "Stage: A Tough, Sad Play." *Newsday*, Feb. 10, 1976: 9A-10A.

1034. _____. "*Streamers* is Painfully Real." *Los Angeles Times*, May 13, 1976, sec. IV: 15.

1035. Wardle, Irving. "*Streamers*: Round House." *London Times*, Mar. 1, 1978: 9.

1036. Watt, Douglas. "*Streamers* is Worth a Trip to New Haven." *New York Daily News*, Feb. 9, 1976: 25.

Long Wharf Theatre

1037. _____. "*Streamers* Exerts Its Power Anew." *New York Daily News*, Apr. 22, 1976: 91. Rpt. in *NYTCR, 1976*: 264-65.

1038. Weales, Gerald. "The Stage: *Streamers*." *Commonweal*, May 21, 1976: 334-35.

1039. Wehmann, Hale. "*Streamers*." *Gay Community News*, 10, no. 37 (Apr. 9, 1983): 7.

1040. White, Peter. "Canadian *Streamers* U.S.-Dominated." *Globe and Mail* [Toronto], July 5, 1977: 15.

Theatre Plus

1041. Wilson, Edwin. "Time Bomb in an Army Barracks." *The Wall Street Journal*, Apr. 27, 1976: 22. Rpt. in *NYTCR, 1976*: 265-66.

1042. Winer, Linda. "A Couple of New York 'Home Runs' Boost Chicago into the Major Leagues." *Chicago Tribune*, Mar. 27, 1977, sec. VI: 2.

Goodman Theatre

1043. _____. "*Streamers* Has Some Older Blood Relatives." *Chicago Tribune*, Apr. 17, 1977, sec. VI: 2.

Goodman Theatre

1044. _____. "*Streamers* is Compact, Powerful." *Chicago Tribune*, Apr. 1, 1977, sec. II: 3.

Goodman Theatre

1045. Winn, Steven. "Vietnam Revisited, or Maybe We Never Left." *The Weekly* [Seattle], Aug. 10, 1977: 14-15.

A Contemporary Theatre

1046. Winslow, Valerie. "Doings in Bothell." *Daily Journal American* [Bellvue, WA], Aug. 12, 1977: 59.

A Contemporary Theatre

1047. Yamamoto, Ken-ichi. "Seihai—O, Uruwashi no Rakkasan, Hiraite Okure: Hoshikkata Tamashii no Kyusaikan" [Seihai *Streamers*: Stage Lacks a Sense of Salvation from the Agony]. *Ashahi Shinbun* [Tokyo], Evening Edition, June 7, 1979: 13.

1048. Yates, Ray. "Gory New Play Opens At Wharf." *Darien Review* [CT], Feb. 12, 1976: 12.

Long Wharf Theatre

1049. Young, B. A. "*Streamers*." *Financial Times* [London], Feb. 24, 1978: 17.

Round House Playhouse, Liverpool

1050. Young, Holly. "TBS *Streamers* Provocative Vehicle." *Portsmouth Herald* [NH], Jan. 8, 1980: 6.

Theatre by the Sea

1051. Ziff, Anne. "Isolation, Among Others, Tied to *Streamers*." *Fairfield Citizen* [CT], Feb. 18, 1976: 35.

Long Wharf Theatre

STREAMERS (FILM)

1052. Ales, B. "*Streamers*." *Cine-Revue*, 69 (Apr. 5, 1984): 9.

1053. Andrews, Nigel. "*Streamers*." *Financial Times* [London], Mar. 23, 1984: 17.

1054. Anselmi, Michele. "Il mondo rinchiuso in Caserna." *L'Unita* [Milan], Apr. 8, 1984: 5.

1055. Asahina, Robert. "On Screen: Flimsy Fall Lineup." *New Leader*, 66 (Oct. 17, 1983): 18-19.

1056. Baigneres, Claude. "Huis clos." *Cinema Le Figaro*, Apr. 16, 1984: 33.

1057. Baltake, Joe. "Vivid Editing Saves *Streamers*." *Philadelphia Daily News*, June 7, 1984: 47.

1058. Barges, Luc. "*Streamers*." *Cine-Revue*, 64 (Jan. 9, 1984): 55.

1059. Bergson, Phillip. "The Right Stuff." *What's On* [London], Mar. 22, 1984: 37.

1060. _____. "Altman Aloud." *What's On* [London], Mar. 29, 1984: 43.

1061. Bilbow, Marjorie. "*Streamers*." *Screen International* [London], no. 439 (1984): 26.

1062. Blowen, Michael. "Altman's *Streamers* Falls Flat." *Boston Globe*, Nov. 11, 1983, sec. L: 4.

1063. Borelli, Sauro. "Ecco il Vietnam prossimo Venturo." *L'Unita* [Milan], Sept. 6, 1984.

1064. Braun, Eric. "*Streamers*." *Film* [London], no. 4 (1984): 39-40.

1065. Canby, Vincent. "Film Festival: Play *Streamers* Adapted by Altman." *New York Times*, Oct. 9, 1983, sec. I: 73.

1066. Champlin, Charles. "Altman's Getting Back to Basics in *Streamers*." *London Times*, Mar. 24, 1984, "Arts": 21.

1067. Chase, Chris. "At the Movies." *New York Times*, Oct. 28, 1983, sec. III: 8.

1068. Christensen, Johs. H. "For turen til Vietnam." *Kristeligt dagblad* [Copenhagen], Oct. 31, 1984.

1069. Christie, Ian. "*Streamers*." *Daily Express*, Mar. 23, 1984: 37.

1070. Ciment, M. "*Streamers*." *Positif*, 273 (Nov. 1983): 48-50.

1071. Coleman, John. "Films: In the Wings." *New Statesman*, 107 (Mar. 23, 1984): 29-30.

1072. Combs, Richard. "*Streamers*." *Monthly Film Bulletin*, 51 (Apr. 1984): 123-25.

1073. Corliss, Richard. "Raking Up the Autumn Leavings: Seven Films for Fall, from Bond to Beyond." *Time*, Oct. 17, 1983: 89.

1074. Cosford, Bill. "*Streamers* Makes Uneasy Transition from Stage to Film." *Miami Herald*, Apr. 21, 1984, sec. B: 5.

1075. Crist, Judith. "A Fallen Star." *Saturday Review*, Nov. 1983: 43.

1076. Cumbow, R. C. "*Streamers*." *Informer* (May-June 1984): 9.

1077. de Cominges, Jorge. *"Desechos."* *El Periodico* [Barcelona], Nov. 6, 1985, "Cine critica": 55.

1078. de Pracontal, Mona and Andre Cornand. "Sur quelques inedits americains au New York Film Festivals." *La revue du cinema*, no. 390 (Jan. 1984): 80-81.

1079. de Saint-Angel, Eric. "Robert Altman: 'La Guerre, C'est Le Comb le Du Mauvais Gout.'" *Le Matin*, Apr. 10, 1984: 29.

1080. De Santi, G. *"Streamers."* *Cineforum*, 24 (May 1984): 51-55.

1081. Dignam, Virginia. "Military Machines." *Morning Star* [London], Mar. 23, 1984: 2.

1082. Dumont, Pierre. *"Streamers."* *Cinema*, no. 305 (May 1984): 47.

1083. Ebert, Roger. *"Streamers."* *Roger Ebert's Movie Home Companion.* Kansas City, KS: Andrews, McMeel, 1985. 313.

1084. Elhem, P. "Les nus et les morts (bis repetita)." *Visions*, 21/22 (Oct. 1984): 38.

1085. Esteve, M. "Contre La Guerre." *Espirit* (May 1984): 173-74.

1086. Fabre, Maurice. *"Streamers*: Guerre de chambree." *France-Soir*, Apr. 16, 1984, "Critique De Cinema": 21.

1087. Fainaru, Dan. "A New Altman." *Jerusalem Post Magazine*, Aug. 17, 1984: E.

1088. Feingold, Michael. "Film: Masterpiece Theatre." *Village Voice*, Nov. 22, 1983: 62.

1089. "Filmspiegel *Streamers.*" *Neue Zurcher Zeitung* [Zurich], Sept. 21, 1984: 51.

1090. Fontenla, Cesar Santos. "Robert Altman va al teatro." *Cambio 16* [Madrid], Sept. 1, 1986: 97.

1091. French, Philip. *"Streamers."* *Observer*, Mar. 25, 1984: 20.

1092. Gibbs, Patrick. *"Streamers." Daily Telegram*, Mar. 23, 1984: 19.

1093. Girard, M. *"Streamers." Sequences*, 117 (July 1984): 52-53.

1094. Grier, David Alan. "Altman's *Streamers* Set for Film Festival." *New York Times*, Aug. 16, 1983, sec. C: 15.

1095. Guthmann, Edward. "60-Film Retrospective/Stage Gems That Glittered on the Screen." *San Francisco Chronicle*, Nov. 24, 1985: 24.

1096. Harvey, Stephen. "The 21st New York Film Festival: The Age of Calligraphy." *Film Comment*, 19 (Nov.-Dec. 1983): 66-67.

1097. Hey, K. R. "Films." *USA Today*, 112 (Jan. 1984): 95-97.

1098. Hibbin, S. *"Streamers." Films and Filming*, 355 (Apr. 1984): 42.

1099. Hinxman, Margaret. *"Streamers." Daily Mail*, Mar. 23, 1984: 28.

1100. Hogsbro, Helle. "Om bosser og krig." *Land og Folk* [Copenhagen], Oct. 26, 1984: 8.

1101. Hutchinson, T. *"Streamers." Photoplay*, 35 (June 1984): 20.

1102. "Interview with Robert Altman." *Streamers*. Press leaflet. See #165: 12-15.

1103. Jackson, Paul. *"Streamers." Western Mail* [Cardiff], June 2, 1984: 8.

1104. Janusonis, Michael. "Movie Review: Contrived World of War Rips *Streamers* to Shreds." *Providence Journal* [RI], Aug. 21, 1984, sec. A: 12.

1105. Jensen, Sten. "For fa billeder for Manage ord." *Politiken* [Copenhagen], Oct. 26, 1984.

1106. Jorgensen, Henning. "Altman pa teatralsk hojtryk." *Information Fredag*, Oct. 26, 1984: 7.

1107. Kell. [Keller, J. R. K.] *"Streamers."* *Variety*, Sept. 7, 1983: 17.

1108. Kerner, F. "Deux morts, le sang par terre, mais le pluie tombe encore. Un homme chante." *Positif*, 280 (June 1984): 19-20.

1109. Kopf, Bilba. "The Army Game (Part One)." *New Musical Express*, Mar. 24, 1984: 24.

1110. Krohn, Bill. *"Streamers."* *Boxoffice* [Chicago], 120 (Jan. 1984): 47-48.

1111. _____. "Fiches Films—*Streamers*." *Le Film Français*, Mar. 16, 1984: 42.

1112. Kroll, Jack. "Movies: Citizen Army." *Newsweek*, Nov. 7, 1983: 131.

1113. J. P. L. "Les points de mire." *Premiere*, Apr. 1984: 53-54.

1114. Lally, K. "Altman and Mileti on *Streamers*." *Film Journal*, 86 (Oct. 28, 1983): 16-17.

1115. Larsen, Jan Kornum. "Krigere." *Weekend-Avisen* [Copenhagen], Oct. 26, 1984.

1116. Le Roux, H. "Bidasses en folie." *Cahiers du Cinema*, 358 (Apr. 1984): 50-51.

1117. Loynd, R. "Mileti Ankles SLM to Solo, Buys *Streamers* for $3-mil." *Variety*, July 6, 1983: 6, 34.

1118. Lyman, Rick. "Film Altman's *Jimmy Dean* Finally Makes It to Phila." *Philadelphia Inquirer*, Sept. 2, 1983, sec. E: 20.

1119. Malcolm, Derek. *"Streamers."* *Guardian*, Mar. 22, 1984: 11.

1120. Marcorelles, Louis. "Les masques tombent." *Le Monde*, Apr. 14, 1984, "Cinema": 11-12.

1121. Marinero, Francisco. "*Desechos*, de Robert Altman." *Diario 16* [Madrid] (Aug. 23, 1986), "Supplemento": III.

1122. Marti, Octavi. "La envidia de 'Estudio 1.'" *El Pais*, Aug. 27, 1986, "Espectaculos": 21.

1123. Martini, Emmanuela. "L'America della spettacolarita." *Cineform*, no. 9 (1983): 7-8.

1124. _____. "Nouveaux films a Paris—*Streamers*." *Cine-Revue*, no. 14 (1984): 9.

1125. Menil, Alain. "*Streamers*." *Cinematographie*, 99 (Apr. 1984): 32-33.

1126. Michiels, D. "*Streamers*: claustrofobische microcosmos." *Film et Televisie*, 329 (Oct. 1984): 29.

1127. Montaigne, Pierre. "A propos de *Streamers*: Altman: le parachute ne s'ouvrepas." *Le Figaro*, Apr. 11, 1984: 25.

1128. Morsiani, A. "*Streamers*." *Segno*, 10 (Nov. 1983): 29.

1129. _____. "*Streamers*." *Segno*, 13 (May 1984): 64-65.

1130. Murat, Piere. "*Streamers*: La peur a huis-clos." *Telerama* (Apr. 4, 1984): 21-22.

1131. O'Toole, Lawrence. "Broadway to Hollywood." *Film Comment*, 17 (Nov./Dec. 1981): 22-25.

1132. _____. "*Streamers*." *Maclean's*, Nov. 28, 1983: 70.

1133. Pantel, Monique. "Robert Altman ràve d'engager Adjani et Depardieu." *France-Soir,* Apr. 2, 1984: 18.

1134. Philbert, B. "Robert Altman." *Cinematographie*, 99 (Apr. 1984): 29-32.

1135. Ringel, Eleanor. "*Streamers*." *Atlanta Constitution*, Sept. 14, 1984, sec. P: 3.

1136. Robinson, David. "Profound Vision with the Eyes of Tragedy." *Times* [London], Mar. 23, 1984: 21.

1137. Roy, Jean. "L'espace de la chambree." *L'Humanité* [Paris], Apr. 25, 1984: 9.

1138. Russell, William. "*Streamers.*" *Glasgow Herald*, June 8, 1985: 8.

1139. Ryan, Desmond. "Robert Altman Takes a Quieter Tack Against War." *Philadelphia Inquirer*, June 8, 1984, sec. E: 6.

1140. Sauvaget, D. "*Streamers*: Altman retrouve." *Revue du Cinema*, 393 (Apr. 1984): 25-26.

1141. Sinyard, Neil. "*Streamers.*" *Sunday Telegram* [London], Mar. 25, 1984: 14.

1142. Stein, Elliot. "The 21st New York Film Festival: Forbidden Revelations." *Film Comment*, 19 (Nov./Dec. 1983): 74.

1143. "*Streamers.*" *Boston Globe*, Aug. 12, 1980, sec. L: 5.

1144. "*Streamers.*" *New Orleans Times-Picayune*, July 6-12, 1986, "TV Focus": 62.

1145. "*Streamers.*" *Film Français*, Mar. 16, 1984: 7.

1146. "*Streamers.*" *Kol Ha'ir* [Jerusalem], Sept. 26, 1984: 35.

1147. "*Streamers.*" *Tablet* [London], Mar. 31, 1984: 320.

1148. "*Streamers*—ein bedeutender film Robert Altmans." *Neue Zurcher Zeitung*, Sept. 28, 1984: 65.

1149. "*Streamers* de Robert Altman." *Le Monde*, Apr. 12, 1984, "Cinema": 14.

1150. "*Streamers.*" *Variety*, Apr. 11, 1984: 98.

1151. Summers, Sue. "Clowning Glory." *Sunday Times* [London], Mar. 25, 1984: 55.

1152. Thirkell, Arthur. "*Streamers.*" *Daily Mirror*, Mar. 23, 1984: 23.

1153. Thygesen, E. "Snadhedens time." *Levende Billeder*, 10 (Nov. 15, 1984): 57.

1154. Tomic, Milica. "Predstavlyamo vam filmove Festa." *Politika* [Belgrade], Feb. 2, 1984: 10.

1155. Toubiana, S. "Les 'monstrables.'" *Cahiers*, 352 (Oct. 1983): 8-13.

1156. Tourigny, M. "Robert Altman, l'Amerique dans tous ses etats." *24 Images*, 19 (Winter 1983-1984): 26-32.

1157. Walker, Alexander. "*Streamers.*" *Standard*, Sept. 8, 1983: 23.

1158. _____. "*Streamers.*" *Standard*, Mar. 22, 1984: 23.

1159. Weinstein, W. "*Streamers.*" *Film Journal,* 86 (Oct. 28, 1983): 61-63.

1160. Wimphen, Catherine. "Huis clos: *Streamers.*" *Elle*, Apr. 3, 1984: 39.

I'M DANCING AS FAST AS I CAN

1161. Anser, D. "Movies: Kicking the Pill Habit." *Newsweek*, Mar. 8, 1982: 90.

1162. Baron, David. "*Dancing* Not Worth All Those Steps to the Theatre." *New Orleans Times-Picayune*, Sept. 9, 1982, sec. 6: 7.

1163. Benson, Sheila. "Dancing on the Edge of a Whirlpool of Success." *Los Angeles Times*, Mar. 4, 1982, sec. 6: 1.

1164. Callahan, J. "Drug Company Down on Valium Movie." *American Film*, 7 (May 1982): 9.

1165. Cart [McCarthy, T.]. "*I'm Dancing as Fast as I Can*." *Variety*, Mar. 3, 1982: 16.

1166. Chanko, K. M. "*I'm Dancing as Fast as I Can*." *Films in Review*, 33 (May 1982): 307.

1167. Chase, Chris. "At the Movies: Busy Director Turns Out His First Movie." *New York Times*, Mar. 5, 1982, sec. C: 8.

1168. Clareas, Carlos. *Song News*, Mar. 9, 1982: 45.

1169. Collins, Glenn. "Jill Clayburgh—Acting on the Edge." *New York Times*, Mar. 7, 1982, sec. 2 : 1+.

1170. Denby, David. "Movies: Princess Val." *New York*, 15 (Mar. 15, 1982): 58-61.

1171. Hall, Margaret. "The Dangers of the Happiness Pill." *Daily Mirror* [London], Mar. 11, 1982: 9.

1172. Haller, Scott. "Jill Clayburgh: The Fine Art of Coping." *Saturday Review*, Mar. 1982: 28-30, 32-33.

1173. Haskell, Molly. "*I'm Dancing as Fast as I Can* and the Jill Clayburgh Backlash." *Vogue*, May 1982: 50, 53.

1174. Hatch, Robert. "Films: *I'm Dancing as Fast as I Can.*" *Nation*, 234 (Mar. 20, 1982): 346-48.

1175. Hey, K. R. "Films." *USA Today*, Apr. 9, 1982: 68.

1176. "*I'm Dancing as Fast as I Can.*" *Halliwell's Film Guide,* 4th ed. New York: Scribner's, 1985. 699.

1177. "*I'm Dancing . . .*" *Variety*, Sept. 7, 1983: 17.

1178. *Jill Clayburgh. I'm Dancing as Fast as I Can. Handbook of Production Information.* Paramount Pictures Corporation, 1981.

1179. Kane, M. "*I'm Dancing as Fast as I Can.*" *Film Journal*, 85 (Mar. 8, 1982): 23-24.

1180. Kauffmann, Stanley. "Fine Farce, Dreary Drama." *New Republic*, 186 (Mar. 24, 1984): 24-26.

1181. Linck, David. "*I'm Dancing as Fast as I Can.*" *Boxoffice* [Chicago], 118 (Apr. 1982): 92-93.

1182. Maslin, J. "Screen: Jill Clayburgh in *Fast as I Can.*" *New York Times*, Mar. 5, 1982, sec. C: 10.

1183. O'Toole, Lawrence. "A Walk on the Fine Line Between Calm and Vertigo." *Maclean's*, Mar. 22, 1982: 60.

1184. Quindlen, Anna. "An Independent Woman." *Washington Post*, Apr. 4, 1982, "Parade": 16, 17, 19.

1185. Sarris, A. "Films in Focus: Valium of the Dolls." *Village Voice*, 27 (Mar. 16, 1982): 45.

1186. Scheuer, Steven, ed. *"I'm Dancing as Fast as I Can."* In *Movies on TV, 1986-87.* New York: Bantam, 1985. 308.

1187. Sorelli, Leila. "Ucleczka od zaleznosci." *Film* [Warsaw], no. 32 (1982): 8.

1188. Sragow, M. "Movies: Clayburgh Trips in *Dancing.*" *Rolling Stone*, Apr. 4, 1982: 71.

1189. Sterritt, David. *"I'm Dancing* as Fast as I Can." *Christian Science Monitor*, Mar. 25, 1982, "Arts/Entertainment": 19.

1190. Wolf, William. "On Film: the Five Million Dollar Directing Lesson." *New York*, 15 (Mar. 29, 1982): 82-83.

GOOSE AND TOMTOM

1191. Corry, John. "Rabe Disavows the *Goose* He Thought He Had Closed." *New York Times*, May 8, 1982: 17.

1192. Gussow, Mel. "Theatre: *Goose and Tom Tom* Opens." *New York Times*, May 8, 1982: 17.

1193. Haun, Harry. *Philadelphia Inquirer*, Sept. 2, 1986, sec. C: 2.

1194. Kolin, Philip. "*Goose and Tomtom.*" *World Literature Today*, 62 (Winter 1988).

    Book review

1195. "Newsmakers." *Philadelphia Inquirer*, Aug. 6, 1986, sec. E: 2.

1196. "Show Business." *Milwaukee Journal*, May 13, 1982, sec. II: 1.

1197. Speers, William. "Maybe Yes, Maybe No." *Philadelphia Inquirer*, Aug. 8, 1986, sec. D: 2.

1198. _____. "Material Girl's Debut Is Back On." *Philadelphia Inquirer*, Aug. 14, 1986, sec. C: 2.

HURLYBURLY

1199. "Actress Sigourney Weaver Interviewed." *CBS Morning News Transcript*, Aug. 13, 1984: 49.

1200. "A Shark in Hollywood." *Scene* (weekly magazine of the *Melbourne Herald* and *Weekly Times, Ltd.*), Aug. 23, 1986: 23.

1201. Bailey, Norma. "Big People?" *Newport This Week* [RI], Dec. 25, 1986, "Arts and Entertainment": 12, 25.

   Trinity Repertory Company

1202. Barnes, Clive. "Rabe's *Hurlyburly* Pins Hollywood to the Wall." *New York Post*, June 22, 1984: 43. Rpt. in *NYTCR, 1984*: 236.

1203. Beaufort, John. "*Hurlyburly* is Confused Comedy." *Christian Science Monitor*, July 3, 1984: 27. Rpt. in *NYTCR, 1984*: 237.

1204. Bennetts, Leslie. "Broadway." *New York Times*, Nov. 16, 1984, sec. III: 2.

1205. _____. "Inside the Ensemble Play *Hurlyburly*." *New York Times*, July 18, 1984, sec. C: 17.

1206. _____. "Rabe's New Play Due Next Month on Upper West Side." *New York Times*, May 11, 1984, sec. III: 2.

1207. _____. "Second Adolescence Theme of Rabe's All-Star Play." *Houston Chronicle*, May 14, 1984, sec. 4: 5.

1208. Berman, Paul. "Theater: *Hurlyburly*." *Nation*, Oct. 6, 1984: 330.

1209. Blau, Eleanor. "American Plays Open to Chicago Audiences." *Cincinnati Enquirer*, Dec. 6, 1983, sec. D: 16.

1210. Bosworth, Patricia. "Sigourney Weaver, Rising Star." *Working Woman*, July 1984: 100.

1211. Brustein, Robert. "*Hurlyburly*: Painless Dentistry." *New Republic*, Aug. 6, 1984: 27.

1212. _____. "Musical Chairs." *New Republic*, Apr. 29, 1985: 28.

   Commentary on the Off-Broadway theatre and *Hurlyburly*

1213. A. C. "Hollywood Gone Mad." *Scene* [Melbourne], Sept. 12, 1986: 23.

   Melbourne Theatre Company, Russell Street

1214. Cedrone, Lou. "Former Dubuquer Hits on Broadway with Play." *Dubuque Telegraph Herald*, Sept. 13, 1984: 9.

1215. Christiansen, Richard. "Hubbub and *Hurlyburly*. Why the Stars Came to Goodman Studio." *Chicago Tribune*, May 6, 1984, sec. XIII: 8-10.

1216. _____. "Rabe's *Hurlyburly* Probes the Depths but Hits the Heights." *Chicago Tribune*, Apr. 4, 1984, sec. 5: 1, 3.

1217. _____. "Is Our Destiny Our Doom? Playwrights Give an Answer." *Chicago Tribune*, May 20, 1984, sec. 13: 16.

1218. Clay, Carolyn. "Man and Hyperman: *Hurlyburly*'s Depraved New World." *Boston Phoenix*, Jan. 6, 1987: 7, 13.

1219. Coale, Sam. "*Hurlyburly*." *Studies in American Drama, 1945-Present*, 2 (1987): 131-33.

   Trinity Repertory Company

1220. Colby, Douglas. "Buzzing Off-Broadway." *Plays and Players*, Feb. 1985: 16-17.

1221. Collins, William B. "Theater: N.Y. *Hurlyburly* Directed by Mike Nichols." *Philadelphia Inquirer*, June 23, 1984, sec. C: 3.

1222. Cornell, Phil. "Shakespeare Festival's Staging of *Hurlyburly* Has People Talking." *Courier News* [Bridgewater, NJ], Nov. 26, 1986: A14.

     New Jersey Shakespeare Festival

1223. Craig, William M. Jr. "California Vice: *Hurlyburly* Tells About Ugly Life in the Fast Lane," *Valley News* [Lebanon, NH], May 19, 1987: 13.

     Dartmouth Players directed by Mara Sabinson

1224. Crimeen, Bob. "*Hurly Burly*, What a Bunch of Beasts." *The Sun* [Melbourne], Aug. 30, 1986: 15.

     Melbourne Theatre Company, Russell Street

1225. Crossett, Allen. "*Hurlyburly* is Effectively Offensive and Excellent." *Bernardsville News* [NJ], Dec. 4, 1986: 7.

     New Jersey Shakespeare Festival

1226. Daniels, Robert L. "Punchy *Hurlyburly* in Madison; Sad Smile on Broadway." *Good Times* [Chatham, NJ], Dec. 10, 1986: 5.

     New Jersey Shakespeare Festival

1227. Davison, Dennis. "Pomposity that Needs Puncturing." *The Australian*, Aug. 25, 1986: 13.

     Melbourne Theatre Company, Russell Street

1228. Dolan, Doug. "Herd of Talented Actors Drives Play Toward Tonys." *Toronto Star*, Oct. 6, 1984, "Entertainment," sec. F: 3.

1229. Dolan, Frank. "*Hurlyburly* at the Trinity Repertory Theatre, Providence." WEEI, 590 **am** Radio. Boston, Dec. 22, 1986.

1230. Dunlop, Don. "As Offensive as Life Itself." *The Herald* [Melbourne], Aug. 26, 1986, "Theatre": 19.

   Melbourne Theatre Company, Russell Street

1231. Ellison, Jennifer. "Men and the Babble about Relationships." *The Bulletin* [Melbourne], Sept. 9, 1986: 108.

   Melbourne Theatre Company, Russell Street.

1232. Engstrom, John. "Raves For *Hurlyburly* at Trinity Rep." *Boston Globe*, Dec. 19, 1986, "Stage": 46.

1233. Feingold, Michael. "Moving Experiences." *Village Voice*, Oct. 9, 1984: 6.

1234. Fiumara, Carmen. "*Hurlyburly* Looks at Relationships." *Mansfield News* [MA], Dec. 31, 1986: 5.

   Trinity Repertory Company

1235. Fowler, Don. "*Hurlyburly* . . . an Endurance Test That's Worth Enduring." *Cranston Herald* [RI], Dec. 25, 1986: 8.

   Trinity Repertory Company

1236. Freedman, Samuel G. "Sacrifices of Many Yield Two Untraditional Plays." *New York Times*, July 2, 1984, sec. III: 12.

1237. Friedman, Arthur. "Rep Finds Riches in Rabe." *Boston Herald*, Dec. 23, 1986: 29.

   Trinity Repertory Company

1238. Gale, William K. "Broadway's Best Not Good Enough." *Providence Sunday Journal* [RI], June 2, 1985, sec T: 6.

Hurlyburly is a strong "contender" in Gale's "predictions" for "Best Play" of the year.

1239. _____. "*Hurlyburly* a Long Look at Unlikeable People." *Providence Journal-Bulletin* [RI], Dec. 18, 1986, sec. B: 9.

Trinity Repertory Company

1240. Game, Peter. "*Hurlyburly* Language." *The Herald* [Melbourne], Aug. 22, 1986: 1, 16.

Melbourne Theatre Company, Russell Street

1241. Gelb, Barbara. "Mike Nichols: The Special Risks and Rewards of the Director's Art." *New York Times*, May 27, 1984, sec. VI: 20.

1242. Haywood, Laura W. "*Hurlyburly*." *Princeton Packet*, Nov. 28, 1986, "Time Off": 9.

New Jersey Shakespeare Festival

1243. Healy-North, Jo. "*Hurlyburly*." *Knox Sherbrooke News*, Sept. 2, 1986, "Stepping Out": 1.

Melbourne Theatre Company, Russell Street

1244. Heath, Sally. "Witty Play on Men Who Want to Hate Women." *The Melbourne Times*, Aug. 27, 1986, "Arts and Entertainment": 13.

Melbourne Theatre Company, Russell Street

1245. Humm. "Off-Broadway Review." *Variety*, July 4, 1984: 83.

1246. "*Hurlyburly*." *San Francisco Review of Books*, 11 (Spring 1986): 17.

Book review

1247. "*Hurlyburly*." *Booklist*, 82 (Sept. 1, 1985): 20.

Book review

1248. *Hurlyburly. Showbill*, June 1984, Promenade Theatre.

1249. *Hurlyburly. Playbill*, 3, no. 3 (1984), Ethel Barrymore Theatre.

1250. *"Hurlyburly." Miami Herald*, Feb. 10, 1985, sec. L: 3.

1251. *"Hurlyburly." Miami Herald*, Feb. 17, 1985, sec. L: 2.

1252. *"Hurlyburly." Miami Herald*, May 25, 1985, sec. L: 3.

1253. *"Hurlyburly* At Shakespeare Festival." *Plainfield Today* [NJ], Nov. 27, 1986: 8.

    New Jersey Shakespeare Festival

1254. *"Hurlyburly* Raunchy and Powerful." *Daily Record, Northwest NJ*, Nov. 25, 1986, sec. A: 12.

1255. Israel, Bob. *"Hurlyburly*: The Bruise that Blisters and Heals." *The New Paper* [Providence, RI], Dec. 23-30, 1986: 8.

    Trinity Repertory Company

1256. Janis, Stefan. "A Foul Aftertaste Remains When *Hurlyburly*s Done." *The Star-Ledger* [NJ], Nov. 25, 1986: 57.

1257. Kelly, Kevin. *"Hurlyburly* Examines the Dark Side of Love." *Boston Globe*, Oct. 8, 1984, sec. L: 1.

1258. Kim, Jeanhee. "Players Shine in Rabe's *Hurlyburly." The Dartmouth*, May 19, 1987, "Arts and Leisure": 8.

    Dartmouth Players directed by Mara Sabinson

1259. Kissel, Howard. *"Hurlyburly." Women's Wear Daily*, June 22, 1984: 20. Rpt. in *NYTCR, 1984*: 237.

1260. _____. "The Year in Drama." *Dictionary of Literary Biography Yearbook, 1984.* Detroit: Gale, 1985. 130.

1261. Kroll, Jack. "Hollywood Wasteland: Off-Broadway, and All-Star Cast Makes Theater History." *Newsweek*, July 2, 1984: 65, 67. Rpt. in *NYTCR, 1984*: 238.

1262. Larkin, John. "The Horrors of Hollywood." *The Sunday Press* [Melbourne], Sept. 14, 1986, "Stage": 39.

    Melbourne Theatre Company, Russell Street

1263. Leiter, Robert. "Theatre Chronicles." *Hudson Review*, 38 (Summer 1985): 297-99.

1264. Levett, Karl. "New York Jungles and Buried Treasure." *Drama*, 154, 4th Quarter (1984): 46-47.

1265. Mansfield, Stephanie. "On Stage, On Screen, In Real Life, She's a Smash." *Philadelphia Inquirer*, Sept. 19, 1984, sec. D: 1.

    About Sigourney Weaver

1266. Mercurio, Gregory. Review of *Hurlyburly*. *Best Sellers*, 45 (Sept. 1985): 232.

1267. Mor. "Resident Legit Reviews." *Variety*, Apr. 6, 1984: 98.

1268. Mount, Betty. "*Hurlyburly* is Harrowing but Honest." *The Independent Press* [NJ], Dec. 10, 1986: 21.

    New Jersey Shakespeare Festival

1269. Nelson, Nels. "Postscript: More on Nonprofit Theater Strategy." *Philadelphia Daily News*, July 30, 1984: 40.

1270. Nemy, Enid. "Broadway." *New York Times*, May 25, 1984, sec. III: 2.

1271. "News." *Theatergoer*, 4, no. 4 (Apr. 1985): 3.

1272. Nightingale, Benedict. "David Rabe Explores a Different Kind of Jungle." *New York Times*, July 1, 1984, sec. II: 3, 11.

1273. _____. "Hollow Cheek." *New Statesman*, Aug. 17, 1984: 24.

1274. O'Connor, Kevin P. "*Hurlyburly* Lasts Too Loooooooong."
Evening Times [Pawtucket, RI], Dec. 19, 1986: 20.

   Trinity Repertory Company

1275. Oliver, Edith. "*Hurlyburly*." *New Yorker*, July 2, 1984: 82.

1276. "On the Way." *Theatergoer*, 4, no. 10 (Oct. 1985): 3.

1277. Pacheco, Patrick. "On and Off the Boards." *Miami Herald*, Sept. 12,
1984, sec. L: 1.

1278. Perry, Bruce. "Trinity's *Hurlyburly* Makes for Compelling Drama."
Sunday Independent [Acton, MA], Jan. 11, 1987: 12.

1279. Phelps, Brad. "*Hurlyburly* is Well-Directed Anger." *Tulsa Tribune*,
June 14, 1986, sec. B: 1.

   Phoenix Theatre

1280. Plaut, Jon. "*Hurlyburly* is Tough." *Madison Eagle* [NJ], Dec. 4,
1986: 35.

   New Jersey Shakespeare Festival

1281. "Plays to Premiere at Chicago Theater." *New Orleans Times-
Picayune*, Dec 5, 1983, sec. V: 7.

1282. "Play with Nasty Theme." *Geelong News* [Victoria, Australia], Aug.
29, 1986: 20.

   Melbourne Theatre Company, Russell Street

1283. Radic, Leonard. "*Hurlyburly* in the Hills of Hollywood." *The Age*
[Melbourne], Aug. 26, 1986, "Arts": 14.

   Melbourne Theatre Company, Russell Street

1284. Rebello, Stephen. "The Real People Who Inspired the Movies." *San Francisco Chronicle*, July 5, 1985: 25.

1285. Reidenberg, Diane. "*Hurly Burly* at NJSF." *The Journal* [NJ], Dec. 10, 1986: 20.

New Jersey Shakespeare Festival

1286. Renold, Evelyn. "Candice Bergen Drops Facade in *Hurlyburly*." *Chicago Tribune*, Dec. 29, 1984, sec. I: 13.

1287. Rich, Frank. "Theater: *Hurlyburly*." *New York Times*, June 22, 1984, sec. C: 3. Rpt. in *NYTCR, 1984*: 234-35.

1288. _____. "Great Cast in New Rabe Play." *San Francisco Chronicle*, June 26, 1984: 38.

1289. _____. "Theatre's Gender Gap is a Chasm." *New York Times*, Sept. 30, 1984, "Arts and Leisure," sec. 2: 1, 4.

1290. Richards, David. "Where's the Drama?" *Washington Post*, July 8, 1984, sec. H: 1.

1291. Rosenberg, Scott. "Marathon of Negative Emotions." *San Francisco Examiner*, Mar. 31, 1987, sec. E: 1, 6.

1292. _____. "The Search for Carnal Redemption." *San Francisco Examiner*, Apr. 5, 1987, sec. E: 2.

1293. St. Edmund, Bury. "Theatre." *The Chicago Reader*, Apr. 13, 1984, sec. 1: 38-39.

Goodman Theatre

1294. Samson, Suzanne. "*Hurlyburly* at Drew: Wrongly Maligned." *Time Out* [NJ], Dec. 10, 1986: 3.

New Jersey Shakespeare Festival

1295. Sanders, Vicki. "*Big River* Rolls to Tony Sweep." *Miami Herald*, June 3, 1985, sec. B: 1.

1296. Sasso, Laurence. "*Hurlyburly* is Like Watching a Train Wreck." *The Observer* [Greenville, RI], Dec. 25, 1986, sec. B: 5.

Trinity Repertory Company

1297. Schickel, Richard. "Failing Words." *Time*, July 2, 1984: 86-87. Rpt. in *NYTCR, 1984*: 239.

1298. Schiro, Anne-Marie. "The Evening Hours." *New York Times*, Aug. 10, 1984, sec. II: 6.

1299. Simon, John. "Slow Thinker, Fast Talkers." *New York*, Dec. 17, 1984: 71-72.

1300. _____. "War Games." *New York*, July 16, 1984: 42-44.

1301. Solomon, Steve. "*Hurlyburly* Not that Strong." *The Ridgewood News* [NJ], Dec. 4, 1986: 32.

New Jersey Shakespeare Festival

1302. Springer, P. Gregory. "Sex, Violence, and blah blah blah." *Champaign-Urbana News-Gazette Weekend*, June 6, 1986: 15.

Station Theatre production directed by John Hightower

1303. "Susan Anton on Auditioning for *Hurlyburly*." *CBS Morning News Transcript*, Feb. 14, 1985: 40.

1304. Syse, Glenna. "Acting Saves a Nowhere *Hurlyburly*." *Houston Chronicle*, Apr. 7, 1984, sec. 4: 7.

Goodman Theatre

1305. _____. "*Hurlyburly*: Talent Without Heart or Pain." *Chicago Sun-Times*, Apr. 4, 1984, "Show": 47.

1306. Taylor, Clarke. "*Hollywood Wives/* A Tinseltown Potboiler is Bergen's *Junk Food*." *San Francisco Chronicle*, Feb. 17, 1985: 51.

1307. "Tonys for *Big River* and *Biloxi Blues*." *San Francisco Chronicle*, June 3, 1985: 54.

1308. "Tony Nominees: Few Musicals." *San Francisco Chronicle*, May 7, 1985: 58.

1309. Tranchant, Marie-Noelle. "*Hurlyburly*." *Le Figaro*, June 12, 1984: 37.

1310. "Two Drifters." *American Theatre*, 1 (July/Aug. 1984): 22.

1311. Vallins, Naomi. "Problems at Pace." *The Jewish News* [Melbourne], Aug. 29, 1986: 14.

1312. Watt, Douglas. "*Hurlyburly*: A Vicious View of Hollywood." *New York Daily News*, June 22, 1984: 25. Rpt. in *NYTCR, 1984*: 235.

1313. Weales, Gerald. "Pleasant Dreams." *Commonweal*, 111 (Oct. 1984): 558-60.

1314. _____. "Theatre Watch." *Georgia Review*, 39 (Fall 1985): 620-21.

1315. Weiner, Bernard. "West Coast Premiere of David Rabe's *Hurlyburly*." *San Francisco Chronicle*, Apr. 1, 1987: 48.

Addison Stage Company

1316. Wilson, David. "Review: *Hurlyburly*." *Tulsa World*, June 14, 1986, sec. D: 4.

Phoenix Theatre

1317. Wilson, Edwin. "On Theater: Rambling Rabe." *The Wall Street Journal*, June 26, 1984: 32. Rpt. in *NYTCR, 1984*: 235-36.

1318. Wohlsen, Theodore O., Jr. *Library Journal*, Aug. 1985: 112.

Book review

INDEX

This index contains two types of numbers. Those in Roman type, appearing first, refer to page numbers in the stage history and biography; those numbers following in boldface refer to entry numbers in the bibliography.